'A worthy successor to Nancy Friday's groundbreaking work.'

Rob Page, founder of *The Lovers' Guide*

'What's so wonderful about *Garden of Desires* is the array of female voices. By taking into account all genders and sexual orientations, it perfectly demonstrates just how vast and varied female fantasies are. This is what makes *Garden of Desires* feel like it has fully bloomed.'

Rose Crompton, sex writer and journalist

'A must read for anyone who has ever wondered what really goes on in a woman's head!'

Suzanne Portnoy, bestselling author of erotic memoir
The Butcher, the Baker, the Candlestick Maker

'With *Garden of Desires*, Emily Dubberley offers us not only the sexual fantasies of modern-day women, but also a widely informed and deeply thoughtful analysis of what those fantasies represent. Dubberley, like Friday before her, has changed the world-view of the female gender.'

Susan Quilliam, relationship psychologist and
author of the new *The Joy of Sex*

T0314640

Garden of Desires

The Evolution of
WOMEN'S SEXUAL FANTASIES

Emily Dubberley

BLACK
LACE

1 3 5 7 9 10 8 6 4 2

First published in the UK in 2013 by Black Lace,
an imprint of Ebury Publishing
A Random House Group Company

The Random House Group Limited Reg. No. 954009

Addresses for companies within the Random House Group can be found at
www.randomhouse.co.uk

A CIP catalogue record for this book is available from
the British Library

Penguin Random House is committed to a sustainable future for
our business, our readers and our planet. This book is made from
Forest Stewardship Council® certified paper.

Printed and bound in Great Britain by Clays Ltd, Elcograf S.p.A.

ISBN 9780352347688

To buy books by your favourite authors and register for offers visit
www.randomhouse.co.uk
www.blacklace.co.uk

Thanks to Nancy Friday for planting the first seed –
and all the women who've shared their fantasies and
helped the garden grow.

Contents

Part One

Prologue:
A Brief History of
Female Sexual Fantasy

Female sexual fantasy began in 1973. That may sound ridiculous, but until Nancy Friday wrote *My Secret Garden*, female sexual fantasy did not officially exist. Not even in the pages of women's magazines.

Anaïs Nin may have achieved a certain measure of renown for *Delta of Venus* and *Little Birds*, but these erotic classics were published posthumously in 1978. *The Story of O* pre-empted *Fifty Shades of Grey* by 58 years – and has sold millions of copies – but Anne Desclos hid behind her pseudonym for forty years, only eventually revealed as Pauline Réage at 87 years of age. More significantly they, and the handful of openly sexual female writers before them, all wrote fiction. Friday was the first woman to collect women's real sexual fantasies and, in doing so, show that women had a sexuality of their own – a highly contentious idea in 1973.

In the month of *My Secret Garden*'s release Helen Gurley Brown (then editor of *Cosmo*) ran a feature written by her in-house psychiatrist, with the opening line, 'Women do not have sexual fantasies, period. Men do.'

And it wasn't just *Cosmo*. At the time Friday wrote *My Secret Garden*, the mainstream thinking of sex therapists, psychologists or psychiatrists was that women didn't have sexual fantasies.

Friday was conflicted by this information, as she fantasised, and set out to discover whether she was the only woman who did. Apparently, even when talking to 'some of the most sexually active women in New York and London', she was met by confusion. Only her persistence, placing discreet classified ads and interviewing rare, open friends helped prove that, for some women at least, sexual fantasy existed.

After *My Secret Garden* achieved popularity – and notoriety – Friday said, 'It's important for people to realize how new this subject is. But we have come to accept that women do have private, erotic thoughts.'[1]

What she was too modest to admit is that this acceptance is largely as a result of her own pioneering work.

Fantasy After Friday

*O*f course, women have always had a private sexuality – but until 1973 the idea that they did was stifled by the media, medical establishment and society alike. Once Friday opened the door to the secret garden, she was joined by similarly sex positive writers: Erica Jong, whose 1974 book *Fear of Flying* coined the term 'zipless fuck' (talking about a woman's desire for casual sex with a stranger) and whose novels included masturbation, rape fantasy and unashamed oral exploits involving a tampon; Shere Hite, whose 1974 book *Sexual Honesty By Women, For Women* was the precursor to her international best-seller, *The Hite Report* – one of the first books to report that women found climax through penetrative sex harder than orgasm through masturbation, posited the now generally accepted view that clitoral stimulation is key to female climax, and suggested that sex needed redefining for true sexual equality; and Betty Dodson, whose 1974 book, *Sex for One: The Joy of Selfloving*, presented an unashamed guide to masturbation, heavily laced with anecdotes about group, public and otherwise non-normative sex.

1 NancyFriday.com, 1 Jan, 2008

Dodson also ran interactive masturbation classes for those who wanted to take things further.

These revolutionary texts reflected the changes in society: a new willingness to talk about – and maybe engage in – sex. In 1973, Margot St Clare created sex-worker activist group COYOTE (Call off Your Tired Old Ethics), a 'loose women's organisation' dedicated to decriminalising sex work. In 1979, Tuppy Owens created Outsiders, a charity that helps disabled people socialise and find partners, offering open-minded support for people who want to talk about – and have – sex; and funded in part through the decadent and inclusive 'Sex Maniacs' Ball'. And these were far from the only organisations and activist groups that bubbled up, helping to broaden the scope of sexual discussion.

Most pivotally, the contraceptive pill was made available to unmarried women in the US for the first time in 1973 (the UK had introduced access for all women in 1961), and Roe vs Wade made abortion legal too. For the first time, female sexuality was separated from motherhood. Being childless became a choice – albeit one still frowned on by society (as demonstrated by Rita having to hide her contraceptive pills from her husband in the 1980 film *Educating Rita*). In a 2000 interview for *Shabhala Sun* magazine, bell hooks said, 'I can remember the sheer bliss that sound birth control offered us. For it meant we did not have to fear the penis. We could embrace our curiosity about it, our wonder and our passion.'

However, it was not all positive. Susan Quilliam, co-author of the new *The Joy of Sex* says, 'The hype of "the Swinging Sixties" and seventies gave the message that having sex was what all young people should be and were doing, so a lot of girls in particular did what they were expected or were pressured to do, not what they really wanted to do. The boys still ruled, and now they had fashion and the Pill on their side – if you didn't put out you were uptight or frigid.'

Women were certainly still judged for their sexuality – Hustler's infamous 'meat grinder' cover in 1978, depicting a naked woman being turned into mincemeat gives an idea of the perception of sexual women – but for the first time, it was accepted that women had a private sexuality in the same way that men do. The sexual revolution was taking seed.

Bonkbusters and Ballsy Women

*T*he 1980s saw the garden of desires grow. Judith Krantz was declared a pornographer for her 'sex and shopping' novels and was unashamed to admit the sex scenes were designed with arousal in mind. Shirley Conran's *Lace* shocked the world and topped the charts with its graphic depictions of under-age porn, teenage abortion, BDSM and a memorable sex scene with a gold-fish. Jackie Collins wrote sexy female characters often portrayed by her sister, Joan, on screen: confident, desirable, voracious women who weren't scared to demand what they wanted – and use their sexuality to get it. Jilly Cooper ensured country living was seen as no less racy than international jet-setting with her 'bonkbusters'. Titles were strong and sexy: *Riders*; *The Bitch*; and *Scruples*.

With the bonkbuster, came the ballbuster. Women weren't just presented with images of sexual empowerment, but with coined liberty. Many books revolved around strong women striving to create business empires or otherwise achieve independence. The books were career-focussed and unafraid to tackle harsh issues. Underneath the glitter and fabulous parties were stories of abortion, rape, racism, abuse and surviving adversity: and most of the glamorous heroines used intelligence, tenacity, sisterhood and sexuality to help them overcome these obstacles. Though the books were romantic, the 'happily ever after' ending was rarely simply the acquisition of a husband. The heroine of the bonkbuster achieved fulfilment through work-life balance: professional success went hand in hand with self-development, romance and friendship.

In addition to graphic and wild sex, these books dripped with consumerism. Money, sex and power intertwined between the bonkbusters' gold glinting covers, introducing women to a new trifecta of happiness that was rapidly seized on – and exploited

– by the media. Such books were dismissively referred to as 'soft porn' but the capitalism within their pages was at least as gratuitous as the sex. The bonkbuster was the precursor of *Sex and the City* – thematically, sexually and aspirationally.

It wasn't just hot writing that was encouraging women to accept and admit to their sexuality. In 1983, Madonna released her first album and soon, her confidence and sexual openness had lifted her to stardom – complete with complaints that *Like a Virgin* corrupted young minds and endorsed sex outside marriage: an accusation still levelled at many sexually open female musicians today (particularly if they are women of colour). Madonna's unashamed sexuality certainly provided a generation of women with a new icon – and fantasy figure. As one *Garden of Desires* survey respondent said, 'My earliest fantasies, aged six, were triggered by a Madonna video full of androgynous people writhing against one another.' And she was far from the only person to be sexually inspired by Madonna.

In 1984, Candida Royalle launched *Femme Productions* – a sex-positive porn production company, targeting narrative-led erotic films at women and making films designed to enhance couples' sex lives. This brought female fantasy further out of the closet – and deeper into some couples' lives.

Though initially resistant, women's magazines finally decided to nurture the seed of female solo sexuality, which in turn increased the amount of women who would admit to having fantasies. The garden was growing faster with every passing day.

Changes in the Garden

*I*n 1991, Nancy Friday revisited female fantasy in her book *Women on Top*. While she had surmised the fantasies within the pages of *My Secret Garden* were strongly linked with guilt, she found that the new fantasies, collated between 1980 and 1990, were more driven by anger. Women were starting to demand pleasure rather than feel ashamed of themselves for seeking it. Guilt still remained to a degree, but it was fading. Friday said in her Introduction, 'I learned the power of permission that comes from other voices. Only women can liberate other women; and only women's voices grant permission to be sexual; to be free to be anything we want, when enough of us tell each other it is OK.' Many women who filled in the survey for *Garden of Desires* supported this idea – as one woman said, 'I loved Nancy Friday's books as a young girl. It made what I thought was shameful and weird acceptable.'

However, there were also increasing concerns that the garden was getting out of control. Mary Whitehouse and other censorship groups tried to tame the beast of sexuality. Sex-positive feminists crossed swords with anti-porn feminists, who conflated sexual expression and open female sexuality with violence and sexual exploitation. In 1986, Linda Lovelace released her book *Out of Bondage*, asserting that her appearance in *Deep Throat* was non-consensual as she had a gun held to her head, and viewers were watching her getting raped. Dark reality started to seep through the glossy fantasy. And it was about to get worse.

The Naughty Nineties?

*B*y the 1990s, HIV/AIDS was casting its shadow over sexual freedom. The excess of the 1980s woman – confident, sexy and shoulder-padded – was replaced with the Zen earth-mother of the 1990s. Tantra started to attract media interest. Rather than fighting or fantasising, the modern woman was a victim, to be helped through her trauma with therapy – and possibly a healing crystal. Scaremongering stories about career women who'd 'left it too late' to get married or, worse, have children became an increasingly insidious media narrative. Strong and athletically sexy supermodels were replaced with vulnerable waifs; ballbusters were replaced by supermums 'having it all' – or downsizing to enjoy more quality time with the kids.

As the 1990s progressed, the bonkbuster was tamed, replaced by 'chick lit'. Designer orgies were thrown out in favour of 'comedy of errors' dinner parties, and characters obsessed about their cellulite rather than trying to create a business empire from scratch. Instead of tackling issues such as abortion, war, rape, class, racial discrimination, feminism and domestic violence, characters had to struggle against being a few dress sizes larger than their peers; having credit-card debt; or merely being single. Women were encouraged to nurture their insecurities and navelgaze rather than confront larger issues facing 'the sisterhood' as a whole. Sexual guilt and paranoia replaced the confident sexual desire of the 1980s. *Basic Instinct* was arguably one of the most iconic sexual films of the 1990s – and perpetuated the myth of the dangerous overtly (bi)sexual woman, much as *Fatal Attraction* had in 1987.

However, it wasn't all bad news for female sexual expression. Madonna was still pushing boundaries. Her video for *Justify My Love* featured sub/dom, bondage and same-sex kissing; her 1992 book, *Sex*, featured her in a number of fantasy-inspired photographs; and her album *Erotica* explored numerous sexual themes, as did her (poorly regarded) film *Body of Evidence*. However, when she handed her panties to popular TV host David Letterman and urged him to sniff them, it was a step too far: she faced harsh media criticism and subsequently started to de-sexualise her image and embrace a more spiritual persona, more in keeping with the 1990s (and expectations of women her age).

Salt'n'Pepa raised awareness of safer sex issues with their international hit, 'Let's Talk About Sex': a subversive rallying call, as sex had historically been used to oppress people of colour. Hypersexualisation had been used under slavery to justify the rape and impregnation of women of colour by (mostly) white slave owners, as was stereotyping of people of colour as bestial and 'other' in an attempt to legitimise their oppression; being a sexual woman of colour was dangerous. Black women had long been stereotyped as the 'hoochie', 'jezebel', or the 'gold digger' and as such, sex was a contentious subject for discussion. Kelly Brown Douglas spoke of the black community's unwillingness to enter into sexual discourse. 'For Blacks, to discuss sex publicly is like eating a watermelon in front of White people. All you do is confirm their images of you.'

However, with HIV/AIDS affecting all communities, it was a potentially life-saving message. Salt'n'Pepa's subsequent single, 'Shoop', was similarly sexually open, encouraging women to admit their desires and be sexually dominant. Over time, Christina Aguilera, Mary J Blige, Erykah Badu, Missy Elliot and Destiny's Child added to their rallying call, encouraging women to be honest and open about their emotional and physical desires.

Innovative publishers and publishing imprints such as Cleis (founded in 1980 in the US) and Black Lace (founded in the UK in 1993) kept female fantasies growing – albeit in dark corners – by creating erotic books specifically aimed at women. In its early days, female-oriented erotica was heavily biased towards the historical 'romance' – possibly inspired by early historical 'bonk-buster' *Forever Amber* – but over time, pioneering editors such as Kerri Sharp at Black Lace introduced more contemporary themes, stronger female characters and a vivid array of fetish. Paranormal fantasy also started entering the scene: one of the most popular erotic sub-genres in recent years (giving a possible hint as to the secret of the success of 'Twilight'-inspired *Fifty Shades*). The erotica market kept diversifying to attract an ever-growing female audience – and a spattering of porn magazines aimed at women also started to appear on the market, including *For Women* and *Playgirl*. The couple-oriented *Lovers' Guide* became the first UK film to legally feature erections, ejaculation and penetrative sex, with the objective of education. It became the first non-fiction film to sell over a million copies, in part down to the outraged newspaper headlines declaring it filth – and a reported 75 per cent of the 1.3 million buyers were women.

While female sexuality was finally recognised, it was still some-thing to be talked about in hushed whispers rather than openly discussed. Although porn mags for women were available, the buff, pumped men between their pages, smiling out underneath the caption, 'He's an able seaman', seemed far more appealing to the gay male than heterosexual female market; and, more to the point, they couldn't show an erection, under the visually repre-sentative 'Mull of Kintyre' guideline (the angle at which the Mull of Kintyre protrudes from Scotland – a limp 'semi-' at best).

Couple-oriented porn was still decidedly niche. Most erotic writers still hid behind pseudonyms – much as Anne Desclos had done forty years before. And though Black Lace was one of the biggest players in the female erotica market, total book sales across two hundred and fifty titles of around three million books were nothing compared to E. L. James's record-breaking sales a decade later. Few erotic writers could expect to reach a large audience – or to pay the bills from the product of their imagination.

Though attitudes were more liberal than before, female sexual fantasy was still largely the preserve of the sex-positive feminist movement, early adopters and – of course, as had always been the case – women in the privacy of their own homes, keeping their 'filthy' ideas to themselves. Most women still needed permission from the mainstream to be truly and openly sexual.

In her prescient paper written in 1987, 'Whatever Happened to the Sexual Revolution', Maxine Holz says, 'According to the pendulum theory of historical change, sexual attitudes periodically shift from one extreme to the other. Thus the 40s and 50s were characterized by uptight, moralistic attitudes toward sex. In the 60s and 70s a cycle of sexual permissiveness followed, while now in the mid-80s, the pendulum appears to be in full swing back to the repressive extreme. Presumably, by the late 90s we can expect yet another reversal.' Sure enough, that reversal was just around the corner.

00-pening Up? Millennial Sex

*F*emale sexuality burst back into public consciousness in the 2000s, with *Sex and the City* (*SATC*) leading the way in 1998. Suddenly, we saw women on mainstream television talking about casual sex, vibrators and anal play. Samantha happily threw herself into her sexual adventures without guilt or remorse (though it was no huge surprise to feminist viewers when she was punished with cancer in the later series: no slut should go unpunished in media, after all). More significantly, Charlotte, the 'good girl', had a sexual side. When she developed a fixation with her Rampant Rabbit in

'The Turtle and the Hare', the toy became the first ever sex toy to sell a million in a year (and inspire the mockumentary *Rabbit Fever* in 2006, about women hooked on their toys attempting to 'kick the rabbit habit'). It was official. Good girls liked sex too. With every new *SATC* came new items to buy. Newspapers and magazines devoted endless column inches to 'getting Carrie's look'. Her fashion sense attracted at least as much attention as her sex advice. Female sexuality was teamed with fabulous shoes. Sex, power and money were together again.

And that was far from the show's only influence. In 2001, I founded female erotica site Cliterati.co.uk and after every episode of *Sex and the City*, we saw a huge boost in fantasies submitted to the site based around the episode's theme, from using toys to watersports. The show gave permission to women to admit their desires – and Cliterati gave them a forum to share them, allowing me to see first-hand the power the media has over our sexuality: if you can see it on 'normal' TV, it must be OK.

However, female sexuality was still not entirely accepted. When I launched Cliterati, I thought female sexual desire was taken as a given. I thought that helping women share their sexual fantasies would be seen as sex-positive. I was wrong. We got hate mail from men threatening to rape us for being 'filthy sluts', and women saying we must be men hiding behind a facade because women wouldn't write 'that kind of thing'. However, we also got grateful letters from women thanking us for providing something they'd wanted for years: and in some cases, helping them climax for the first time ever. So I removed our email addresses from the site, masked our physical address in the domain records and continued.

After *Sex and the City*, the garden of desire ran rampant. I was approached by publisher Gavin Griffiths, who liked what he saw on Cliterati and wanted to create an offline equivalent: and so *Scarlet* magazine was born, featuring erotica, sex education, sex-toy reviews and features on sexual penchants of all kinds. (Aptly, it ceased publication at issue 69.)

Female porn producers including Anna Span, Erica Lust, Petra Joy and Jennifer Lyons Bell followed in the footsteps of Candida

Royalle, making porn for women – but rather than simply accept-ing the idea that women required romance and narrative, they each brought their own perspectives to 'female friendly' porn. There was a common core of treating performers with respect, but they and other female – mostly feminist – and queer pornogra-phers also brought greater variety to a previously male-dominated industry. There was a greater diversity of body types, sex acts and scenarios. Some female pornographers subverted tired old tropes such as 'pizza delivery man gets sex' and 'doctors and nurses', presenting them from a female perspective, while others ripped up the porn rule-book altogether. Female fantasies were increasingly used to inform porn, rather than remaining in women's heads.

Buy, Buy Baby

Burlesque hit the mainstream, moving from working men's clubs to glamorous supper clubs. Initially, the burlesque scene featured a diverse range of performers of numerous body types. However, as time went on, fat and queer performers became more marginalised, replaced by the slender Dita von Teese and glamorous 'beauties'; satire became increasingly replaced with striptease; and the initially subversive art form was replaced by a magazine-friendly sanitised version of burlesque, accessorised with designer corsets, crystal pasties and vintage make up. The neo-burlesque movement still offered an alternative to the consumer led 'corporate' scene but the mainstream view of burlesque was informed by glossy stereotypical depictions of the industry through films such as *Moulin Rouge* and *Burlesque*. The seductive call that 'sex sells' was reaching deafening levels.

Ann Summers exploded, cashing in on the popularity of the rabbit and building the profile of sex toys on the high street: sex toy sales were no longer something to be conducted secretly – though many women still enjoyed the female camaraderie of the Ann Summers Party. The erotic boutique developed as more companies flocked to satisfy women's growing desire for sexual exploration, and with it came solid gold vibrators, discreet sex toys disguised as lipsticks and rubber ducks, and a growing acceptance that women masturbated.

Toy companies finally realised that if they wanted women to use their devices, actually designing and packaging them with women in mind would probably be a good idea. They developed a strange attachment to producing pink or mauve vibrators featuring 'cute' animal heads – with the objective of 'feminising' the products – and to a degree, it worked, as the products were non-sexual enough to be featured in mainstream women's magazines. The phrase, 'by women, for women' – as used by Shere Hite back in the 1970s – became ubiquitous with female-targeted sex toy companies, to such a degree that the phrase is now all but meaningless. Over time, innovative companies produced less patronising, more design-led sex toys for women. Brands including Lelo, Shiri Zinn and Fun Factory created tasteful, ergonomically designed toys that looked as beautiful as they felt. The sex toy market was no longer the preserve of seedy back-streets: sisters were doing it for themselves.

The media also reflected this new sexual freedom. *Buffy The Vampire Slayer* brought a greater variety of accepted sexual relationship models into the mainstream, introducing lesbianism and BDSM relationships into popular TV narrative. Soap operas and drama shows started to feature gay and lesbian characters, and before long bicuriosity became the latest label to wear. Though this did introduce new stereotypes such as the 'lipstick lesbian' it also gave implicit endorsement to those who had previously been afraid to be honest about their sexuality.

Films such as *Secretary*, *The Notorious Bettie Page* and *Shortbus* made new generations curious about the fetish scene, while Jean Paul Gaultier was just one designer to draw inspiration from fetish wear. This saw a rise in fetish clubs: a mainstreaming of the 'perverted' – though only at its most stylised and least sexual. BDSM still entered the courts on several occasions when the powers that be deemed people had transgressed from 'acceptable' sexuality and the porn-and-violence debate became ever more heated. Elsewhere, the sexual revolution was gaining traction too: trans women (and men) were finally protected on the basis of gender-reassignment sex-discrimination under the UK Sex

Discrimination Act in 1999 – an important step towards acceptance (though sadly, discrimination is still rife).

The internet flourished with chat forums, adult dating websites, online fantasy games, and messaging programmes that made cybersex a new way to play. Women could not just share fantasies but create avatars to interact in 'alternative reality' environments; or hook up a web cam and put on a sex show for a lover or stranger. Fetishists found each other in forums and newsgroups and the gap between reality and fantasy started to close. People's dirtiest dreams were coming true on a daily basis: and at the very least, if you couldn't do it, you could almost certainly read about it or watch it online.

Sex for Sale

Sex parties were also entering the mainstream. Fetish and swinging parties became increasingly common, albeit mainly in cities. Designer orgies attracted media coverage, giving 'beautiful people' (with equally beautiful wallets) the chance to live out their fantasies for one night only, at least. For the first time, women were as able to buy sexual pleasure as easily as men.

However, Belle de Jour still attracted outrage in 2005 when she wrote her memoir about being a sex worker. Her honest book showed her selling and enjoying sex – and money – attracting claims that she must be a man – and accusations that it was a fantasy. When she was finally 'outed', it turned out she had indeed been a female sex worker before writing the book – and used her earnings to fund her academic career. The so-called 'fantasy' was a reality. (Today, the UK's National Union of Students reports growing numbers of students are becoming sex workers – and the English Collective of Prostitutes agree that they have seen increased numbers of calls from students since tuition fees were brought in. As such, the fantasy of the middle-class, academic sex worker is most definitely a reality.)

The book was turned into a popular television programme in 2007 and, as her fame grew, Belle de Jour was accused of glamorising sex work, by representing her genuine experience in the industry. It seemed that the trifecta of sex, power and money could only be attained by women in fiction. However, there was an opportunity for sexually open women to cash in once Belle de Jour opened the door. For a while, sex confessionals became the 'next big thing', offering titillation along with true-life stories of being an escort, dominatrix, swinger or simply a sexually active single woman. This ran parallel with a grubby trend for papers to 'out' anonymous sex writers. Female sexual memoirists including Girl with a One Track Mind, Belle de Jour and The Bride Laid Bare all saw their books top the sales charts – and all were later stripped of anonymity against their will. The media might have been open to women sharing their sexual thoughts but not without a generous side dish of slut-shaming.[2]

Suzanne Portnoy, author of *The Butcher, the Baker, the Candlestick Maker* (a frank memoir about a mother in her forties enjoying casual sex and swinging while running her own business) spoke of this slut-shaming in an interview with Kay Jaybee, about the online response to her book. '"Is her name down in the dictionary next to the word 'slut?'" was a typical posting. I skimmed through the three dozen other comments. "One thing this woman will probably never get from a man . . . respect. I hope she regularly gets tested for AIDs." I've never been much of a masochist but somehow felt compelled to check back 24 hours later. Nearly one hundred people had posted responses, all but one echoing the original sentiment, only in increasingly stronger language.' Portnoy was philosophical about the comments. 'It's not just that imagining a middle-aged woman having sex is the discomfiting equivalent of thinking about your parents still "doing it".' It's that a mother having sex is wrong, bad, evil, immoral, scandalous. That this belief is still prevalent, even today, shows the virgin/whore myth is still well

2 Belle de Jour and Girl With a One Track Mind were punished by the press for daring to write about their sexual experiences far more rapidly than Pauline Réage, fifty years after she wrote *The Story of O*. In Belle de Jour's case it took six years before she was 'outed'. In the case of Girl With a One Track Mind, less than three.

and truly alive – and being used as an excuse to stifle women's sexual freedom.

For a while, the book market was awash with stories from women prepared to share their sexual experiences, and in doing so show that women liked sex too. However this trend was short-lived and soon the sex-memoir market died down to be replaced by the 'misery memoir' – but not before it had inspired thousands of 'normal' women to create sex blogs of their own, and share their fantasies, realities or both.

Sex Sells

As women became more open about sex, manufacturers and advertisers rushed to exploit our fears and desires, and in doing so make a profit. By defining 'normal' sexuality, whole new markets were opened up: every new 'disorder' and 'dysfunction' was accompanied by a treatment, pill or product to buy to solve the 'problem'. And by defining 'sexy' in ever more stringent terms, the same was true for the beauty industry.

Referencing Ariel Levy, author of anti-'porn culture' book, *Female Chauvenist Pigs*, Ros Gill says, 'Raunch culture [referring to the media representation of sex] isn't about opening our minds to the possibilities and mysteries of sexuality. It's about endlessly reiterating one particular – and particularly saleable – shorthand for sexiness.'[3] One enlightening survey reported, '*Playboy* addresses men and *Cosmopolitan* addresses women, yet the visual rhetorics of both magazines reflect the male gaze and promote the idea that women should primarily concern themselves with attracting and sexually satisfying men.'[4]

The increasing media focus on celebrity only added to the problem. 'Sex trend' reports became increasingly common in

3 *Spicing It Up: Sexual Entrepreneurs and The Sex Inspectors, Laura Harvey and Rosalind Gill*, 2011, (p.29)
4 *Boxing Helena and Corseting Eunice: Sexual Rhetoric in* Cosmopolitan *and* Playboy *Magazines*, Nicole R. Krassas, Joan M. Blauwkamp, Peggy Wesselink, 2001

women's media – thus influencing what women 'should' and 'shouldn't' fantasise about (or, indeed, do). In the vast majority of cases, these weren't based on genuine research but instead on whatever the female celebrity *du jour* was endorsing (or being judged for) whether with her words or her behaviour.

Spend to Be Sexy

As sex has increasingly featured in women's magazines, we have been pushed to pursue ever higher standards of sexual attractiveness – as dictated by the media – who in turn are all too willing to sell us products to help us conform to the media ideal of sexual attractiveness. Meg Barker says, 'In the last decade or two we've witnessed the invention of cellulite, the seven signs of ageing, muffin tops, bingo wings and, more recently, increased attention on the genitals.' This 'genital beauty' market started with the Brazilian wax, in 1994, rapidly expanding into 'designer vaginas'. By 2009, the American Society for Aesthetic Plastic Surgery reported American women were spending $6.8 million on designer-vagina surgeries, and in 2008, the NHS carried out 1,118 labiaplasty surgeries – an increase of seventy per cent from 2007. Many blame porn for pressures on women to have 'conformist' bodies – and more recently genitals. However, like many other cosmetic treatments blamed on pornography, the Brazilian was actually popularised through the media. Celebrities including Gwyneth Paltrow and Paula Yates raved about the sexual benefits of a hair free pudenda and, as with the rabbit vibrator, after being featured in a storyline on *SATC*, it really shot to fame, attracting an explosion of coverage in women's magazines that still continues to the present day.

Although the Brazilian trend no doubt fed into porn as it became increasingly normalised (with the added 'bonus' that being hairless makes the genitals easier to see in their intimate detail on camera), it was women's magazines who benefited from advertising for waxing salons, plastic surgeons and 'vajazzles'; and as such, they had the most to benefit from in commercialising female genitalia by representing anything other than the pink, 'groomed', 'neat' vagina as ugly. (Indeed, one surgeon claimed his most popular surgery was 'the Barbie' which made a woman's genitalia resemble that of the infamous doll.)

Over time, yet more intimate procedures have sprung up, from labial dyes and anal bleaching to the G-spot injection – which was condemned by numerous doctors and led to one doctor being struck off, after 'effectively amputating' parts of women's anatomy with lasers during the surgery.

For a woman to be sexy, she is expected to spend more time and money than ever before: fake tan, fake teeth, fake tits – women are being urged to buy their way to sexiness, 'because you're worth it'. And the glut of products and services designed to alter our sexuality in some way only looks set to continue. Much as Viagra changed male sexuality by offering the option of 'an unpoppable balloon', now 'female Viagra' is just a few years away. In June 2013, the UK's *Daily Telegraph* reported, 'A Dutch company called Emotional Brain claims that early clinical trials of a new drug, Lybrido, shows promise in the treatment of hypoactive sexual desire disorder (HSDD), defined as a lack of sexual fantasies or desire for sexual activity.' That female sexual fantasies were not thought to exist forty years ago, and now a lack of female sexual fantasies is used to diagnose women as having a sexual disorder just goes to show how much judgement and control is still imposed over our sexuality today. In 1973 people were shocked at the idea that women fantasised at all. Now women with a low libido who don't fantasise are being told that they need a medical cure for their 'condition'. Attitudes to female sexuality may have moved on – but possibly not as much as we might think.

Fifty Shades Freed?

Fifty Shades is the latest series to bring female sexual fantasy to the fore. E. L. James freely admits to sharing her own fantasies through the book – without any idea of the impact it would have. In doing so, she commoditised her fantasies in perhaps the

most lucrative way any woman has to date: the film rights sold
for five million dollars, on top of weekly book sales amounting
to £800,000 per week at the book's peak – before you take into
account any merchandising deals – and she was listed by *Time*
magazine as one of the hundred most influential people of 2012.
E. L. James's fantasies have resulted in the reality of a bulging
bank balance and a lot more power – for her at least.

But it's not just her own reality that James has changed. Since
the book burst onto the scene, sales of jiggle balls and spank
paddles – as featured in the book – have shot up. Kinky-sex
classes have seen a boost (as has interest in erotic writing) and the
sex industry has been rubbing its hands together in glee at the
increase in profits. However, this was not her intent: E. L. James
was simply putting her *Twilight*-inspired ideas down in words.
'Everything about Fifty Shades is fantasy: fantasy man, fantasy
sex. It made me feel slightly less of a pervert when other people
enjoyed the fantasy as well.'[5]

'Less of a pervert': even today, the stigma of fantasy sex still
lingers, echoing that faced by Friday forty years ago. James has
been quoted as saying, 'All female fantasy is derided. It's an
insight into how misogynist the world is.' BDSM may have
replaced mortgages as acceptable dinner party conversation and
the phrase 'mummy porn' might have entered the vernacular, but
that doesn't mean female solo sexuality is completely accepted.
Indeed, the dismissive phrase 'mummy porn' surely reinforces
the fact that people are still shocked at the idea that women –
particularly mothers – fantasise. We still have a long way to go
before a woman sharing her erotic ideas won't automatically be
greeted with slut-shaming, concern for her mental health or cries
that she's a man.

Women are as guilty of this slut-shaming as men. On her site,
Plasticdollheads.wordpress.com, Gemma Ahearne says, 'Female
tweeters admit that they join in slut-shaming/slut-bashing because
they are just glad it isn't them being victimised, and because by
slut-shaming someone else, you are distancing yourself from the

5 Telegraph.co.uk, 7 Dec, 2012

action.' However, our relationships also have a lot to answer for. As one survey respondent, a 39-year-old currently building her coaching practice said, 'I feel that many women have been told what they should do and how they should feel, many of them by their husbands, and especially with regards to sex and sexual feelings. They get out of these relationships and get divorced in their forties and have no clue who they are or what they want. Then one day they have sex with someone amazing and loving and the whole world changes for them. They start dreaming, they open up, they realize what they like and what they don't like and that it's okay to be a sexual person with all of these feelings and emotions. And with that comes the sadness of realizing that they were never really free to be who they are, until now.'

Sexual Freedom?

That this is still an issue, forty years after *My Secret Garden* came out, is a sad sign of women's sexual oppression – how little things have changed. Female sexual fantasy may be more accepted but there is no doubt that it is still judged harshly.

History shows us that, to date, female sexual freedom has been very much 'two steps forward, one step back'. Every time women have put their head above the parapet and been honest about their sexual desires, they've been disbelieved, shouted down (often with accompanying sexual threats) and judged harshly by the 'moral majority' before much time has elapsed. Even now, the threat of further sexual oppression hangs over us, with censorship on the increase and many minorities seeing their voices being silenced, whether through online bullying or, more seriously, assault and murder for something as simple as wearing clothes that are somehow deemed inappropriate.

However, more women than ever before are prepared to face that judgement if the reward is sexual liberation. Girl on the Net said, in a column for the *New Statesman*, 'Keeping our sexual desires secret doesn't make us alluring: it makes us weak . . . Understanding female sexual desire, and having an open and honest discussion about it, gives women more power to shape our entire outlook on sex.'

Every honest sexual confession and erotic story we share helps water down the mainstream, controlling image of sexuality. By sharing their fantasies, the women who contributed to *Garden of Desires* are showing the reality of female sexual desire – and in doing so, shining a light on the myths that are fed to us by society. Though the media would like to pretend otherwise, women's sexuality does not fit into a neat little box: we are diverse, with different libidos, fantasies and realities. Only when that is truly understood, respected and represented will women be truly sexually free.

Part Two

Introduction: Exploring Fantasy

*W*hile the idea that female sexual fantasy was only accepted as existing in 1973 may seem shocking, exploring sexual fantasy *at all* is a relatively new field. Freud is widely credited as bringing the topic out into the open, in the early 1900s, and Kinsey's second report *Sexual Behavior in the Human Female,* published in 1953 added evidence, albeit scant, that many people had active fantasy lives.

Initially, sexual fantasy was viewed negatively: a product of a damaged mind. However, over time, fantasy has become (broadly) accepted as a normal and healthy part of sexuality that can help increase sexual pleasure and offer an opportunity for lovers to deepen their bond.

Now, sex inspires everything from porn films and erotic books to advertising campaigns and computer games. As a result, we are more used to seeing media-created sexual fantasies than ever before. What level this inspires our fantasies or confuses our ideas about what we want by defining what is 'normal' and directing our sexuality is still open to debate.

What is a Sexual Fantasy?

*S*exual fantasies can take many forms. They can be whispers of thoughts that pop in and out of a woman's head or complex narratives that have evolved over time; they can be used for arousal during sex, masturbation, both or neither; they can be used to escape reality with no physical sexual stimulation at all. They can be romantic, clinical, sensual, violent, all of the above or something else entirely. They can be used to inform erotic stories, whether as a form of intellectual exhibitionism or as a means to make money – possibly both. A sexual fantasy can be inspired by reality, can inspire reality or could be something that the woman concerned would never wish to make come true at all. In short, every woman has her own experience of fantasy, defining her own inner world for herself.

Dr Susan Block said, in an article for counterpunch.org, 'Fantasy – the original "theatre of the mind" – makes up a huge portion of human consciousness. Memory, as it filters through the mind's eye, is a kind of fantasy that gazes backward, into the past. Hope, anticipation, fear and ambition are fantasies that look toward the future. Our sexuality is fuelled by fantasies of the past and the future, as well as "pure" fantasies – wild dreams that never happened and that you never really want to have happen – that haunt and stimulate you like a kinky parallel universe. A sexual fantasy can be a long, complicated story, a quick mental flash of erotic imagery or something in between. Whatever form it takes, it arouses your sexual feelings. As such, your favourite fantasy is the G-spot of your mind.'

Similarly, Dr Michael Bader says in his book on fantasy, *Arousal*, 'Sexual fantasies might be likened to microchips in which complex information is reduced and contained in a tiny, nearly invisible space.' The degree to which anyone else is allowed to access these microchips varies from woman to woman. Some women prefer to keep their fantasies to themselves. Others are happy to share anonymously, and some women gain an exhibitionist (or otherwise) thrill out of sharing their fantasies with other people.

How Women Share

When reading the fantasies submitted to Garden of Desires, there were marked differences between the ways in which women reported their fantasies. Some submitted elaborate stories. Some submitted brief outlines. Some simply submitted single words. While every woman is different, and as such may have myriad reasons for the way in which she communicates, it is interesting to note that research has found women who felt guilty about sex and/or their fantasies tended to produce 'more restricted content and shorter fantasies'.[6] This may explain why certain fantasy categories such as group sex attracted shorter responses. Fantasies deemed acceptable by society can be elaborated on. Those that are more taboo are more likely to elicit guilt.

In her paper, 'Women and Erotic Rape Fantasies', Jenny Bivona says, 'Sexual fantasies give women a context for actively exploring their sexuality in a manner that is relatively free from social consequence. In fantasy, there are limitless possibilities for what can be imagined, and because it takes place in the privacy of one's own mind there is little reason for inhibition (Shulman & Horne, 2006).' She adds, 'Ellis and Symons (1990) ... have argued that, since sexual fantasies are relatively unconstrained by social consequences, they may reveal underlying psychological processes, predispositions, and motives more clearly than does overt behavior."

In short, a fantasy allows the fantasiser freedom to exist outside the limitations of the everyday world; and gives her a way to access her subconscious if she so desires.

Where Do Fantasies Come From?

Our fantasies don't necessarily bear any relation to things we'd like to happen in real life, though some people do have 'wish fulfilment' fantasies. However, psychoanalysts suggest that sexual fantasies may be used by the brain to process our emotions and experiences. In *Your Brain on Sex: How Smarter Sex Can Change Your Life*, Stanley Siegel says, 'Among the mind's most

---

6 'Sex fantasies revisited: An expansion and further clarification of variables affecting sex fantasy production,' Diane R. Follingstad Ph.D, C. Dawne Kimbrell, *Archives of Sexual Behavior*, Volume 15, Issue 6, 1986

inventive weapons in the battle for recovery and reconciliation are our fantasies. We create them to counteract anxiety and pain, substituting pleasure where conflict exists.'

However, to assume fantasy is simply a form of therapy is an oversimplification as fantasies can serve multiple purposes – and indeed, different purposes for different people. While some people's fantasies may help them come to terms with any psychological issues they may have, a fantasy can equally be the mental equivalent of watching porn: an easy way to spur arousal, whether by remembering a pleasurable experience or imagining something new. Some women say they enjoy the creative process involved in fantasies, seeing it as a form of adult 'play' – escaping into their imagination much like children's make-believe games.

It is also important to consider the social construction of fantasy. A woman cannot be removed from society. As such, fantasy cannot be removed from reality but may instead be seen as a reflection of women's experience. Changing fantasies reflect changes in society – and the recurrence of certain themes such as submission and exhibitionism may reflect the role that women are expected to play in society. Only an analysis over time can truly show the effect of our reality on our fantasy mind. However, academic studies into sexuality are still judged negatively – if allowed at all – by many universities, and funding is thin on the ground, even if a sexual study gets through the rigors of an ethics committee, and few women keep diaries of the way in which their sexual fantasies change over the years. Luckily, the rise of sex bloggers means that more women are now tracking their desires over time, offering scope for exciting research in the future.

Porn Power?

In examining where our fantasies come from, it would be remiss to omit pornography from the equation. The debate about the level to which pornography affects people's behaviour – if at all – is still ongoing, with the bulk of research focussing on potential negative effects. However, to date, most research suggests that people are only influenced by pornography if it reflects acts and behaviours they already endorse. Violent pornography only encourages violence when shown to people who are already predisposed towards violent behaviour, and a 2000 study into the effects of porn on the way men view women found that the 'amount of exposure to internet pornography *per se* had no detectable relationship with the dependent measures of misogynist attitudes'.[7] That does not mean that pornography has no effect on our sexual behaviour, however. Academic and sex researcher Feona Attwood found that people use porn, 'as a source of knowledge, a resource for intimate practices, a site for identity construction, and an occasion for performing gender and sexuality.'[8] And other research has shown that eroticised use of condoms encourages real-life safe-sex practise.

However, only a handful of women who contributed to *Garden of Desires* directly referenced porn as an inspiration for their fantasies. While some surveys have suggested women form around a third of porn consumers, the female-oriented porn market is still in relative infancy compared to 'mainstream' porn, and consuming porn is far from a universal female experience. It will be interesting to see if women's fantasies change as the stigma regarding women watching porn decreases – and the material made with female viewers in mind grows.

Many more women drew fantasy inspiration from mainstream media. These inspirations are often borne out of childhood, making for an intriguing list. In their earliest fantasies, women admitted to being inspired by: Barbie; Thomas the Tank Engine; Davy Jones; Snoopy; McGyver and Disney princesses. As adults, many were inspired by fantasies within Nancy Friday's books,

7 'Effects of Internet Pornography and Individual Differences on Men's Attitudes Toward Women,' Azy Barak Ph.D, William A. Fisher Ph.D, Sandra Belfry BA & Darryl R. Lashambe BA, *DATb*, 2008
8 'What do people do with porn? Qualitative research into the comsumption, use, and experience of pornography and other sexually explicit media,' Feona Attwood, *Sexuality and Culture*, 2005

referencing *My Secret Garden* and *Women on Top*, though TV and the media still played a part with women fantasising about everyone from music stars including Madonna and David Bowie, to Simon Amstell and Nick Grimshaw (together).

Though pornography may influence some women's fantasies, the diversity of inspiration shows that women don't need to see graphic sex in order to find fuel for a fantasy. The erotic imagination is fertile enough on its own.

Acceptance and Growth

As more people share their desires, a wider range of activities are becoming normalised. This has certainly been the case with BDSM recently: as a result of *Fifty Shades*, people are more open about their sadomasochistic desires. Increased acceptance of the queer community has seen heteronormativity (finally) challenged. Many fantasies submitted to *Garden of Desires* showed gender and sexual fluidity, perhaps supporting the idea that many people need permission from society to admit their desires; as gender and sexual fluidity are increasingly accepted, more people are willing to put their hands up and say, 'me too'. The idea of 'normal' is being increasingly challenged as more people talk openly about their innermost desires.

We may still have a long way to go before sex is accurately represented by society, but the changing nature of people's shared desires, experiences and confessions suggests that society may affect our sexual fantasies – and realities – more than we might like to admit.

When Do Fantasies Start?

The press may be filled with panic stories about 'child sexualisation', but most women who submitted fantasies to *Garden of Desires* reported having active fantasy lives as children – regardless of their current age. That women aged from 18 to

78 said they had pre-pubescent fantasies suggests that this is not a reflection of increasingly 'lax' morals but instead suggests that fantasy starts far younger than we may feel comfortable accepting – or be willing to talk about.

This attitude is dangerous. Pretending that nobody thinks about sex until they are legally 'of age' protects no one. Instead, we need to ensure that children have the correct level of sexual education for their age – including, crucially, consent – to help them deal with any sexual activity they encounter, be it an abusive threat or a consensual relationship. Sadly, many parents shy away from talking to their children about sex, even though it is a major concern.

Partly as a result in some cases, many children have nowhere other than the internet to turn to for solid sex education. This is more true than ever in the UK since it was announced in March 2013 that sex education would not be compulsory in schools (despite Prime Minister David Cameron previously – and rightly – saying in 2007 that sex education 'must mean teaching young people about consent: that "no" means "no". At the moment, this is not even compulsory in the sex education curriculum. This has to change – and it will change with a Conservative government.')

It is a disappointing – and worrying – u-turn. As the responses to the *Garden of Desires* survey clearly show, whatever we may like to believe, our sexual awareness doesn't begin the morning of our sixteenth birthdays. Given that, there seems little justification to deny children accurate and honest sex education, and plenty of evidence to suggest that it would provide social – and economic – benefits to society.

Think of the Children

In admitting that children fantasise, there is a fear that this somehow endorses juvenile sexual activity – or worse, paedophilia – though the childhood fantasies are generally far more innocent and less tainted by societal pressures than most of the adult fantasies submitted to the survey.

As Nancy Friday says, 'Women's earliest fantasies are often a natural extension of daydreaming, make-believe or other childhood play. Role-playing and imaginative play are the tools children intuitively use to make sense of the world and tackle developmental challenges.' (p.52, *My Secret Garden*). She adds, 'A woman's fantasy life is often a reflection of her search for sexual power, pleasure and identity that started in childhood.' (p.77, *My Secret Garden*.)

Children's toys certainly inspired many women's earliest remembered fantasies, with Barbie cropping up in several different ways. Childhood TV shows are a common feature of childhood fantasies, as shown below.

Anon

'I remember fantasies from when I was at primary school, perhaps six or seven. My earliest fantasy was about Thomas the Tank Engine, a character to whom I related strongly. He had a problem – wasp's nest in his engine, I think, or something of the kind – and required extensive help to fix it. I imagined this process in detail while masturbating.'

Anon

'Playing with Barbies, I'd simulate the male and female dolls having sex.'

Robin Sweet

'I was about 9 or 10. I used to play "Barbie brothel" with a friend. Ken was involved. Skipper too. Sometimes the horse. Does that count as a sexual fantasy? If not, then probably something to do with being forced to join a harem and perform sexual favours for the Sultan.'

Heather, 27, heterosexual

'I used to fantasise about my Barbie dolls and teddy bears and doing sexual things with them. I was in the bath with Barbie and she came to life and wanted to walk all over my clit with her little feet so I helped her. Over time, my fantasies have "grown up" and become more amorphous – now sometimes I fantasise about balls of coloured light or adult people.'

Anon, straight, cisfemale, switch, college student, possibly genderqueer

'My fantasies involved acting out stories about my favorite fictional characters after I'd been sent to bed, usually because I couldn't sleep. Han and Leia from Star Wars were an early favorite, though I cooked up come interesting Legend of Zelda, Pokemon, and Harry Potter ones too. Most of said fantasies took place over three episodes: a wedding scene, a sex scene, and a baby-delivery scene. When I was a kid, that was the progression my semi-conservative Christian parents taught: marriage, sex, babies. Somehow, that progression turned into fantasy fuel.'

Ruth

'My earliest sexual fantasy was derived from an Enid Blyton story where a mad teacher (Dame Slap) unjustly spanks some children.'

Cheeky Minx, erotic writer and sensual self-portraitist at lovehate-sexcake.com, hetero redhead (with a healthy dash of bi-curiosity); Eastern European background; single

'My cultural background – and my father's side of the family in particular – is very passionate generally. We love to dance, eat well, engage with the body and its sensual pleasures (in a non-sexual way with each other obviously!). Fantasies were a natural extension of exploring my body and nascent sexuality. And although I've always had a very vivid imagination, I do remember being drawn to my older sister's books and magazines (complete with sealed sex sections) from this age. I do have a strong recollection of flicking through one of her bodice-ripper novels one summer afternoon and stumbling across a section that had my entire body blushing and my mind racing.'

Amber

'I remember my first ever erotic dream – I was about five or six – and it was about a boy called Billy. I didn't even know a boy called Billy back then – it's all very mysterious. My first fantasy was before that dream, and it was inspired by an extreme version of playground kiss-chase we used to play: we were about four or five – very young – and when the boys caught a girl the rest of us would all have to stand around in a circle so that the teachers couldn't see the boys pull down the girl's pants and massage and play with her genitals. I always wanted to be that girl, but although I came close I never got caught, as even then I knew it wasn't acceptable for us to behave like that, and I didn't know if I'd be able to go through with it in reality because I knew it was perceived as wrong. I still desperately wanted to have that experience though, and was ashamed just how much . . . In retrospect it shocks me that we were so young – I'm not exaggerating about our age – and I can only put it down to scenes that some of the other kids had seen in their home lives. Otherwise, how did they know what to do? We were just starting out at school – we didn't know anything yet!'

Deborah, 48, bisexual, cis, never married

My earliest sexual fantasy was something about Donny Osmond's clothes being ripped off while he was onstage. Hilarious, I know. I think I actually drew pictures of this. I was seven and had no art talent. I'm not into Donny Osmond any more.

Morgan

'I remember playing "show me your bits" around age 4 and masturbating around age 6. My first orgasm around age 10 really blew my tiny mind. I think I might have had a wet dream about my best friend at the time and I lying on a hammock in the summer time, then the two boys we each had crushes on laying on top of us and sticking their tongues in our mouths. I only remember this because I wrote it in my diary. Also, possibly Britney Spears' ass.'

Anon, 36, writer, straight, cis, white, born/raised in South Africa but now British, living with a partner, no children, Masters

'I'm not sure if I knew it was sexual – I did, but not with the understanding I have of that now. It was a fantasy setting, a brutal desert landscape, where most of the people were prisoners. Large obelisk structures were used for punishment and the person being punished would be on a ledge, extremely high up, strapped facing inwards. Buttons at the bottom controlled various whips. This very early fantasy continues to shock me.

When I was nine, almost ten, we were staying in a holiday home which had a novel about a girl who got pregnant and suffered resulting horrid fallout. The "sex scene" described her arriving at this chap's house, drenched from the rain, and taking all her clothes off to dry them and getting into the bed to stay warm and covered. The last line of the chapter read, "It took him ten seconds to join her under the covers." The rest of the page was white space. The next chapter opened with her pregnancy. I read that white space more times than I could count and masturbated to it repeatedly.'

Anon, 22, student

'The earliest fantasy I remember is watching *Saved by the Bell* and imagining a different, pornographic plot-line – triggered by Kelly's short shorts!'

Rhiann

'I started fantasising properly at around 12, inspired by boys in bands and the abundance of boobs at my school. Oh and *Charmed*.'

Anon, 29, 'Ph.D student and virgin'

'I can remember having sexual fantasies when I was seven or eight and talking about them with my friends. Sometimes at sleepovers we would tell each other elaborate fantasies even though none of us had a very clear idea of what sex actually entailed.'

Anon, 48, married for 18 years

'I fantasised about Davy Jones of the Monkees, so I know I was very young. I merely thought of him touching me.'

Amy, 36, single, academic

'I would have been about ten when I started fantasising. I remember reading a story in reading class, about a boy who found a magic pebble that granted wishes. He accidentally wished he was a donkey, and the story described the process of his transformation. I remember being aroused (although I didn't know that's what it was at the time) by the thought of him being changed against his will, and specifically I wondered what would happen to his penis. I knew what penises were at that age, but I hadn't really given them any specific thought before.'

Anon, 46, poly, kinky college professor

'My earliest memory is actually of a Snoopy cartoon in which Lucy tickles Snoopy's feet. I whited out the dialogue and wrote in my own, with Snoopy begging her to stop and Lucy refusing.'

Anon, asexual student blogger

'I started fantasizing at seven or eight – although they were rather innocent compared to my current attitudes, but they did have a sexual nature. I remember being fascinated by the idea of a man and a woman being locked up in a cave for winter that was only big enough for the two of them, and what they would end up doing in there.'

Anon, 48, white female, married for 18 years, with two children

'When I was about ten, Patricia Hearst was kidnapped and I heard the news stories of how she was kept in a closet until her captors brought her out for sex. For many years I had vague fantasies of being kidnapped or held in a confined space. I did and still do have fantasies of being trapped somewhere with a desirable partner. However these are basically romantic fantasies in nature, not the orgasmic sort. I also recall seeing a page in a *Playboy* magazine of a white woman being held down by a number of "native" black hands. I think this interested me because she was apparently being held down, but the interracial aspect didn't interest me.'

Sally, 29, single, happy

'I used to find watching old films with women tied to railway tracks hot and as I got older, I found my stepdad's porn collection which was a collection of erotic stories with a fairytale theme. I started reading them because I thought they were normal fairy tales and remember feeling the same "flippy tummy" feeling. As I got older – maybe 8 or 9 – I masturbated to my stepdad's porn when I had the house to myself – I used to feel really excited at the build up, knowing I was going to be reading it soon, and still feel excited anticipation when I buy a new erotic book.'

Anon, 42, blonde, slightly overweight, 18 years with same male partner

'I remember one when I was very little – under 4. I would lay on the bed with my bum in the air and wait for a baker to put a cake on my bum. I remember the feeling mostly – they way I felt it was naughty and only when I was older could I equate that feeling to sexual arousal. I didn't know it felt sexual at the time as I was so young.'

Kalika Gold, erotic writer

'I first started fantasising aged 8 years 11 months. I started off doing comics two weeks before I turned nine. After about two months I started creating little illustrated books. It was my sex drive expressing itself through my mental processes, and expressing itself through writing – the mode of expression I have always been comfortable with, and it was triggered by the *Song of the South* video tape and the Calamity James strip in the *Beano*. My earliest fantasy was boys aged 9 and 10 (I was 8, remember) being spanked, burned, stung or stabbed in their bums. And publicly humiliated.'

Jess, 30, queer/bisexual teacher, white, mental health issues, Ph.D candidate

'I think I was ten when I started having sexual fantasies. I didn't really hit puberty until sixteen, so I wasn't particularly sexual before then, but I had romantic quasi-sexual fantasies then. I remember being fascinated by a scene of sexual threat on a soap opera my babysitter watched (*Days of Our Lives*), where a white woman was surrounded by non-white "tribal" men. (This is at around age ten.) I thought about it a lot, and made up stories about how the woman escaped or was captured or how she interacted with the men (befriending them, oddly).'

Anon, 40, physician, married, no children

'I remember being very young, 6 or 7, and climbing a tree. Suddenly, something felt very good and that started me looking for other ways to find that sensation. I would start fantasizing about ways to get that sensation, usually about being restrained and being forced to have that sensation over and over again. I can't think of any books, magazines, or TV shows that would have triggered it, most just came out of imagination.'

As children, we have far greater fluidity, and can explore fantasies that suit our own unique needs. As we become more aware of sexual norms as adults, it can be easy for sexuality to become influenced and shaped by society. Perhaps the common ground between our childhood and adult fantasies holds the core of our desires? Aged 78, bisexual divorcée Rose still fantasises about an experience from her youth:

Rose, retired but active in the Lions, tenth-grade education, two grown children and grandchildren

'When I was five or six, a few boys in the neighborhood who were about 13 used to have sex with me. I liked it, but we got caught, and I got beaten. Also a dog licked me somewhere around that time. It happened only once, but I can't forget it, and find it a turn on to think about. I also fantasise about those guys and me.'

Anon, bisexual, 26, in an long-term open relationship (with a man).
Artist, BA, blonde hair and blue eyes

'I started fantasising at 10 or 11. I read teen magazines and books my mum bought me and learnt about sex around that time too, and I remember wanting to grow up as quickly as possible so I could be like the girls I looked up to. I think I started out by just imagining kissing boys & what they might say to me during a date/foreplay/sex, but the earliest full-blown fantasy went something along the lines of some older girls at school (sort of sixth form age) locking themselves in a classroom with a load of us year 7 girls (I went to a girls' school) and making us lie on the desks in a row and masturbate so they could watch … It was some kind of "initiation" to join their (imaginary) gang, I think. It was always very clinical, with them sitting there with a clip board and pencil, as if it was an exam. I would masturbate in front of them with the other girls, and none of us would be allowed to leave until we'd come!'

Though most women said they started fantasising between the ages of eight and 11, some found fantasy a little later.

Anon, middle aged female writer, campaigner

'My fantasies started when I was around 12, inspired by *Batman* and *Dr Who*. 1960s *Batman* always had that cliffhanger on the Saturday night, usually with Batman, Robin or both tied up and in peril. I used to play Batman with my brothers … and we all wanted to be Batman, not cause he was the hero, but cause he got tied up. And *Dr Who*, again, of the 1960s, had a lot of mind-control stuff … Very crude, but it piqued some sort of interest that was non-sexual at the time, and became so later.

Going to sleep at night, I kept a sort of mini-narrative going from night to night which involved a long journey through a jungle and all manner of traps along the way. And of course, I always got caught, stripped, left helpless. Yum!'

Anon, I'm genderqueer (androgyne), currently struggling to transition and am attracted to those who are not my gender (namely, binary gender presentation). I'm a masochistic sub who likes BDSM all the way up to far more extreme fetishes like gore and snuff.

'My explicitly "sexual" fantasies started quite late, about 15–16. When I was younger (about eight or nine) my burgeoning attraction to female bodies horrified me, so I avoided thinking about sex for as long as I could. I do remember when I was very, very young – under five – I would get sleep paralysis and wake up unable to move, but feeling good about it and enjoying it; and before falling asleep, pretending to be unable to move to try and recreate the feeling. Looking back at it, it seems sexual, but I doubt it was at the time. Blue skin was always a trigger. Cartoon characters, monsters in video games, South Asian art. Depictions of helplessness, too – damsels in distress, that sort of thing. Generally, anything that turned me on – whereas now I can knowingly wink or nudge my partner, or enjoy it and remember it for later, back then I would just scuttle off to my room to be confused for a while.

In my earliest fantasy I was a lady thief, breaking into a wizard's palace to steal one of his Tomes Of Power; of course, he caught me in the act. He cast a spell on me that prevented me from moving anything below my neck, taunted me for a while, moved closer, and . . . then it petered out, because I was too young to really know what came next.'

Anon, 64 year old mother of two

'I started fantasising at around 13. I imagined having a man suspended above me by a series of ropes and pulleys so that he could impregnate me.'

Anon

'My first fantasy, in my early teens, was about being tied up, naked, and covered in draped fabric above the waist, being examined in the area of my genitals by a group of people, one of whom owned me. I don't know how old I was, but I did not have pubic hair. I don't think I was aware of this as a particularly sexual fantasy – I didn't masturbate till I was in my twenties, despite engaging in BDSM sexual play (stylised violence, objectification, massaging breasts, no genital touching) with a female friend at about 14 and losing my heterosexual virginity at 17.'

Anon, 40, single mom of two

'I believe I was about 14 or 15 when I started fantasising. I think it was triggered by some of the movies that my parents would bring home for us to watch. We watched *The Last American Virgin, Porky's* and *The Best Little Whorehouse in Texas.*'

Anon, 18, Asian university student

'I remember fantasising as a teenager – about 14 or 15 – about having sex with a guy I liked at the time. He would kiss my lips tenderly at first, and then harder. I respond in kind, and we would fall onto the bed, making out passionately. I guess I didn't really think about whether I had clothes on or not, so I'm just going to assume that we were already undressed.

He runs his lips from my mouth to my ear, sensually, kissing me in that spot behind my earlobe. He moves down my neck, as I moan softly and writhe. From there, he trails his mouth down in between my breasts. He stops, and then proceeds to take my breasts into his hands. He massages and plays with them for a bit while kissing my lips, my face and my neck again. Then, he licks and sucks one of my nipples; I am moaning louder at this point.

He moves to lavish attention on my other nipple, with his hands stroking up and down my stomach. He continues his sensual seduction down my body, inching his lips down my stomach, his hands stroking my waist and hips.

Since I didn't know about oral sex at the time, I thought that he would just kiss back up my body and we would make out. He eases himself into me, and we would slowly and romantically make love.

That's as far as my imagination went. Since then they've gotten more detailed, included oral sex, toys, BDSM, different positions, different locations. They also include what I would do to him.'

No matter what age our sexual fantasies start, many women have fantasised long before they have any form of sexual encounter. But with every sexual – and indeed, life – experience comes potential for those fantasies to adapt.

Do Fantasies Change?

Though some people claim that sexual fantasies are static, this runs contrary to the idea that they reflect our inner state – assuming, of course, that people change over the course of their lifetime. The responses to the *Garden of Desires* survey would certainly suggest that there is variation in women's fantasies over the course of their lifetime – and even on a day-to-day basis.

Anon, 34 year old Swedish female

'My first fantasies were triggered by Ursula in *The Little Mermaid*, of all things. During 'Poor Unfortunate Souls', she shakes her breasts. I remember finding that just really . . . interesting. And feeling a little embarrassed that I liked seeing it. I knew that was not something I should be talking about. I wished I had large breasts. I think the fantasy went on from that, but it was the breasts that were the constant feature. Over time my fantasies have become more elaborate, of course. Also, now that I have breasts, I don't really fantasise about having larger ones.'

Joy, 27, bisexual, about to start Ph.D

'I was fascinated by sex from an early age and found any form of gender-bending exciting. From when I was 12 til 17 many of my fantasies were inspired/shaped by the *Rocky Horror Picture Show*. My first ever sex-dream (at age 5) was inspired by a cartoon (the 3 little pigs short at the end of *Dumbo*) and a school play (Jack and the Beanstalk) but was about being helpless/submissive – it also included spanking. An early conscious fantasy involved multiple male partners at around 11 or 12. I now have a range of almost exclusively female oriented fantasies. BDSM is still a big part of sexual fantasy for me – with a large focus on power-play. Most if not all of my fantasies are related to my partner now.'

Anon, 26, bi, heteromantic, polyamorous, sub-nomadic female educator with a handful of lovers in various cities and a BA in English

'My first fantasies were inspired by choose-your-own-adventure books. I noticed around age 11 that if I pressed on my vagina while reading "my" adventure, that it felt "more real". By 12, I was imagining my own adventures while masturbating, and the adventures became sexual. The earliest sexual fantasy I remember is being tied onto a table while a man touched my body, including my vagina. This might be related to my first orgasm happening while reading a choose-your-own-adventure book that ended with me being wrapped up like a mummy alive and put on display. Just the touching happened – I hadn't seen many penises, nor had I any idea how they were used. This fantasy also lacked romance; there was no kissing. I didn't associate sexual pleasure with the romance I saw in the media at that time.

My fantasies changed over time in some ways. They progressed through my teen years to being tied down and having multiple people use me for sexual pleasure at once. I've also fantasised about being "forced" to give oral sex (the reality is that I enjoy giving it, so it's never really forced, but the idea of a man taking control is exciting), or performing oral sex while the man does another task, such as playing video games or working on the computer, so that I'm not the centre of attention, just a source of pleasure while he does something else. I have also fantasised about forced anal, which I in real life usually do not enjoy and insist on very clear, sober consent for. As a teen, I began fantasising about women, which still happens from time to time, but much less often than fantasies about men.

My most recent fantasy was about having PIV (penis-in-vagina) sex with a new co-worker. This is pretty standard for me when I'm attracted to someone new and I have enough interactions with them to think it might go somewhere. I imagined taking him into my bedroom, going through the awkward moment where we both know we're up there to "do something", but unsure of how to start, then just kissing him to get started, taking clothes off, and lying back on the bed with him on top. I tend to fantasise with the other person being in control still, even if the sex itself is pretty tame, and often the fantasy ends with me rolled over on my stomach while my partner enters me from behind to finish.

Currently, I often fantasise about one of my lovers unzipping his pants and asking for oral without even bothering to undress or perform any kind of foreplay with me. He might take off my shirt to play with my breasts during this, and if I'm lucky, he might take off his own shirt so I can look up at his (very nice) abdominal muscles, chest, and face while I'm on my knees. Then he'll have me stand, and lift me to toss me onto my back onto a bed or couch, quickly removing my pants and underwear to "return the favour" for a short time before taking off his own pants and entering me. The fantasy often ends with him turning me over to have anal sex with me, which I wouldn't do in real life due to his size, but the fantasy of him doing what he wants even the possibility of it hurting me a bit excites me. I often focus on the idea that he is lubricated from being inside my vagina, and have detailed visuals in my head.'

Anon, female heteroflexible married business-owner, 49, one child, submissive and play BDSM games in secret with a number of doms

'When younger I probably augmented my core diet of BDSM fantasies with vanilla fantasies about film stars etc, but I doubt that I would have "got off" on these. Over time have incorporated more activities into my basic repertoire, but there is a core of sure fire fantasies I retain still from adolescence. I have some quite subtle ones now, and some very complicated ones involving large groups of people, weird steam punk machines etc.'

Robin

'I think my fantasies have become more varied and better informed over time. I like historical settings and my knowledge of social history is much better these days than when I was ten. I think during my teens they became progressively more extreme as I explored the possibilities of my imagination and pushed the limits of my sexual interests. Then I reached a natural level for me and they've stayed at that level probably since my early twenties.'

Anon, 40, heterosexual bi-curious professional graduate. Chinese, from Hong Kong. Australia-resident, three kids

'I remember touching and masturbating before I even knew what sex was, I'd have fantasies of being taken, kidnapped against my will, and that would trigger a response in me. But proper sexual fantasies with intercourse came later when I was around 11, when I found my parents' erotic-fiction collection. The first stirrings of sexual feeling were just associated with being wanted and desired so much that I was taken against my will – I still remember it, it was a damsel-in-distress fantasy, taken by a villain, restrained and eventually rescued. It wasn't even sexual in nature at the time but that changed as I learnt more about sex.

Strangely enough, the essential theme hasn't changed over time, but as my sexual experience grew more garnish is added to the fantasies, there is a strong sense of power and control by the men, and this helplessness and submission on my end. Over time, there has been an increase in the number of men, and the perversity of the sexual act involved. While at the beginning it was mere suggestion, it continued onto extensive and varied sexual behaviours.

Today I fantasied about being taken by two men. It didn't matter who they were, just two strangers that found me attractive and irresistible, taking me in turns and spilling their seeds inside me. The idea of being filled completely with their penis and semen was extremely arousing.

My favourite fantasy is one of being abducted by an admirer, blindfolded, and restrained. Slowly being introduced to the pleasures of the flesh. He'd teach me slowly, how to enjoy all my body, use all my orifices, with objects or other men if he pleased. And I think underneath it all, his control frees me from being responsible. And I'd be free to enjoy, uninhibited, whatever my body takes pleasure in.'

Anon, 39, lesbian, lifelong sufferer of severe depression and agoraphobia, unmarried, no kids. Combination of emotionally abusive (all female) partners, and medication taken to treat mental health crisis have lead to anorgasmia

'Growing up with an awareness of my sexual orientation long before I had a word for it, and having no experience of being LGBT . . . I was mostly dealing with knowing I was different, and picturing women – often teachers – in a proximity situation, but not necessarily a sexual one, since I had no understanding whatsoever of female on female sexuality. I have no memory of when those thoughts turned sexual. For a long time the mere thought of romantic contact with women was sufficient without engaging sexual activity.

Access to erotic fiction triggered my early fantasies. First heterosexual, but only stimulated by the woman's experience and response, and coping with an unwanted masculine presence by mentally editing it out. A lot of this came from the "letters" pages of adult magazines belonging to a brother. The pictures didn't do much for me (and still don't to this day) but reading about how women became aroused and experience sex was a trigger.

My fantasies have changed significantly over the years. It helps to have at least some understanding of how women love women, rather than borrowing a masculine proxy in early experiences with reading erotic fiction. To going on into my own sex life and beyond. My most recent fantasy

INTRODUCTION: EXPLORING FANTASY

was a mild DS game with another woman, leading to her using a toy on me.

Anon, 31, queer boi

'I'm a masochist but I don't usually fantasise about being beaten so much as the aroused state I'm usually in afterwards. My most recent fantasy involved a school headmistress bringing each of her charges to orgasm while they sat on her desk in turn, before inserting an inflatable ball that they would have to keep in for the entire day.

In the past I found it very difficult to have sex with men because it was always filtered through my own misogynistic fantasies. Now my fantasies anticipate enjoyably what I might do with a female play partner or recall something we've done together, and I no longer feel ashamed of the nature of my fantasies. In a world of queer sex they lose their anti-feminist slant entirely.

Since realising I'm gay I really enjoy fantasising and can enjoy a range of erotic ideas, from the gentle and loving to the sadistic. Until I was 28 I could only come thinking about a man forcing a woman, and I would identify with the man. I couldn't make myself come without a vibrator until I started fantasising about lesbian encounters and then the men dropped out of my fantasies altogether as I realised *I* wanted to fuck women.

I wish I'd realised that the complete absence of interest in men's bodies but the fixation on women's mouths and cunts wasn't because I objectified women but because I just really wanted to be with women!'

Summer, 35, bisexual female, in an open marriage to a man, poly-amorous, homeschooling mom to 4 children, Masters degree

'I remember fantasising with my Barbies that they were captured and forced to be pleasured sexually, starting around age 10. I also fantasised that my stuffed animals were boyfriends, that we went to the prom, and then had sex. I began fantasising about being intimate with a woman once I became an adult. I also had more fantasies about having sex with two men.'

Nicola

'I read a lot about puberty, early-teenage body changes etc. This naturally lead to a curiosity about what my body was preparing for ... then to the Mills and Boon section of the secondhand book store. My earliest fantasies were very much influenced by the romance novels I was reading in my early teens, it was about a tall handsome stranger, who falls deeply and wildly in love with me – after sweeping me off my feet we make tender love and he takes my virginity in a strong yet gentle way. I come over and over again.

Over time, the narrative of my fantasies has become far less full, or romantically grounded. I will fixate on a single act, smell, touch or person and very narrowly fantasise about just that. I am far more attuned to the subtleties of the act than creating an in-depth story.

Anon, 23, female European/Maori woman from New Zealand. I live with my partner and have an honours bachelors degree

'My earliest fantasies involved meeting a lover in the middle of the day when I am meant to be at work, etc. and exploring somewhere like an abandoned warehouse before having sex here. I fantasised that I would be blindfolded and my lover would take his time pleasing me, building tension before having sex.

Over time, some have become more realistic, as in meeting a stranger at a bar and fucking with wild abandon at his apartment or mine, through to other elaborations of my earliest sexual fantasy, of being blindfolded/tied and being seduced and teased before fucking. I recently dreamed that I was having a threeway with two other girls. There was sexy lingerie and I was being dominant of the other girls getting them to touch and finger each other before I joined in.

My favourite fantasy is that I am being fucked by a group of men, maybe two or three. They are using me as their sexual slave, tying me up, blindfolding me and fucking me. Every time I have this fantasy I imagine myself enjoying it.'

Anon, 36, writer

'My fantasies change continually and my favourites also vary. I distinguish between several key kinds. One kind is "never-events" – things I have no desire to pursue in real life, don't actively pursue in my imaginary life, but find intensely erotic in the throes of arousal. These tend to feature extreme objectification. Another kind is "fads" – a particular trope that I'll fantasise about for a while, then that phase passes. For some time at university, the teacher-pupil dynamic seemed very erotic (with me being the virginal pupil), but now it leaves me cold. The third and main kind is the realistic "story" fantasy, which is mostly what I put myself to sleep with. This is based on real-life desires that I'd like to pursue but don't intend to (for instance, an affair) or actively want to happen (furtherance of a current relationship/interest). They are meticulously realised and all the usual real-life constraints are considered and addressed within the set-up. I fantasise them almost in real time, though not quite obviously, and play them out in my mind extremely slowly. Often I'll fall asleep part of the way through, and continue the next night (overlapping from where I left off), so a good one will last several nights. My fantasies (and desires) also change across my cycle – the dirtiest, darkest, most extreme ones being in the run-up to my period. This is also when my desire is most impersonal – I don't want all the touchy-feely gazy stuff then, I want the hard dark intense stuff.'

Anon

'Themes within my fantasies have remained the same since early puberty – these include objectification, bondage, submission, ownership, non-consensual touch (medical type play, sexual contact), object insertion, body modification, slave training, enjoyment of the rape/sexual assault.

After a period of self-judgemental puritanism that lasted most of my twenties, I've become much more comfortable with my fantasies and much more realising of the fact that fantasy and reality are not the same thing. I can think whatever I want in my own head, that's not the same as reality. My fantasies may – along with many other factors – influence and inform my interactions with other people, but only to the extent I choose to allow. '

Anon

'I started fantasising at around 10 or 11, I think. Maybe younger. I can't recall specific triggers for fantasies. I remember playing "doctor" once when I was a young girl with one of my friends. A lot of looking, but we touched ourselves and not each other. I was in elementary school. I think it only happened one time and it didn't change our friendship. I used to imagine doing that more, I liked it and the thought of it always got me excited.

In high school my fantasies were just about my current boyfriend or someone I was interested in and it was always just sex, wondering about what they were like. When I was in my twenties it seemed to amp up in intensity. I was unhappily married and I used to fantasise about sex with other men, and in them the sex was always much different from what I was used to. Less polite, more engaged, more exciting.

Now that I'm 39 I feel like they're about a lot of different things, using objects to masturbate with in front of others, imagining sex in different situations, being sprayed with water until I have an orgasm. I also don't feel guilty for fantasising any more, which may be why they are more varied.'

Jess, 26, white single American

'I do know that I began having sexual fantasies and masturbating at an early age. Although I did not know what I was really doing at the time. I did not know these were 'sexual fantasies' or even that it was something that other people did. I would fantasise about playing "doctor" together with the little boys from my neighbourhood. I would also sometimes fantasise that they had "captured" me and were inspecting me. In my fantasies they would restrain me somehow and touch my body in different places with their mouths. I had no knowledge of oral sex (or sex at all), and didn't get exposed to that until my teenage years, so I'm not sure where the idea came from. I just imagined them doing that and in my fantasy it felt good. I did this while letting the water from the bath faucet run over my clitoris (which back then I had no idea what that was). I hope I'm not a weirdo!

As I have gotten older, learned what sex was, and have had sexual relationships with boyfriends, my fantasies have become more informed. Obviously I know what both oral sex and penetration are now, and know what they actually feel like. But my fantasies do still tend to revolve around being restrained, with an element of being dominated, but never in an overly violent way.'

As women learn more about and accept their sexuality, their fantasies seem to reflect these changes. The professor whose childhood fantasies revolved around tickling Snoopy said, 'In my 20s my fantasies became more violent and involved with SM. Once I started actually engaging in kink, the fantasies became more realistic, less "kidnapped slave forced to have sex 20 times a day while tied to a stake" and more a ramped up version of the things I was doing in real life.' Another survey respondent said, 'My fantasies have become a lot less innocent and a lot more perverted as I've become more experienced. Normal sex doesn't do the trick for me at all any more.'

Perhaps fantasies offer some people a way to track their sexual progression through life, offering a way to steer and mentally document their way through their sexual experiences. Or perhaps they change simply because, over time, we want to explore something new.

Why Do We Fantasise?

Freud initially believed that sexual fantasies were repressed memories of childhood abuse, later changing his opinion and deciding they were unconscious fantasies instead. Though some of the women who submitted surveys to *Garden of Desires* said that abuse had influenced their fantasies, many more – particularly those with submissive fantasies – were adamant that no traumatic experiences had influenced their desires.

In his fascinating study of sexual fantasy, *Arousal* (Virgin Books, 2003), Dr Michael Bader says, 'While I have come to reject many assumptions of psychoanalysis about the nature of sexual desire, one fact is irrefutable. Psychoanalysis, more than any other theory, has helped us appreciate the power of the unconscious mind and informed our attempt to unlock the meaning of sexual excitement.' He continues, 'Our feelings about the how, where and why of sexual excitement are often a window into the deepest levels of our psyches and the deepest sources of our suffering and pleasure.'

It certainly makes sense that a woman's fantasies give a level of insight into what she values, the way she feels about herself and possibly her sexual desires. Some women fantasise about real-life sexual encounters with a current or previous partner, whether as a way to feel close to a partner, cling on to a relationship that is long gone, or simply provide masturbatory fodder. And some women consciously use their fantasies to take control of their insecurities. As Dr Susan Block says at Counterpoint.org, 'Your sexual fantasies are keys that unlock the doors of your repressed personal history. They can help you to cope with your real-life problems, just as your dreams do. But they tend to do it when you're awake.'

Anon

'Being shy and inexperienced, I think that I fantasise about situations in which I have no control because it is a way I can overcome that shyness. I don't have to worry about what to do because I have no choice. It's kind of relaxing. They can also provide a sexual surrogate. I find it difficult to meet single men who I am attracted to so at the moment they substitute for sex and help me achieve orgasm while masturbating.'

Anon, asexual student blogger prone to wild flights of fancy with hair style and colour

'My fantasy is being tied down nude, unable to move or to touch anything, while a man performs oral sex on me.

Everything is done for me, so that I don't have to make a decision or feel under pressure. The man is older than I am. With my asexuality, it feels like a conflict between what I know I am and how I believe I should behave. I know and understand that I can fantasise as an asexual but I feel that I shouldn't – that if I am unable to be sexually attracted to people, then I should not have sexual feeling. It's crap, but there you go.'

However, even this does not allow for the full complexity of female fantasies. Though some women may use their fantasies as a form of therapy – or be inspired to seek therapy by their fantasies – other women use their fantasies as a way to 'try out' a new sexual idea, in a safe and non-threatening way. Sexual fantasy also offers a form of 'outercourse': sexual play without penetration or fluid exchange – making it a form of safe sex. Some say that the rise of BDSM in the 1990s was as a result of the HIV/AIDS crisis – people searching for new ways to enjoy sexual play with less risk of infection. Perhaps women's fantasies offer them similarly safe scope to play. And of course, fantasy also offers an easy way to sate the libido.

Cheeky Minx is a 'writer of erotica, sensual self-portraitist; authoress of the site Love Hate Sex Cake (lovehatesexcake.com)'. She says, 'Even though my sexual desire has always been *very* healthy, around 2008 my libido hit the roof. It was all I could think about. At the time I was having a gorgeous fling with a much younger man and even our sex (as well as masturbation) wasn't enough. There was a real need to work through some of this desire through writing (and shortly after, self-portraiture).'

Basically, fantasies can serve many functions. As a 48-year-old mother of two says, 'I fantasise to have orgasms, to relieve boredom. Sometimes in the middle of a boring meeting at work, for example, I'll spin fantasies about the people at the conference table all starting to have sex with each other. Sometimes I use them to lull myself to sleep.'

However, they seem to largely serve a practical – sexual – purpose. Almost all the women who submitted their surveys to

Garden of Desires said they use their fantasies to increase their chances of orgasm during masturbation and/or sex.

Anon

'Fantasies are an aid to masturbation and inspiration for what I want to do in real life – I try to find the core of the fantasy. It's really fun to tell my husband my crazy fantasies, I'm totally embarrassed, but we can laugh about them, and when he teases me about them later, I get totally turned on.'

Anon

'Fantasies make me feel better. They help me relieve the stress of everyday life and I can't function without orgasming at least three times a week.'

Anon

'I use fantasies to get aroused or to increase arousal when masturbating. I do use a significant amount of my stray thoughts for thinking about sex as well. That's either when I'm very busy, angry and/or impatient (but more abstract, it just really makes me horny, which usually just makes me more annoyed), or for comfort.

I call up fantasies quite frequently on toilet breaks because toilets are usually intensely private and separate spaces, safe spaces. It is comforting to think of sex then (a very specific kind, always tied in with an established or emerging strong emotional attachment). I think in that regard, sexual fantasies help me get through the day; if I don't have this kind of loving support from a partner myself, then I can at least imagine (and thereby, feel) scenes in which that happens. It's a bit like seeing something beautiful and being reminded that life is not all sad and dark and frightening. Even if it's not "real", I can imagine emotions into being, and because that happens in my head, I can feel them, too.

I sometimes think I won't ever feel love, affection and sexual attraction to anyone ever again (this happens to me extremely rarely). I want to feel these things for somebody and have them felt "back", but I have no concept of ever making that happen, so I guess "fantasies" are a sort of surrogate support.'

Anon

'My fantasies are useful for sexual arousal, psychological/emotional self-awareness, and processing stress. I've noticed increased stress results in more extreme and violent fantasies so now sometimes proactively use more extreme fantasy to dispel stress. My evolving sexual fantasies, together with other life events of the last twenty years: six to seven years of therapy in several tranches, entering sex work ten years ago (something that I found really positive), a wider and less repressive friendship, (to some degree) changing social attitudes, learning more about sexuality and social constructions of sexual behaviour – have enabled me to act out, to some extent, my sexual fantasies (excluding those that are morally wrong – for example, non-consensual – and rightly illegal). I look forward to further exploring this as I have the opportunity, within SSC/RACK boundaries. Increased acceptance of my fantasies has lead to greater self-acceptance generally. Increased self-awareness has resulted in greater comfort communicating about sexual matters. I am more comfortable exploring fantasy play with others (both in my sex work and my private life). It's made me more sexually adventurous and happier.'

Anon, 30, mother of two and 'homemaker with disabilities'

'My mind has to be turned on as well as my body for me to be able to orgasm. If he is giving me oral sex for example, there is not much mental stimulus happening except knowing what he is doing but this isn't enough. Fantasising during times like this helps me to reach orgasm.'

That women use fantasies to climax is hardly surprising given the 'orgasm gap' that exists between men and women. *The Social Organization of Sexuality: Sexual Practices in the United States* (2000) found that heterosexual women have one orgasm to every three that their partner has, while *The Handbook of Sexuality in Close Relationships* (2003) found that women who have sex with women have many more orgasms than heterosexual women – almost as many as heterosexual men. Orgasm is rarely easy for most women through penis-in-vagina sex, but fantasy allows many women to take control over closing the orgasm gap for themselves: not only can they imagine sex on their own terms during masturbation, but during sex, their mind can provide stimulation that penis-in-vagina sex alone cannot. As a woman who identified herself as 'J' said, 'It's a guaranteed efficient pathway to satisfaction: to climax and get the most relaxation and enjoyment out of sex.'

Sharing Fantasies

*F*antasy can also bring relationship benefits – and be used to cope with issues within a relationship. Sharing fantasies has been shown to help some couples feel closer, helping build intimacy. Xcite books founder, Hazel Cushion, says, 'Many sex therapists recommend Xcite Books, especially the short-story collections because they help to introduce new themes and ideas into a relationship. I think reading or listening to erotica really helps a relationship keep fresh and many couples find it more stimulating than watching porn.'

Many relationship therapists recommend fantasy sharing – and indeed, reading *My Secret Garden* – as a way to help couples deal with libido differences and intimacy issues. Leading physician, and specialist in sexual health, Dr Malcolm VandenBurg says, 'Erotic literature can be empowering and helpful to marriage. It may be educational to teach safe sex, avoiding infections, teaching about BDSM contracts and safe words. I have used Nancy Friday's books *Women On Top*, *Men in Love* and *My Secret Garden* for about twenty years to help women feel comfortable with their fantasies and rid them of guilt as a path to recovery.'

To Share or Not to Share?

Several contributors to *Garden of Desires* use fantasies in this way. One said, 'My husband and I have been together for 16 years. We have a family and from the outside probably look like the "normal" couple. But we have a very active sex life (every day if not twice a day, except at "that" time of the month) and think that it is because we talk about what we want, what we like and we are constantly in love with each other. We don't swing or partner-swap. Communication is the key. Looking back now we wished that we were this open with each other when we were younger!'

However, while some women who fantasise about sex choose to share their fantasies with a partner, many choose to keep their fantasies to themselves, often to protect their partner's ego, or because they feel embarrassed about their desires. 33-year-old Robin says, 'A recent partner and I talked a lot about our sexual fantasies and needs and I made it clear in those conversations that if we weren't having kinky sex then I would probably fantasise about it during sex. Before "coming out" as kinky, though, I always fantasised during sex (which was always vanilla) and never told my boyfriend or anyone else!'

A number of women thought that fantasising during sex reduced intimacy, distanced them from a partner or was 'cheating': 'If I'm not sharing fantasies with my partner/s, it's because the sex isn't very good; my preference is to share to turn us both on more.'

It can also help avoid other issues. As a thirty-five-year-old 'bisexual genderqueer' respondent says, 'My partner is more likely to fantasise about specific people. I am more likely to fantasise about specific scenarios. So sometimes I feel like that doesn't match up and he would like me to say more about people I'm attracted to.'

There is no right or wrong when it comes to sharing fantasies. Some people find it useful, bonding and intimate. Others prefer their fantasies to remain in their head. Only the individuals involved in a relationship can decide whether it's something that's right for them – and if they want their fantasies to come true.

Anon, I'm 31, have a doctorate, think bisexual is the best word available to describe my sexuality but also think it's a dumb word. I'd prefer to just be 'sexual', or maybe 'omnisexual' because it sounds playful and open-minded. I'm single, though I've mostly been in relationships over the past 13 years – usually lasting between 2 and 4 years each. Always guys, though I have slept with a woman once too. I'm white.

'I've only had one partner who asked me about my fantasies and I actually found it a little draining. It's nice to have sovereignty over your fantasies, and not have to open your head for your lover to peer inside. On the other hand it's also nice to feel able to share fantasies, if and when you want to.

With the one guy who I did this with – he was excited by them, but I felt I always had to provide him with a certain sort of fantasy (i.e. my fantasies about women) and I found I resented that a bit. It felt like he was taking my fantasies away from me – appropriating them, and demanding more at a rate I wasn't able to supply.

I'm afraid my fantasies will scare my lovers. Telling a guy that I'm imagining I'm a guy, having sex with him – isn't going to go down well with many Kiwi men.'

Do We Want Our Dreams to Come True?

*W*hile some women are happy to keep their fantasies in their imagination alone, others use them to inform real life sex.

Anon, 25, heterosexual, Anglo-Saxon (New Zealander raised in Australia with European heritage). Single medical student

'I've had fantasies about being restrained or forced into sex. However, once I was restrained and having no control scared me so I don't fantasise about that. Another time I was sexually assaulted while I was sleeping and woke up during the act, which stopped me from ever fantasising about unwilling sex again. Other experiences have been positive though – I've fantasised about threesomes (2 girls 1 guy and 2 guys 1 girl) and those have come true, and I've enjoyed those experiences. Multiple sex partners is something I've always fantasised about and enjoy in real life. Overall I feel OK about sexual fantasies coming true because even when it goes badly, I learn something about my sexuality and I'm good at accepting the silver lining rather than dwelling too much on the bad parts (although I make sure I deal with those as well).'

Anon, 39, reference assistant, Florida, single.

'I am getting to a point where I want to tell partners what I fantasise about so they know how to treat me in bed. I also want to know about them so I can make as much of their fantasy life a reality as possible. I think women deserve to have what they want in the bedroom and not always be held back by some dork who's really uncomfortable with a woman who actually has a brain and has sexual feelings.

Real life is starting to influence my fantasies. I met someone, two people actually, who I can be truthful with about what I want. I am more attracted to one of them and so I've been talking to him about how I feel, what I want, what makes me excited. The first time we had a sexual experience he made one fantasy come true, right away, and he did it without asking permission. That was huge for me. It made me feel comfortable with him on many different levels and now I know I can tell him the truth about what I want without judgement.

The last conversation I had about this with the person I'm interested in was very positive, the most positive I've ever had and it was the most comfortable I've ever been sharing something like that. We shared, he told me one of his, I told him one of mine. The best part was that we were laughing and holding hands in the dark, and we both really loved what the other was saying. It definitely made me feel much more confident in telling him what I want in my sex life and gave me a pretty good indication that he is more than willing to keep me satisfied and happy.

I made some of my partner's fantasies come true and it was amazing. The emails, texts and looks I got from him over the next few days brought us closer together, made us both feel excited, and God, it was so worth it. Can't wait to do that again for him. He was really grateful and happy about it, and for me, just seeing his face and expression was enough for me to get really excited.'

Anon

'I've pretended to be a sex doll, or turned the lights out and let my partner imagine that I was someone else he was attracted to. I was in a long-term relationship and was very open to trying new sexual experiences. I voice my fantasies with my lovers, and they usually want to fulfil them as long as they are ones that I want fulfilled in reality. For the most part, I get positive responses and/or questions about "what that does for me," which to me shows a desire to understand my sexuality better. It brings me closer to my lovers and I have positive associations with fantasies because of it. If we all were more open about our fantasies, and knew more about one another's fantasies, we'd be less scared of our own and more understanding of the diversity in sexuality around us.'

Anon, Bi potentially poly Black female Christian Adult Life Skills and Sexuality Researcher and Educator

'I've made a fantasy come true and had a man and woman individually join my relationship, one a male friend of his and one a female friend of mine – she looked like one of the women from *National Geographic*. [This contributor's earliest fantasies were inspired in part by pictures in *National Geographic* magazine.] It's was great having his friend join us! Zero regrets. As well as using various toys, he enjoyed using one on me in front of his friend to show him that female ejaculation is a possibility. Loved it!'

Robin

'During my twenties I felt driven to explore my interest in BDSM and had lots of experiences on that scene, trying everything I encountered that appealed to me. I felt as though it was something I needed to do to understand myself. Through those experiences I met a few amazing people who in many ways made me who I am today – showed me what the possibilities were for me and my life, not just sexually but in so many other ways. I have always felt very fulfilled (and orgasmic) as a result of making my fantasies come true. For me, fantasy is a very poor second to living a BDSM lifestyle in reality.'

Louise, Erotic writer

'I've made most of my fantasies come true. Group sex was mostly disappointing though I do have fond memories of a couple of FFM experiences. I've tried most BDSM I wanted to and have loved it though it depends on my mood – sometimes I just want cuddly vanilla sex and BDSM is a huge turn off. I've had sex with men, women, both at the same time, anal sex and been watched during sex (way less arousing than I thought it would be). I made a porn film with my partner too but that moved it from fantasy into reality and ceased to turn me on because the technical stuff – making sure the camera was working properly and filmed us well – got in the way. However, watching the film back together was a turn on that made me feel extra close to my partner.'

Anon

'Since my husband and I started exploring our fantasies together, our sex life has improved a TON. We always had good sex, but it got really boring and I knew there were other things that would turn me on. Now, we are really open and honest with each other which has positively effected our communication in other areas. We are also generally more affectionate and happier now.'

Anon

'I am a lot more sexually driven than my boyfriend and initially he didn't really understand where I was coming from. So I talk with him often about what I'm feeling and thinking and he does the same. Sometimes he looks at me very strangely but he is willing to try most fantasies.'

However, several women who'd made their fantasies come true reported that in doing so the fantasy lost its power.

Some women feel pressured to make their fantasies come true after sharing them with a partner, and many women report that they have no desire to turn fantasy into reality or have had disappointing experiences in doing so. Catherine has lived out some of her fantasies and although she describes the experience as 'awesome', she adds a cautionary note:

Catherine

'Some of the best sexual experiences I've had have been when my fantasies were fulfilled organically rather than specifically planning to do so (which can lead to disappointment and resentment if things aren't quite right). And sharing fantasies does not always go to plan.'

Anon

'I blurted out a scat [scatology – sex involving defecation] fantasy to my vanilla husband when we were young and new together and it disgusted him, which felt shaming for me, and also confirmed for me that scat is beyond the pale for many, even as a fantasy. I am more circumspect about checking and gauging likely responses before I share more extreme fantasy material with sexual partners now.'

Anon, bisexual potentially polyamorous Black female Christian, Adult Life Skills and Sexuality Researcher and Educator

'One or two partners loved and encouraged my fantasies but then added many of his own that he wanted me to act out. A few were great but most were just downright weird! So his ideas took over and I barely got to get a fantasy in there. The next guy I was with long term. He was open to ideas and talk but only when I initiated and he even enjoyed having one male and one female each separate into our relationship. They were both great, we referred to it a few times but after 8 years was back to basic sex. I even tried to make it work by asking, "So, how often and when do you masturbate?" His answer, "It's not as often as you think!" Keep in mind, I had just sent him a sexy video of myself masturbating to spice things up.'

Anon, 30 year old

'I'm glad to finally come to the realisation that my fantasies do not have to define me, and that it's okay in the heat of the moment to think of something that might be wrong by normal standards to help me get off. I really enjoy helping others achieve their fantasies, but I would never want one of mine enacted. But honestly, mine tend to be violent, and I wonder if that's a product of my past (family with lots of violence).'

Anon

'I found my fantasies to be quite dangerous to ask the men in my life to role play. One ended up raping me and causing my second pregnancy, and the other became violent towards me. Now I don't share my fantasies with my lover, and will not role play.'

Anon

'Fantasy allows us to explore aspects of sexuality that would be painful, embarrassing or risky to put into practice. I don't agree that we should try to live out our fantasies – they exist as an escape, but reality often brings consequences, hurt for people we love, or disappointment. I think it's also fine that they stay private – my partner knows a little, but certainly not everything. They are for me, not him, and I also wouldn't ask about his unless he wants to tell me.'

As Friday said in *Beyond My Control*, fantasy can be stage-managed to perfection: reality is messy and uncontrollable by comparison. Treating fantasy and reality as interchangeable is not without its risks.

Are Fantasies Normal?

One of the most common questions asked of agony aunts is, 'Am I normal?' and there is a lot of stigma attached to fantasies and desires which are deemed 'abnormal'. However, the desire to be normal primarily benefits the advertising industry and capitalism as a whole: it's easy to market a product to a clearly defined group of homogeneous people – and almost as easy to drive the desire for people to be homogeneous, simply by positioning anyone 'other' as being undesirably outside the norm. It's far harder to market a product to people who feel comfortable in their own skin and aren't looking to solve a problem.

In reading other people's fantasies, it may be tempting to make assumptions about what is or is not normal. However, in reality, normality is defined by society: why it is acceptable to fetishise a woman in stockings and suspenders but not one wearing gum boots? Why is it permissible to fantasise about a man's strong arms but not his armpit? These are arbitrary rules based on a host of factors from culture and religion to media and history.

While real life is diverse, within the pages of magazines white heteronormativity is the order of the day: lesbians, bisexuals, trans women, women of colour, fat women, disabled women and people who opt out of the gender binary but identify towards female, are all invisible. In addition, media representations of sexuality tend to have a solo focus: emotional *or* physical – but never the twain shall meet. Most magazine articles tend to focus either on 'relationships' or 'sex', rarely recognising the interaction between the two. This leads to a limited sexual narrative that magazines use to present a view of 'normal' sex.

What is 'Normal' Sex

- 'Normal' sex takes place within monogamous relationships. Non-monogamy is abnormal (or a juicy TV plotline), as is sex outside relationships.
- 'Normal' sex involves the man having a higher sex drive than the woman. Men want sex. Women want love.
- 'Normal' sex is something that women can use as a bargaining tool. Men will do anything for it (particularly oral sex). However, buying and selling it is abnormal.

- Normal sex does not combine the physical and spiritual (excluding articles about Tantra).
- 'Normal' sex (grudgingly) accepts that not everyone is hetero-sexual, but same-sex encounters are only discussed within the framework of experimentation and/or pleasing a man. Women can be 'bi-curious' but the expectation that she will return to 'normality' underlies the label.
- 'Normal' sex involves two people. Group sex may occasionally be mentioned, particularly if a celebrity does it, but is gener-ally presented as something that damages relationships. 'Trend' pieces on designer orgies occasionally make swinging briefly fashionable. However, in general group sex is abnormal.
- 'Normal' sex always involves the penis-in-vagina. (This ambi-guity was highlighted by Bill 'I did not have sexual relations with that woman' Clinton.)
- 'Normal' sex is not kinky. It may involve light bondage, dress-ing up or spanking but if you can't buy a luxury product for a kink then it's probably abnormal.
- 'Normal' sex is not something that mothers or women over forty do (unless they are 'cougars').
- 'Normal' sex is not something that teenagers do (unless they're 'from deprived areas' or 'damaged' in which case it is bad).
- 'Normal' sex is not something that trans women, fat women, disabled women and women of colour do.
- 'Normal' sex focuses on the importance of a large phallus to women (despite research covering 60 years' worth of studies finding that men care far more about penis size than women).
- 'Normal' sex sees orgasm as essential to sex (unless a woman has a 'dysfunction').
- 'Normal' sex involves easy male orgasm and complicated female orgasm.
- 'Normal' sex involves solving sexual problems with a pill, a new toy or a new kind of orgasm.

These are just a few of the myths perpetuated in the quest for normality. Almost all of these 'norms' reinforce family values, male dominance and capitalism. However, 'normal' sex is far from central in the fantasies submitted to *Garden of Desires* – or previous collections of female fantasies, so perhaps 'normal' is not so 'normal' after all. Instead, it reflects norms that have been perpetuated throughout history – no matter how limiting these can be.

While some might argue that 'normal' sex reflects what is 'natural', again, this is something defined by society. All kinds of behaviour are apparent in nature (and indeed human history), from group sex to polyamory, homosexuality to necrophilia (an ornithologist documented a case of a homosexual, necrophiliac mallard). Defining behaviours as 'normal' and 'natural' only works on the basis that everything and everyone is the same.

However, this infinite variety of sexual diversity is not reflected by society. The media, religion and individuals' judgemental attitudes all serve to constrain sexuality within boxes. Certain acts, sexualities and genders are deemed 'acceptable' or 'unacceptable'. Some are deemed 'dysfunctional'. Over time, the *Diagnostic and Statistical Manual (DSM)*, used to list psychiatric conditions, particularly in the US, has fallen under increasing scrutiny. Homosexuality is no longer medicalised, and transgender categorisation is now under the spotlight. Many previous paraphilias have been declassified as societal attitudes towards fetish have become more open. However, there is still some way to go before sex and the *DSM* have an unproblematic relationship.

Similarly, the way in which we define sex has a direct effect on the way in which we feel about it – and possibly experience it. While the word 'sex' is commonly used to refer to 'penis-in-vagina' sex, in reality, many people's sexual desires are far more diverse than that, so it does not truly represent many people's lived experience of sex. Indeed, the entire idea of 'normal' sex is limiting as it means many people who don't particularly enjoy penis-in-vagina sex may feel abnormal. As Mia More, Editor of Cliterati, points out: 'The very fact that we've had to employ a term for penis-in-vagina sex is just as indicative of the sex happening outside these confines as within them – as the widely used three letter acronym "PIV" would suggest.' It ignores the massive scope of people's sexuality, which is so clearly demonstrated by the diversity of female fantasies.

As such, no matter what you fantasise about, you can rest assured that you are normal.

Have Women's Fantasies Changed Over the Last Forty Years?

*I*n *My Secret Garden*, Nancy Friday surmised that female fantasies and guilt were heavily interconnected as women needed coping mechanisms in order to get round the pressure to be 'good girls'. This was fading by the time she wrote *Women on Top* in 1988, and, in the responses to the *Garden of Desires* survey, few women felt guilty about their desires (excluding some feminist-identified women who admitted to feeling guilty about having submissive fantasies; and a few women who consider it 'cheating' on a lover). So if women are able to be sexual with less guilt than ever before, has what they fantasise about changed? Or has the increasing conversation about fantasies led to certain ideas becoming normalised and commonplace while others are marginalised and rejected?

Research to date shows a huge range of diversity in women's fantasies, along with several popular themes. As with *My Secret Garden*, women are still fantasising about their lovers; group sex; domination and submission; and experiences outside their 'normal' sex play. Voyeurism and exhibitionism are still abundant in women's imaginations. Passionate sex, forbidden sex, animalistic sex and slutty sex all crop up as often today as they did when Friday published her first book.

However, my research found several new themes emerging. Gender is becoming increasingly fluid: women fantasising about being gay men; growing a penis with which to penetrate a partner; or simply wearing a strap-on and assuming a penetrative role in sex. Sexuality is also becoming increasingly fluid. A woman's 'real' sexuality gives no indication as to the gender of her fantasy lovers – if, indeed, those lovers are human at all, as animals, plants and inanimate objects all featured in fantasies submitted to this book.

In the privacy of her own mind, a woman can be whoever she wants to be – and women's desires have remained surprisingly and remarkably consistent – and 'dirty' – over the last forty years. However, while it may be reassuring to believe the past was a more innocent time, and sexuality becomes more open as the years progress, some of the fantasies Friday first published still have the potential to shock or surprise; a woman having sex with an Alsatian as a 14-year-old male observes; having her vagina ripped and arms wrenched from their sockets; and the 'most atrocious vivisection' to name just a few. If anything, since fantasies have become more accepted, the content has become less extreme. Friday found many women fantasised about animals in her research but there were very few animal fantasies submitted to *Garden of Desires*. Similarly, there were some extremely violent themes within the fantasies submitted to *My Secret Garden*, but very few submitted to *Garden of Desires*.

This could be because women with violent fantasies didn't feel comfortable about sharing them for some reason. However, it could also indicate a change in women's desires over the last forty years. Maybe, if everything is forbidden, that repression has to come out somewhere; if everything is allowed, there is nothing to rebel against and women's fantasies can be enjoyed in a steady flow rather than burst in frustration from their imagination. If society returns to a more sexually repressive state, we will find out soon enough.

Why Study Female Fantasy?

Following in the footsteps of Nancy Friday is an intimidating task – albeit one made much easier by the sexual fantasy revolution she helped to kick-start. I was born in 1974. I am lucky enough to have lived my entire life in a world that accepts female sexual fantasy exists. I even studied it for my psychology dissertation, exploring whether women wanted their fantasies to come true (finding, unsurprisingly, that it depended on the fantasy). Over the last few decades, I've seen the way in which women's openness about and access to fantasies – and sexual content in general – has evolved and grown.

It is easy to forget that the sexual freedom women currently experience is new: it is only forty years ago that female solo sexuality was even accepted as existing. We may have more vibrators and erotic accessories than ever before but we have still got a long way to go before women have universal rights over their bodies. There are still women all over the world being forced to breed or have contraceptive implants; being subjected to genital mutilation as punishment for 'sorcery', part of a religious tradition, or to fit with societally 'acceptable' views of what a woman is (sometimes even paying cosmetic surgeons thousands for the privilege); being shamed for revealing, concealing or 'selling' their bodies. This is not something for those in developed countries to feel superior about: sexual controls affect the developed and developing world alike.

Women's sexuality is often drowned out by the increasingly insidious 'sex sells' narrative, which presents a pastiche of real sex in an effort to sell solutions to invented problems. Instead of being listened to, women are being medicalised: 75 per cent of women can't climax through penetrative PIV sex alone – yet rather than reconsidering the definition of sex, doctors instead label them as 'dysfunctional'. In a piece for the *Daily Telegraph*, Glenda Cooper says, 'The journalist Ray Moynihan, author of *Sex, Lies and Pharmaceuticals* (2010) has called female sexual dysfunction the clearest example yet of the "corporate-sponsored creation of a disease".'

Dr Petra Boynton, a psychologist and sex researcher from University College London, argues that a flagging female libido should not necessarily be viewed as a medical disorder. '"Good" sex is now presented as lots of sex and mind-blowing multiple orgasms. So you end up with people going to their GPs thinking they have sexual problems, when they may be misinformed, or may have relationship rather than sexual problems.'

In examining women's fantasies today, we can see the way in which society influences sexuality and understand the infinite variety within women's sexual imagination; and explore the full range of female desires rather than a media-friendly edited version of sex. If women's true sexuality is to be represented, it needs to be shared. As Alfred Kinsey wrote in 1953, 'We do not believe that the happiness of individual men, and the good of the total social organization, is ever furthered by the perpetuation of ignorance.'

We should not take female sexuality for granted – or allow it to become synonymous with media representations of 'sexy' women. It is only by being honest that we can deal with the sexual issues that really affect us – and this is something that is now within. As erotic author Nicci Gemmell said on UK BBC Radio 4's 'Woman's Hour', '*Fifty Shades* led to an explosion of honesty at the school gate.' In harnessing the power of that honesty, and sharing their true desires, women are more likely to get what they really want.

From Here to Diversity

By far the biggest finding of my research was that women's fantasies are incredibly diverse: even if two women share a similar fantasy, its inspiration, their motivations and the way in which they use their fantasy can be very different. Similarly, few women had fantasies that contained a single theme. Though many fitted within broad categories of, say, domination, a lot also included exhibitionism or group sex. Many of the fantasies could have fitted comfortably in numerous chapters within the book, just going to show how complex sexual fantasy can be. I have grouped fantasies together with others that seem most complimentary but please don't consider the labels to be static: one person's exhibitionist thrill is another's submissive treat.

No matter how complex they are and how the common themes of women's fantasies have changed over the last forty years, they still serve the same purpose as ever: inspiring arousal. It's true: some women find their fantasies help them work through sexual issues. Some women see them as a form of creative escape. Some women use their fantasies to mentally 'try out' new experiences and gauge their willingness to indulge for real. But almost all women use their fantasies to increase their chances of orgasm, no matter what those fantasies may be.

A Note Before Reading:
Judge Not Lest Ye Be Judged

*W*hile we may have a long way to go before female sexuality is fully understood and accepted, there is no doubting that many women have a fertile erotic imagination. As Nancy Friday said, women seek approval from other women – and in gaining it, feel happier about their desires. As such, when reading these fantasies, please fight any urge you may have to judge the women who have contributed their innermost intimate thoughts. You may find some fantasies don't match up to your idea of sex, or seem 'perverted', but consider this. Oral sex was only legalised in 13 of the US states in 2003 – and there are still people who believe that it is immoral and 'perverted' today. Sex toys are illegal in some American states, yet over fifty per cent of women in the UK and US own one. It's easy to label anything deviant, particularly if it runs contrary to societal norms, but in fantasy, anything goes – and so it should.

Fantasies reflect our individual (and collective) histories. If your fantasies happen to fit the norm, consider yourself lucky: you are more likely to find resources to help turn you on if your own imagination runs dry. However, it does not make you any better or more 'normal' than those with esoteric fantasies. The only 'normal' in fantasies is that they help the person fantasising to process their experiences and make sense of the world – and even then, some people don't fantasise and find their own ways to assimilate information.

Similarly, if you can't find anything that reflects your fantasies within the pages of this book, please do not consider yourself abnormal. It simply means that your fantasies are tailored to your own needs – or perhaps you're more honest about your desires than most. Why aspire to reach the artificial construct of normal when instead, you can be yourself?

Garden of Desires is the first book to be produced as part of an ongoing research project. If you would like to contribute your fantasies to future books and research, please submit your answers to our questionnaire via http://www.dubberley.com. *You can also share your fantasies in erotic story form at Cliterati.co.uk.*

Chapter One:
Submissive Fantasies

'I know it takes a strong woman to be a true submissive.'

MIA MORE, EDITOR CLITERATI.CO.UK, MOTHER, LATE THIRTIES

*T*he tightrope of female submissive fantasies has straddled the chasm between sexual freedom and patriarchal control ever since Pauline Réage was first accused of being a man back in 1954. When *The Story of O* was first published, the idea of willing female sexual submission was so subversive that a male author projecting his desires through a female pseudonym seemed the only logical explanation. 'Nice girls' couldn't possibly like the idea of being tied up, pinned down, and ravaged unless a bad man made them do it – or so society wanted to believe.

Submissive fantasies cover a broad spectrum. They might entail nothing more than a strong, controlling man – the Mr Darcy and Rhett Butler of classic romance – making his partner acquiesce to his whim with a firm grip and overwhelming sexual chemistry. Kinks including bondage, spanking and dress-up can play a part. Money may provide an added aphrodisiac (maybe with an element of blackmail thrown in), whether through direct payment for performing a 'slutty' act, or less direct but no less gratuitous means, such as Christian Grey's lavish gifts to Anastasia in *Fifty Shades*. And they can span all genders and sexualities.

There might be one dominant lover or a crowded room of sadistic strangers; and the 'punishment' could be part of a loving, consensual submissive relationship, or a wild night with a stranger or acquaintance who pushes a woman to her limits and beyond. At its most extreme, submissive fantasies can also include rape.

Anon, 40, married graduate, still faithful, no kids, bisexual and out to my husband

'I like to fantasise about being controlled and punished although my actual desire for those things isn't strong. But in the past few years my arousal fantasies have been more about making contact with new people and developing an illicit relationship with them – being caught cheating by my husband and being spanked and forced to give him oral sex as a consequence. My favourite fantasy is being forced into sexual submission by my husband and another woman. I imagine I would first play with them willingly, then when I had enough they would trap me and force me to service them while alternately humiliating me.'

Anon, 28, Caucasian, BA

'I have recently met a very dominant man with whom I am not and can not be involved because we are not of the same sexual orientation. But my fantasies involving him are the most vivid, intense, and for lack of a better word "right". than any other. In these fantasies he is in complete control of me, makes softly murmured demands, and withholds the appearance of his own desire except in flashes so brief that I feel later that I may have imagined them.'

Anon, 44 year old mother of two

'One of the fantasies that I have is having sex with my ex. He is married but sex with him was great. With him I tried things that I probably never would have. I often think about him showing up and wanting to have sex with me. In the beginning I tell him no. But I always give in and enjoy it. I don't know if I would really do it, but if the situation comes up I can't say that I wouldn't.'

Anon, Professor
'Spanking.'

J, 49, straight serial monogamist with two daughters and two grand-sons living with me, non live-in partner

'Being captured as a youngish girl, and lured to live with a man who totally dominates and controls me for his pleasure. I live at his house and he is cruel from time to time in order to dominate me. He allows his friends to inspect me and take me off to enjoy my body for their pleasure. I have no rights.

Sometimes he obliterates my personality by punishment, sometimes he gradually erodes my freedom and my confidence in the outside world until I simply live at his house and await his demands.

My fantasies are most often along the theme as above but vary from time to time in their context, sometimes the "owner" is more cruel, sometimes less, sometimes he keeps other women, sometimes it is a paedophile situation where he is in a position of trust with a child (could be sometimes a male child) and abuses them, sometimes he is a slave owner and sells me, sometimes he sells me into prostitution, but more often just ownership, occasionally there is gang rape. I'm embarrassed at how extreme, violent and perverted I get.'

The submission can be emotional (through acquiescing to humiliating acts); physical (through use of restraints, psychological control or pain); or of course sexual (by relinquishing the body to the Dominant's desires) – often all three. And there's no guarantee that a fantasy that starts with submission won't end with the woman turning the tables and dominating her lover instead – also known as being a 'switch' – someone able to become aroused by both dominant and submissive fantasies/behaviour. Indeed, research has repeatedly suggested that people with submissive fantasies are also likely to have dominant fantasies too – and vice versa.

Izabella, 23, bisexual, physical disabilities, artist

'Being forced to submit by a male, dominating a female, being tied up.'

Morgan, 25, bisexual and polyamorous

I fantasise about being restrained, spanked, being helpless, being told what to do, being given orgasm denial and given control. My favourite fantasy is being topped by my dom at the same time as adding another girl in who I, in turn, top. I have blogged about my experiences before, when I've had a good night out. The last one I wrote, I wouldn't have said I fantasise about all the things that happen, but I do now fantasise about a couple of things that did happen. For example, a female domme had me under her control, and I like to think about the way she stroked my neck and what her beautiful blue eyes were like, watching me.'

Many of the submissive fantasies contributed to Cliterati.co.uk often involve a degree of transgression from the norm: experimenting with kink and boundaries rather than simply relinquishing control to a lover. The same was true of fantasies submitted to *Scarlet* magazine's 'Cliterature' section, and can be seen in hundreds of erotic novels – even *Fifty Shades* – giving a good indication that it's not just Cliterati's users who fantasise about pushing their sexual limits. In submitting, a woman is free to enjoy her more animal, base or just plain dirty desires.

The Politics of Submission

Some feminists have admitted to finding their own submissive fantasies problematic, claiming they reinforce negative gender roles and feed into 'rape culture'. Rather than seeing them as freeing the 'good girl', they see them as supporting the 'bad man'. And that is not the only political dynamic. Some people feel that submissive fantasies are damaging, sexualising and eroticising slavery. As a result, many women feel guilty about having submissive desires – let alone sharing or acting on them.

Anon, 26, American

'I think that many women are unfortunately ashamed that they have sexual fantasies, or maybe they don't feel that being sexual is naturally part of their identity as it is for men. Not all women, just many of my close friends. I think they hold themselves back from fantasising, or at least feeling comfortable with expressing that they do this. For example, even when I have heard women talking about *Fifty Shades of Grey* they talk about how sexy Christian Grey is but they never mention the sexual acts and whether or not that turns them on.'

Anon

'I used to worry that I was wrong to think about the things I did, and (emotionally) beat myself up to no purpose. I felt I was betraying my feminism to imagine female submission (as was the case for about twenty to twenty-five years of my fantasy life, from about 12 on). Now, I'm very aware that the things in my head are not reality (most of them shouldn't be) and some are impossible (e.g, male cross-species impregnation). I've come to quite enjoy the sheer outrageousness of my more extreme fantasies. Also, I find it curious that many things I am aware I would not find enjoyable (e.g, rape) and many things I have no wish to attempt in reality (e.g, watching someone forced to defecate) are some of the highlights in fantasy – and many things I enjoy enormously and repeatedly are rarely or never the subject of fantasy. I haven't tried to orgasm without fantasising in some years, but as I recall it I found it impossible.'

Regardless of how 'acceptable' it is, all research into the area has shown that submission is one of women's top sexual fantasies (and is almost as popular with men). More fantasies submitted to this book featured submission than any other theme, though it should be taken into account that submission is a broad category, ranging from traditional 'romance' to BDSM along with the much discussed rape fantasy – which is far less common than the media reports. Submission has long been one of the most popular themes in stories submitted to Cliterati, Nancy Friday devoted pages to submissive fantasies in all three of her books and E. L. James's book sales demonstrated submission is still an intoxicating idea to many women.

Like it or not, some women have submissive fantasies. Even feminists. And even nice girls.

Jemima, mother, wife, collared sub and sex worker

'My most common fantasy, which I have had since I was at least early teens, always involves force. Often I am kidnapped, bundled into a car or van, and end up at some form of "hideaway" where I am told I have to satisfy a group of men. I will be tied to a bed, my arms and legs unable to move, and fucked by each of them, cocks put in my mouth, one man taking over as another comes. Since I became an owned BDSM sub this fantasy has always involved my Master as the guiding hand, and usually concluded with him using me.'

Anon, middle-aged, female, writer and campaigner

'My favourite fantasy is still all tied up with passivity and helplessness and not being in control of myself. I love giving pleasure to others . . . Thinking of setting up a small group of like-minded lesbians to tour lesbian clubs doing massage and just generally being tactile (but not necessarily sexual). And I love to play with situations that teeter on the edge of consciousness or self-control. Sleepy sex: hypno (as subject or as hypnotist); use of "substances" that would leave me aware but really not up to doing anything much about my situation. There's always been a fascination with passivity, helplessness, being unable to control my self, being subject to another's will.'

Anon, 23, lesbian, petite, feminine, brunette, spectacled, white. In a relationship. NOT gold star

'Being dominated by a butch female with a flesh-coloured strap on. And being told to pleasure myself as she fucks me.

The strap-on is one that ejaculates. She fucks me and comes on my back. It's inspired by the power of the women I had sex with before my wife. I had one night stands and "relationships" based on me being the vessel for their sexual needs. It was just sex. I loved some aspects of those transactions. Sex was a transaction. Now I am married and my sex life has changed again for the better in 99% of the ways but my fantasy remains being used like that.'

Gemma, 18, pole dancer (note not sex worker), part-time student. I'm in a relationship, but no serious commitment or children

'To be held down/restrained, not to be incapable of seeing/speaking, just my limbs held down by my partner and marked somehow. I want to be seriously bitten, scratched and bruised on anywhere on my body except my face (somehow its wrong when its my face). I just want my skin to be a physical reminder of when we have sex. I want it rough and I want him to just lose all restraint and take pleasure in my body and enjoy me. I generally want to make people happy in everyday life . . . I guess it kinda carries over that I want to be a source of enjoyment for my partner's sexual needs. I don't know where the desire for some pain comes from, but I guess it just feels good and it me it's like a sign he's not holding back or anything.'

Anon, 26, redhead, student

'A Dominant older woman and I will meet for the first time somewhere non-specific like a coffee shop, and we will start talking. The conversation drifts to sex, gets steamy, and we move in closer. She moves her hand in under my skirt and tells me that if I want her to meet me again, that I must come, but not let it show in any way. She teases me like this, and I follow her rules, until I beg her, in a normal conversation tone, to stop. She then suggests we head off to somewhere more private – we go to her car and I follow her next orders, by eating her out there and then.'

Why Do People Have Submissive Fantasies?

*T*here are numerous common and conflicting beliefs about why women have submissive fantasies. Some see it as positive, others as negative but the bulk of research shows that submissive fantasies are not damaging – though romantic fantasies may be, so it does depend on the content.[9] But broadly speaking, far from disempowering women, submissive fantasies can offer a boost to the ego.

As anyone who's had the mildest brush with the fetish scene will tell you, in reality, it's the submissive who's really in control anyway. Whether real or imagined, the sub can always say the safe word to stop proceedings. Fantasy has the added bonus of allowing women to push their limits beyond levels they're comfortable going to in real life, with no risk of harm. It allows a woman scope to 'try an idea on for size' and decide which ideas she really wants to explore.

There are four pervasive ideas about why women have submissive fantasies: relaxation; therapy; permission-giving; and of course, sexual pleasure.

Relaxation

Many people see submissive fantasies as an outlet for people who have to be in control during their everyday life. In relinquishing control they are also letting go of the responsibility to perform,

9 Rudman and Heppen (*Implicit Romantic Fantasies and Women's Interest in Personal Power: A Glass Slipper Effect*, 2003) found women who had romantic fantasies were less likely to be interested in personal power, including educational attainment, leadership, ambition and projected income. A later study (Power, Desire and Pleasure in Sexual Fantasies, Zurbriggen, 2003) found that women with romantic fantasies were more likely to accept rape myths (e.g., women are 'asking for it') – though submissive fantasies did not correlate with problematic beliefs.

getting to enjoy being pleasured without having to tell a lover what to do.

Amber

'I have a demanding job and I'm a mum too, and I get fed up telling people what to do all the time: it's so boring having to be forever bossy. So being submissive in the bedroom is like a holiday for me. I like this secret juxtaposition, and I'm enjoying exploring my submissive side with my husband while the kids are sleeping and my work colleagues are ... Well, you just don't know what goes on behind closed doors, do you?

For me fantasies are escapism – from real life, stress, worries, everything. They're also where I can explore the part of me I keep hidden from the world – even from myself at times – as it can be a dark place. And I don't mean that negatively, I mean it with regards to deviation from the light, fluffy, "vanilla" side of sex that most people would perceive as normality.'

Anon, 24, female, heterosexual, Australian, engineer

'Being fucked by someone from behind, being tied up or restrained in some way. Working and studying with a lot of men, I have a lot of male friends so half the time my fantasies involve other men and the other half my partner. I would never want to date these guys and I only want to be with my partner but it does turn me on to think about what they would be like in bed. I think it comes from knowing so many different types of men and being in a job where I am always in a role where I am expected to be dominant, the idea of being dominated is appealing.'

Jules, 21, single, straight, blonde, white art graduate

'My most common fantasy is that of a man taking control. I did the whole rough-sex thing with one guy and realised that that wasn't what I wanted. When I talk about a guy taking control, it's more about him knowing what he wants and also knowing exactly what I want. A guy who wants me to orgasm and will do whatever is necessary to achieve that. Someone who will be gentle, but commanding *and not* ask me, "Is that okay?" I think it comes from a life where I've had to be fiercely independent since about age eight. I've always had to take care of myself and have always been the one calling the shots. I'm sick of making decisions all the time and just want to be taken care of. I'd love to give up control and let someone else do all the work for once.'

Therapy

There is also an increasing body of work examining fantasy within psychotherapy. Dr Michael Baden said, in his book *Arousal: The Secret Logic of Sexual Fantasies* (2003), 'The adult indulging in a fantasy of sexual surrender or abasement is actually saying to her or himself, "I'm recreating a terrifying and traumatic scene, but this time I'm in control because I'm scripting the scene" . . . Trauma is turned on its head.'

Zoltan Dienes (Professor of Psychology, Sussex University) found that submissive fantasies correlate with feelings of anxiety both towards being too sexual and too controlling. He says, 'One could see both as worrying about people being difficult to please, one way or the other. Submission means no longer having to worry about others: They will get what they want from you.'

Submissive fantasies can offer an alternative to reality. Amber says, 'My submissive fantasies help me escape from the daily grind – from whatever's going on in my life at that particular time. My head just drifts away as my body endures the pain I inflict on it. It really is escapism – with a sexual kick. What's not to like?'

Some people believe that anyone with submissive desires must be damaged by a traumatic past or be suffering from some form of mental disorder. While exploring the therapeutic benefits of kink is beginning to gain some traction in academia, merely linking sexual trauma and submissive fantasies is intellectually lazy. There is no evidence to support these claims to date, and no way to categorise or group women who have submissive fantasies beyond, 'They fantasise about being submissive.'

Anon, 26, redhead, psychology student. No kids (infertile). Attracted to men and women, only had long term relationships with men. Currently 5 years into a semi-open relationship (women only) with a man ten years older

'An explicit rape fantasy has come about since I was sexually assaulted at 15 (my first experience with a sexual partner, and multiple orgasm) – big fantasy to relive being on the receiving end of his obvious desire to cause that unique blend of survival instinct, fear/panic, "taboo", lust/desire, shame, and pleasure.

I wake up somewhere, blindfolded, tied up, and being fucked in the mouth and pussy at the same time. I'm mid-orgasm, and completely wet – it seems my body was one hundred per cent approving while I was unconscious. There's no way to object to whatever they do to me, or however long they want to continue – and then one squeezes my nipple hard and says "Welcome back bitch". I can hear the grin in his voice as a hand tightens around my neck, and wave after wave of orgasm hits until I pass out once more.

Rape/edge play fantasies serve to provide a safe way to experience those feelings, rather than seeking them out in reality as I did in my later teen years. In my teen years I tried to relive the sexual assault experience with a sex-only relationship, where the man used me as he wanted . . . I still felt unsatisfied, and felt less emotionally secure.

Fantasies fulfil for me what reality cannot. If I made most of mine come true I would feel shame, disgust, and/or put myself (and possibly my partner via STIs) in physical danger. Given their content, experience indicates they are also best kept to myself – as I can enjoy them without judgement or too much in the way of negative emotions.'

Jane, 50s, academic, 'married with children, het, female, able/lucky and Caucasian, with light brown hair'

'I fantasise about domination/forced sex, with me in submissive role being forced to orgasm. There are a huge variety of settings. Often more than one male partner. Bondage is a key element, and sometimes pain/humiliation. It begins with a girl tied up being looked at and described by someone who has wanted her for some time but been rejected. He slowly lays every part of her bare, including her desires, and caresses her, and teases her, sometimes punishes her, and then he takes her, and takes her to orgasm. That's a bit bare-boned but it's the constant elements. Voyeurism. Love. Desire. Acceptance of desire. I'm NOT INTERESTED AT ALL [Jane's capitalisation] in consensual BDSM as per *Fifty Shades* – only in force, tenderly, lovingly and desiringly applied, by someone who really wants me. The trouble he takes to coerce me is proof of devotion in the fantasy. He knows my body and takes complete control. As per *A Child is Being Beaten* (Freud's 1919 exploration of masochism), I am both him and the girl to whom all this is done. It's a perfect OCD control loop. I give him the power to do all this to me, and I am him, so I never let go of control.'

Permission-Giving

Another common reading of submissive fantasies is that they're about permission-giving: if you're 'forced' to commit a 'gross' sex act, it's not your own responsibility, and as such, you have nothing to feel guilty about. If you're 'made' to be sexual, you are free from society's judgemental eye and can be unashamedly sexual.

As one woman, a forty-year-old mother of three, says of her submissive fantasies, 'Obviously I do not want to be raped or be gang banged, and I try to understand the motivation behind it all. So far, I think it's still mainly the shame associated with wanting sex as a woman that I grew up with. Wanting sex and being a slut is just not what good girls do, it's not socially accepted. But that is precisely the place where I want to go but can't, so I'd imagine up men that would come and take me against my will, dominate me, tie me up, force me to be the slut I want to be deep down. It's often not even romantic. Romantic fantasies are separate from sexual ones in my mind.'

Adding an element of submission to a fantasy can help women enjoy desires they may feel are taboo.

Anon, 45, bisexual, 'degreed', and married for 23 years with three older teens

'I work in the medical profession, have been involved in the swinger community for five years with my spouse, and have an interest in kink and BDSM. My most common fantasy is giving up control being bound and used for his pleasure; or being in a club dirty dancing with a handsome man, the music pounding, the sexual tension high – finding the bathroom or dark corner and being taken right there. My fantasy comes from a desire to break boundaries, discover the erotic without shame and live in the moment.'

Anon, 22, white British bisexual student, 'in a long-term relationship with a man'

'Friday's *My Secret Garden* was the very first thing that ever turned me on. The story that begins 'Screaming and scratching and struggling' . . . or something like that. I did this quiz because I owe Friday. My current favourite fantasy is going to visit my ex and end up having really kinky sex with him – being tied up and whipped and having a knife dragged over my skin, as well as oral and vaginal sex. I feel guilty about fantasising about my ex, although I would never actually sleep with him, and in my fantasies he looks and behaves differently! Sometimes I feel my fantasies are really disturbed and wrong. Mostly though they are just exciting and private.'

Sexual Pleasure

Of course, submissive fantasies can just be used as inspiration for a *ménage a moi*, or to enhance sex, without any deeper analysis required. Catherine uses her fantasies, 'to relax; to think about things that turn me on; as sexual input when I'm not having much sex; and to help get me off.'

Catherine, a 'queer, female masochist'

'I don't have a favourite fantasy but elements of SM, power differences, forced orgasms and sustained sexual tension recur. A frequent fantasy is of violence that isn't explicitly sexual (being punched, shoved into walls, slapped, all whilst fully clothed). Another current favourite is reading aloud whilst being touched, undressed and eventually fucked (and being told to keep going as I get more and more turned on).

The people who recur in my fantasies are influenced by my real life (e.g. I fantasised a lot about my previous partner when we were together; not at all now). Sexual/ sadomasochistic acts (or discussion thereof) in real life also influence them, for example when I was doing a lot of rope bondage my fantasies frequently involved that. Following a recent mention of rape play by someone very attractive they currently involve a lot of coercion/line-of-consent stuff.'

Anon

'Most of my favourite fantasies have to do with power. Being taken advantage of, being forced to be a sex slave, being the object of a gang bang, being humiliated and called names. Sometimes I get a thrill for coming up with something so naughty, something that would shock most people who know me.'

Of course, the simplest reading of why women have submissive fantasies could be because women are fantasising about the sex that arouses them in real life. Many women who submitted both submissive and dominant fantasies to *Garden of Desires* admitted to turning their fantasies into reality with one or more partners; and several fantasies were based on real life experiences.

This absolutely does not mean that *every* woman with submissive fantasies wants them to come true – and indeed, many women made a point of stating very clearly that they have no desire to make their fantasies reality – rape fantasies in particular (obviously) being something that no women wanted to happen. However, we would never think to ask why people have romantic fantasies about their partner, assuming that was perfectly 'normal', so it is interesting that we apply so much thought to why women might fantasise about submissive sex. Perhaps the reason that some women fantasise about submissive sex is simply because they enjoy it.

Keely, 24, tea drinker

'Wearing nothing but cat ears my boyfriend pins me on the bed and roughly takes me.'

Common Fantasy Themes

So if women can have multiple reasons for having submissive fantasies, do they have myriad fantasies too? While there is no such thing as a classic submissive fantasy, there are certain themes and strands that are repeated frequently. Submissive fantasies often incorporate numerous other fantasy aspects too: group sex, exhibitionism and 'forced' sexual experimentation, to name just a few. The narratives are often complex, and it can sometimes be hard to gauge how much is fantasy and how much is fond recollection of real sexual encounters.

While the woman may be in an apparently vulnerable situation, she still reaches some form of sexual satisfaction through her fantasy. Whether through repeated forced orgasms, extended periods of teasing with orgasm denial or being 'forced' to relinquish to her 'dirtier' desires, in a submissive fantasy, the woman gets what she wants.

In over a decade at Cliterati.co.uk, in addition to all the research for this book, I have yet to receive a single submissive fantasy that hasn't involved the woman reaching a sexual peak – though the ways in which that can occur vary immensely. Whips and handcuffs play a part, but to a far lesser extent than lewd letters detailing sexual tasks that must be undertaken, thorough spankings, 'forced' lesbian experiences and, most of all, loving but controlling Dominants with vivid and filthy imaginations. Fantasies set within relationships are common, whether past or present lovers. There are several other common submissive themes. In addition, many women with submissive fantasies also enjoy dominant desires.

Anon, 34, bisexual switch in a monogamous relationship

'My sexual fantasies are almost exclusively submissive in nature but I identify as a switch that enjoys topping where I feed off the bottom's reactions through empathy. In my fantasies I am way more confident with other women during sex, whereas in real life I am very shy around other women when it comes to sex.'

Look at Me

Many submissive fantasies contain an element of exhibitionism, much as many of the exhibitionist fantasies (Chapter 3) contain an element of submission. There is vulnerability in opening oneself up to another's gaze, and thus it could be argued that exhibitionism shares some common ground with submission.

Rose de Fer is a happily married writer of erotic fiction. Her website is at poisonthorns.blogspot.com

'I couldn't possibly pick just one favourite fantasy! The slave auction is very much a part of my fantasy repertoire. I am standing in a line with several other girls on the auction block. One by one the slave trader calls us out to the front to inspect us for the audience, exposing our breasts, our bottoms, our sex, stimulating us in various ways to see how responsive we are. I watch nervously as he makes his way down the line of girls, dreading and anticipating my own turn. Some girls resist and he punishes them, which makes me even more frightened and aroused.

There's also the Victorian demonstration where I'm the meek little chambermaid of some wicked Victorian doctor who straps me naked to a table in front of a roomful of frock-coated gentlemen and objectifies me completely. He displays me in every possible way and then tests my responses to various stimuli, commenting dispassionately on everything throughout. (I wrote a couple of variations on this beloved theme in *Lust Ever After*, my kinky retelling of *Bride of Frankenstein*.)

I also love the fantasy I wrote about in my story 'Holding Still' in Mischief Books' *Instructed to Play*. In that one I've been trained to be a human statue. I must hold perfectly still as my master strokes and caresses me, using his riding crop in intimate areas to test my obedience. Or there's the *koonago* – or tiny-woman – fantasy where I'm shrunk down to pocket-size and have all manner of strange and exciting erotic adventures. Or any number of pet-play fantasies. I could go on and on!'

Anon

'My favourite fantasy is that my partner puts me in a situation that would involve him watch me have sex with other men (two or three) or participate in having sex with me and another man. This fantasy often involves elements of me being "forced" or coerced into the situation.'

Anon, 29, bisexual, single, Ph.D student, and a virgin

'In my earliest fantasies I generally appropriated Disney Princesses and they basically ended up as sex slaves, and not any sort of consensual D/s relationship but actual slaves. Over time, I stopped substituting Disney princesses for myself and I now star in them or they happen to characters I made up. Also as I gained an understanding of what sex actually is and started reading romance and erotica, the fantasies became increasingly more detailed.

My most recent fantasy featured a vaguely historical setting (Regency? Medieval? Doesn't really matter but definitely not the modern world). A woman (young, virginal) has just married. After taking her repeatedly orally, vaginally, and anally, while she is restrained her husband blindfolds her and without her consent (or knowledge at first) shares her with his friends.

Most often I have variations on the above fantasy involving forced, but pleasurable, sex, often as an initiation to sex, and often involving multiple male partners. Although I identify as bisexual I do not often fantasise about female only encounters.'

Grace, 46, Irish redhead and a teacher, 'married for 19 years with no children'

'My most common fantasy is that I am sold at a slave auction to the highest bidder but prior to that is the preparation. I am lined up with other captured women for inspection by two or three large, dominant men. I'm selected for auction and then brought to a bath house to be scrubbed clean, all body hair shaved off and then restrained. Finally a gel that stimulates blood flow is smeared over my breasts and vagina, my breasts swell and I become aroused and moist; so much so that I have to be relieved by one of the men before I'm brought to the auction. One of them is told to have sex with me and bring me to orgasm before I can be brought out for sale.'

Katie

'My fantasy involves wearing high heels and a short skirt, bending over, and being taken from behind in an empty but public space. I've had the same fantasy for about four years and it makes me feel willingly dominated.'

Though objectification of women is painted as negative, in fantasy at least, some women, like Rose and Katie, find great pleasure in being objectified – potentially claiming back power over that objectification for themselves.

Tie Me Down

Bondage is a popular female fantasy, and many women also admit to enjoying it in reality. Bondage fantasies can range from being tied with silk ropes and lovingly brought to orgasm again and again to being cruelly bound and violated by multiple people

– and, very occasionally, animals. However, most tend to fall somewhere between these extremes.

Patricia, 27, straight, cerebral paralysism, single

'Being handcuffed and or blindfolded and being told what to do/ control and dominate one's moves and pleasure.'

Leonie, 41, female, caucasian, heterosexual, two children, Masters, single

'Being tied to a dining room chair while in my lingerie.'

Mary, 46, 'straight, never married, no children'

'I fantasise about being taken by a male unknown to me, kidnapped, bound tightly, gagged, blindfolded, taken somewhere unknown to me in the trunk of a vehicle.'

Anon, 26, American

'I imagine being restrained in some way "against my will", but with the person in my fantasy somehow having good intentions and not wanting to hurt me.'

Anon

'Being tied up. The specifics have a tendency to change.'

Anon, 40, physician, married, no children, highly educated and hard working

'My most recent fantasy was having someone tie my hands above my head, my legs tied, spread apart, straddling a man I don't know, being whipped or hit with a belt by one or two men.'

Hannah, 21, student

'I recently fantasised about being dominated by a woman in front of (and at the request of) a man who I imagined was my partner. I identify as straight but sometimes I enjoy fantasising about women. My favourite fantasy is a variation on the theme of being spanked and dominated by a man. Sometimes I'm restrained but often I'm not. Sometimes it progresses to sex but sometimes he just touches or goes down on me.'

Anon

'My most common fantasy would be being tied up in one of those machine, and also blindfolded with a man sucking my nipples, pulling them and also sticking his tongue in my private parts while I scream and enjoy. Also, they could use the whip on my bottom as that will make me even more horny.'

Anon

'I used to fantasise about being fisted. Now it is being tied up, spanked, intense nipple play and then fisting. My favourite fantasy is probably being teased and denied orgasm for a long, long time, while being punished with a rubber flogger.'

Daisy, blogger at Daisydanger.com

'Bondage is a common thread throughout my fantasy life. As I get older, though, I've moved into liking very hardcore bondage, including needle play. My favourite fantasy is to be tied down and used over a course of days. Not necessarily fucked, but beaten, use of vibrators, etc.'

Heather

'In my most recent fantasy I was being topped by my boyfriend who had carefully, safely, and purposefully bound me in shibari style and we were sharing a wonderful connection as he gave me everything I wanted: his body, his tongue, his attention, vibrator, pressure on my abdomen and neck, sensual touch, penetration. My fantasies have become more intricate as rope play has been added but they're also more technical as I will not be turned on if I don't fantasise that the play is safe and consensual.'

Anon

'My favourite fantasy is being tied up on a bed, wrists and ankles while having sex. Since starting to read BDSM fiction,

I am having it more frequently and it's usually the fantasy that is most effective for me when masturbating.'

Anon, female, 41, single, straight-ish, graduate, two kids

'Being overpowered by a powerful and attractive man – possibly in a uniform or workman's clothing – who bends me over or pushes me underneath him and slams me roughly with his big penis.'

Anon, 37 and married

'Some of my earliest fantasies have involved being handcuffed, pinned down etc and then intercourse taking place. In the fantasies I'd be compliant with this and secretly loving it. My fantasies haven't changed much over time. My favourite fantasy is anal sex (receiving) and/or being dominated.'

Be My Boss

Figures of authority are another common theme in submissive fantasies. An 18-year-old student, 'interested in politics, philosophy, history and other humans,' fantasises about 'being a innocent girl, pleasing a dominating, serious, older guy in his workplace.' And she is far from the only woman to imagine being bossed around.

Anon, 49, white woman, married, no kids, psychologist, tertiary ed, ambitious

'I like the idea of a man taking control, but in real life my husband is a gentle man and does not like to dominate, though we have played dom/sub games. I also think that because I am a manager and spend my day making decisions, I like the idea of a man directing the action, being subtly dominated by a professional man, who tells me what to do and I do it. No oral sex, usually we have anal sex, lots of sucking my breasts prior to that. But as with all fantasies, this is a fantasy. In real life, setting the boundaries so that I would feel comfortable in this type of scenario with anyone other than my partner, I do not think would work.'

Anon, 28, cis female, in a loving long-term relationship with a woman. Identify as queer but prefer not to identify at all

'My partner is a librarian and associate lecturer, so I often imagine being a student of hers, made to stay behind after class to pleasure her, get fucked from behind over a desk, ask for help with an essay, and other such things related to student-lecturer relationship. She is dominant, but never cruel; firm and teacherly, rather than a mistress. There is also a sense of stimulation from the academic setting, an environment of intellectualism. I become aroused from the idea of learning from her both academically and sexually. I suppose some of my first feelings of attraction towards women were female teachers. Having spent many years in higher education, I find there is a thin line between intellectual and sexual stimulation. I have also always been very eager to please and impress lecturers and teachers, and respond well to praise and criticism.'

Anon, 27, doctor from New Zealand, married to husband for over ten years. No kids yet.

'Currently, my most common fantasy involves being dominated by my boss – hands tied, bent over and fucked over his examination bed in his clinic room. In "real life" I am not attracted to my boss and have no desire to enter in a sexual relationship with anyone other than my husband. I am interested in BDSM and experimenting a little but can't really imagine doing this with my husband – I think the attraction of envisaging it with my boss is the whole power situation and the thrill of doing something completely illicit at work.'

Anon, late 40s, bisexual professional woman

'Being told to bend over and pull my panties down by an authority figure (sometimes head teacher, sometimes boss). I'm wearing a short skirt. He spanks me with a paddle and then fucks me from behind, while fondling my breasts. I think there is something exciting about apparently being punished but both of us finding it very pleasurable.'

Anon

'I started having fantasies at 14, triggered by a crush on a (female) teacher to whom I was teacher's pet. My earliest fantasy was being made to stand in the corner at school, knickers down and being touched by Mrs S. the teacher mentioned above. I fantasised about being punished by her but never was. I was a good girl. My fantasies have changed over time: I have always fantasised about sex in power relationships, but usually with men these days. My favourite fantasy is being in prison and strip searched by a young male prison officer who finishes off by f**king me in my cell.'

Robin

'My current favourite involves being a serving maid in a big Victorian house and being used as a sex toy by the entire household.'

Anon

'I am a BDSM slave of this guy who is into WS (watersports) and scat. Mostly I dress as he instructs, but one day he lets me pick out my favourite underwear. I am to wear just that. He goes to work and leaves me chained to an office chair at a table with my hands tied so that I can type on a computer but can't move beyond that. He has a webcam set up to get a good view of me. Unbeknownst to me he has slipped me diuretics and laxatives so that at some point during the day I will wet and soil myself. He stays in touch sporadically by Skype and email. As my distress builds, realising I'm going to wet and shit myself, he plays with that, exploiting my feelings of shame, threatening punishments and so on. I must Skype him when I think it's going to happen so that he can watch. When he returns, various punishments ensue, including me being wheeled out to the garden, still tied to my office chair, and left there, to sit uncomfortably in my stinking knickers.'

Anon, 25, heterosexual Masters student, German, living in Cologne

'It's about my history professor. He's like forty or a bit older. And he's so damn attractive, I wanna rip off his clothes every time I see him. So in my fantasy he's doing me really hard with his unbelievable big penis. When I think about it it's like classic porn. We meet by accident and talk about no matter what and suddenly we both can't help it because we want each other so badly.'

Anon

'Being forced to give a blow job and then being whipped with a belt.'

Rebecca

'I fantasised about my teachers throughout middle school and high school. Even if I wasn't attracted to them physically I was attracted to their power and control. If I was repulsed by them I still wanted them to like me, to want me, to think me desirable. I dreamt about them coercing me, touching me, abusing me, taking me into their back room in their classroom and having sex with me. I dreamt of being on the floor beneath them, naked. Or being undressed by them. I dreamt of them shoving their cock into my face, making me feel the bulge in their pants while they fingered me or sucked on my nipples or put their finger up my ass.

I still fantasise about rough sex and punishment. Being gagged by fingers and cock. Choked. Pushed around. Pinned to the wall or ground. Throat fucked. Ass fucked. Finger fucked and made to squirt. Rimming a guy's asshole, licking his balls. Having him sit on my face. Ass in the air, face to the floor. Having clothes ripped off and being groped and touched and having my tits slapped or face slapped. Being forced to tell him that I want to be used and abused. Having a man call me names, whether gently or aggressively. The sound of his voice in my ear. Telling me what to do.'

Anon, 44, single mom of two. 'I have been single for 15 years and haven't had sex for 13.'

'I am looking for a job and see a help wanted sign in a window. I go into the company and am told that the owner will interview me. I go into the owner's office. He is about 75 years old. He starts out the interview asking the normal questions. Why do you want to work here? What do you have to offer the company? Then he asks me what is my favorite sexual position, what makes me horny and if I have seen a porn movie before. He says that I don't have to answer the questions if I don't want to. I do, telling him I haven't tried a position that I don't like and I saw a porn once and it made me horny.

He asks if I will take off my shirt and my bra. I don't really want to but he comes over to me and touches my breast and my nipples go hard. He unbuttons my shirt and undoes my bra. He begins to caress my breast and I can tell that I am getting wet. He goes back over to his desk and sits down.

He asks what I would do to make a man hard so I walk over to him and start to rub his crotch. He takes my hand and puts it down his pants. With his other hand he undoes his belt and unzips his pants. He lifts my skirt, pulls off my underwear and touches me. I am so hot that I turn around and lower myself on him, guiding his erection into me.

Soon he lifts me onto his desk and continues to thrust himself into me. When we have both had an orgasm he leaves me sitting on his desk. He asks me some more questions then asks what is my favourite way to make a man hard again, so I go down on him. Soon he is hard and he takes me to the couch that was in his office. He slowly enters me and continues to have sex with me.

As we are having sex on the couch, his grandson who is about thirty enters his office. We continue to finish while his grandson watches. When we finish he gets up and leaves the office. I am left naked on the couch. His grandson stands in front of me. He takes my hand and puts it on his crotch. With my other hand I unzip his pants and pull out his large hard penis. He takes off his pants and slowly lowers himself on me. I take his erection in my hand and guided it inside of me. He slowly thrusts himself inside me until I am gasping for air and begging for more. We continue for about an hour until we both come.

When we finish he continues to lie on top of me, still inside me. Somewhere in the office a TV comes on and it's showing a porno. I began to get hot again and rub him until he is hard again. We continue in different positions, my favourite being doggie style where he can thrust deep and completely.

Once we finish he says thank you and leaves. I get dressed, everything except my underwear which I can't find, and sit back waiting. Soon the owner returned he asked me to come over to his desk. He asks me a few more questions. Next thing I know his hand is up my skirt and he has two fingers inside of me. His other hand on my behind rubbing it. I am getting all wet again. He turns away from bending me over his desk.

Next thing I know he is hard and inside of me again. He slowly moves in and out of me. At one time he has his penis rubbing against my clit. It's making me so hot that I reach down and direct him back inside of me, thrusting him deep inside of me. He has me bend over touching the floor with my hands as he completely enters me from behind. My body is shaking as I begin to have an orgasm. When I finish he continues to thrust himself deeper inside of me with one hand on my breast and the other on my clit. He then goes harder and harder and deeper and deeper until I explode again. Finally he finishes and thanks me for the interview. He tells me he will contact me about the job.'

Noelle, 22, hetero-flexible Dutch woman living in South Africa with her male partner

'My favourite fantasy is my partner in a leather, comfy chair, sipping whiskey and smoking a cigar, wearing a suit; me, naked or in stockings and corset, collared and on a leash, sitting on a sheepskin on the floor, ready to serve him.'

Maria, heterosexual, cis, in a relationship, not living together, no children

'I imagine having sex in my old workplace with a university professor (I used to work in university admin). In that fantasy I am in a submissive position with the professor as an older, more powerful man who is in control although I enjoy and initiate the encounter.'

Anon, Even though I do not agree with your identifiers in a way that most identifies myself (Which is that I am Owned), I provide the following. My age is 29, I am bisexual, I have depression. I am Caucasian. I am separated from my husband and living with my Master and his wife. I have one child and he is 27 months old. I work in a call centre. No academic qualifications. I have brown hair. I read extensively and on a daily basis I try and improve myself. Being loved is most important to me.

'In my most recent fantasy, I welcome my Master home kneeling in the doorway, arms bound behind my back with an armbinder. I have my hood on my head, which only has a mouth hole. My breasts are bound and sensitive, my nipples are pierced with the thick rings my Master likes so much. My labia are also pierced with those thick rings and padlocked closed – a reminder of my Owner's control over my sexuality and my orgasms. I follow him to his chair and he pulls his pants down and has me kneel and throat his cock in silence. It's very messy because he likes that.

While he enjoys my mouth-hole he tells me how pleasing it is to have me chaste for his pleasure, so that I become more focussed in my service to him. By this stage I have not had an orgasm in quite a while and doesn't look like I'm going to have one any time soon. I like knowing that soon afterward he is going to fuck any one of my holes and come in it, that I will be able to feel all of the pleasure and have to control myself that I do not disobey his wishes and come without permission.

That to me, is lovely service. Giving all that you can towards someone's pleasure without the expectation of receiving what you desire in return.

My favourite fantasy is being reduced to little more than three holes. Usually, this is by wearing a full latex suit, including my hood so that I am dehumanised. Usually my arms are bound behind me and at times I am hobbled. I have a ring gag in my mouth to keep it open and accessible. My genital area is able to be opened by a zipper in the latex suit. It is merely my fantasy that my Owner uses me in any hole, any time his whim takes him.

Because I live in a 24/7 TPE relationship with my Master, I am intrinsically submissive and it has a very heavy emphasis on the way my personality is shaped, how I communicate with people and how I serve my Master. The more dominant my Master is, it seems the more I crave to be dehumanised, objectified and humiliated.

My Master is so welcoming and amazing, that he makes me comfortable in my own skin. I don't feel afraid to tell him things, even the things that are touted to be taboo or extreme. When I'm play-acting as a puppy he makes me feel so loved and cherished that I don't feel stupid or embarrassed. He is very good about making sure that I am able to express myself and my sexual desires.'

Take My Love

Submission is often used to show love in fantasies: the most deviant submissive fantasies can sometimes be the most romantic of all. The appeal of this fantasy is hardly surprising given representations of the female body in the media; women are judged for 'giving away' sex and valued for how 'sexy' they are, while romantic narratives also reinforce the idea that a woman in love 'gives herself' to her partner. As such, 'giving' a body to a lover may be perceived as showing love.

Ella, 36, bisexual, 'In a long term relationship with the man I want to spend the rest of my life with'

'I've always had submissive fantasies but since I met my partner, I've been unable to fantasise about anyone but him – other than the occasional group experience involving women, with him directing proceedings. I imagine being his slave for a weekend, sucking his cock and licking his balls while he watches football – even pissing in my mouth if he needs to. I get off on the idea of there being no limits: I am there to serve him and give him pleasure (in reality, he doesn't like watersports and I do, so when he demeans me in the fantasy, it is on my terms). He pushes my limits, spanking me or sometimes even branding me: the idea of facing up to the pain and overcoming it for him makes me feel strong.

I give him access to my entire body, even though I generally find anal sex painful in real life so don't tend to do it unless I'm in the (rare) mood. He uses all three holes as he sees fit and "forces" me to masturbate for him, telling me how hot I am and how I'm "his slut". He brings me to orgasm after orgasm with a magic-wand vibrator, purely for his own entertainment, and I often imagine him filming me as I indulge his desires – however "disgusting" and base – to blackmail me into pushing my limits even further.

This "blackmail" generally entails being forced to have kinky lesbian sex in front of him, and sometimes being forced to watch as he pleasures the other woman while I'm tied up and unable to masturbate. He comments on how wet I'm getting as I watch, which I find humiliating because I see sex as an intimate thing and the other woman's presence is shameful – he's turning "our" intimacy into "my" slutty behaviour.

Sometimes, he makes the woman and I compete to show who the "best slut" is – either by pleasuring him or, more often, by doing increasingly hardcore things to each other: fisting, squirting all over each other and taking each other with strap ons – whoever manages the biggest dildo "wins". The prize is generally his ejaculate – over my face or sprayed over the other woman's tits for me to lick off. Sometimes I prefer to lose – when I imagine the "loser" will have to lick the "winner" clean after she's been fucked, or even during, lying underneath the woman as my lover has sex with her doggy style, licking her pussy and his balls and arse.

In reality, I'm wary about having group sex with my partner. I've done it before with other people and it's always led to relationship breakdown – I think I'm too jealous to be able to effectively separate out all the feelings. However, mentally, I get off on competing with another woman to "win" his affections. And I always win – unless I don't want to – of course.'

Disgust Me

Much as Ella fantasises about an experience she wouldn't want to happen in real life, some women enjoy fantasising about having sex with men they find physically undesirable. Fear and disgust are both powerful emotions that can feed our fantasies; having sex with someone 'undesirable' can feel like the ultimate transgression for some women.

Amber

'I have fantasies about having sex with men who are generally considered unattractive and undesirable: greasy, ugly men, very obese, seedy, unclean men – men I wouldn't want to sleep with in real life. But it's the fact I don't want to have sex with them that turns me on so much – it brings sex down to the most base level of rutting animals. It's a need-fulfilment rather than romantic desire. I fantasise about fucking these semi-repulsive men more than I fantasise about hot, handsome sexy men. I often fantasise about fucking men I wouldn't in real life.'

Amy, 36, single academic, no children

'A male student of mine (I teach at a university in real life) who is failing all his classes bribes me with money to change his grade from an F to a B, so that he can stay in school. Unfortunately none of his other professors agree, so he will be thrown out anyway. He comes back to my office and uses the fact that I've taken his money as leverage to demand sexual favours – specifically, that I fellate him. He's young, pasty, overweight, and has typically bad freshman hygiene. He's not attractive to me in any way, but I don't feel like I can safely refuse.

I kneel in front of him on the bad carpet in my office. His erection is tenting his dirty sweatpants. I pull them down and take his penis in my mouth. I can taste sweat on it. I realise that he has almost no sexual experience, and that he's going to have his first sexual contact with a woman he's coerced. He ejaculates almost immediately into my mouth. There's a surprising amount of it. As I masturbate to this fantasy, I generally have an orgasm when he does.'

Take Me Fundamentally

Anal sex is a common theme in submissive fantasies, often teamed with simultaneous oral and/or vaginal penetration. While this often forms part of the narrative of contemporary porn, its inclusion in female fantasies pre-dates the rise in hardcore-porn availability. Though pornography *may* help inform people's sexual desires by providing masturbatory stimuli, it's chicken-and-egg, and research, as yet, provides no definitive answers.

Anal sex can be used in many different ways in submissive fantasies. Sometimes it is used to show a man's power over a woman; sometimes to show a woman how 'slutty' she is; sometimes as a way of inflicting 'pleasurable' pain; but generally speaking, the woman sexually enjoys her anal defilement just as much as the man. As 21-year-old Katie says, 'I love to be dominated and love that fine line between pain and pleasure (also in the form of anal sex).'

Perhaps the real taboo is the idea that some women might actually enjoy anal sex just as much as some men. As one woman said of living out a fantasy, 'My partner wanted to try anal sex. It was great and we both enjoy it. I sometimes prefer anal to vaginal sex.'

Isobel, heterosexual with some threesomes, separated mother of two, Ph.D in psychology

'An older man beating me with a cane for being bad and then using his hand, which becomes his finger penetrating my anus which he then has anal sex with.'

Anon, female pansexual

'My favourite fantasy is being subdued and pleasured digitally while the aggressor finishes by popping his cock into my ass.'

Anon, 46, college professor, heterosexual, poly, kinky

'My lover and a friend of ours agrees to help me realise my desire to push my limits, both in terms of pain and anal sex. The friend spanks me while I give my lover a blow-job, hitting me harder and harder until my lover comes. Then they tie my hands to hooks in the ceiling, put in a small butt plug and then my lover flogs me while the friend fucks me.

Next I'm tied to a bench and the butt plug is replaced by a larger, vibrating butt plug. A Hitachi (strong vibrator) is put in place and I come over and over until I beg for a break. I'm allowed a brief rest, but then my lover replaces the butt plug with an almost full sized dildo and offers me a choice. I can finish the scene with ten cane strokes and anal sex, or thirty cane strokes. I choose the fucking and after ten strokes, he removes the butt plug and starts to fuck me. Our friend starts fucking my mouth and the combination is so intense I come one last time.'

Come For Me

Ejaculate features in many female submissive fantasies. While the media has made much of the adult industry's penchant for 'facials' (in which a man ejaculates on a woman's face) and bukkake (in which a woman is covered more rigorously in ejaculate) as a sign of the increasing objectification of women, that is just one reading that can be made.

For some women, accepting semen shows acceptance of sex. Ejaculate represents the male climax, and as such offers a woman validation of her own desirability. These women are not only complicit in sex but positively revelling in being ejaculated on.

Rebecca, 28, single, lives in New York, views her sexuality as being on a continuum, Ph.D

'I've fantasised about being in gangbangs, multiple men at the same time, having every hole filled, being controlled and dominated. I dreamed about being covered in come. Being degraded. I dreamt about being forced to suck on a dog's dick or a horse's cock. To be a slave to someone. To be owned and used. To be called a fuck doll, fuck pig, slut, slave, whore or come slut. I dreamt of being in prison and having to fuck the guards. Being abused by them, taken by them. I fantasised about bondage, breast bondage, mouth gags, tit torture, wax torture, spanking and nipple weights and clamps. I fantasised about being teased, being wet, being made to wait. Being told to come or not to. Being made to submit. Dominated. Humiliated. And then rewarded.'

Amber

'The idea of being used as a mere vessel for someone else's sexual release is a huge turn-on for me: getting down to the nitty-gritty, I yearn to be a come-dump – a receptacle used and abused for my lover(s)' requirements. I find being used for the basest and least controllable of needs – the orgasm – empowering in its animal submissiveness. The mental dichotomy is both exciting and perverse and I relish it.'

Lisa, 28, in a long term relationship and bisexual

'I've always fantasised about being come all over – possibly inspired by Nancy Friday's book *Men in Love*, which has lots of fantasises involving ejaculate (including one with a man whose ejaculate tastes of honey that's seen me through many a long night). Sometimes I imagine my partner masturbating over me, coming over me again and again until I'm covered in his sperm. Other times, I imagine kneeling in a group of men – like you see in porn films – and sucking and licking their cocks until they come all over me. I also imagine my partner masturbating me at a fetish club in front of lots of horny strangers – male and female – who my partner allows to ejaculate all over me at the point he makes me come: it's both my punishment and reward for being slutty. In coming all over me, he and the voyeurs show how sexy they find me.

I've watched some bukkake videos online but I don't like them unless the woman is clearly enjoying herself. I generally read the descriptions of the porno videos and masturbate about them putting myself in the starring role rather than watching the videos: that way, I can make the fantasy work however I want it to without having to worry about a woman being hurt. (I don't like it when men come in your eye because it hurts but lots of men in bukkake videos seem to take pleasure in getting their come in a woman's eye.)

However, my most common fantasy is definitely having my partner's come all over me: I like the idea of being covered in his spunk, and don't find it demeaning at all. To me, it's a compliment that he finds me sexy enough to want to give me his come: and I find the idea of accepting every part of him romantic in a twisted kind of way.'

Rape Fantasies

Rape fantasies are by far the most commonly researched female fantasies – to such a degree that many people believe the rape fantasy is women's most common fantasy. However, contributions to the survey for *Garden of Desires*, *Scarlet* magazine and Cliterati at least do not support this theory. It is far more common to read more sophisticated control fantasies: women being bound and teased; forced to wear specific outfits, or take part in 'depraved' sexual acts; being humiliated or flogged; paid for sex; or being 'forced' to show their slutty side generally with a healthy dose of orgasms thrown into the equation. Indeed, penis-in-vagina sex is far from ubiquitous in submissive fantasies, so if anything, they are often distanced from rape.

Given that kinky sex is only just beginning to enter the mainstream, it is possible that previous studies into female sexual fantasy categorised any fantasies with a theme of male control as 'rape' fantasies, particularly as some studies don't use the word rape but instead 'overpowered', 'coerced' or 'forced' which can all play a part in consensual BDSM play without necessarily indicating a rape fantasy. Now we have a more sophisticated understanding of sex, it is easier to draw the lines between traditional romantic stereotypes, consensual BDSM and rape fantasies (though some people are still unable to separate them and insist on conflating them).

That said, some women do fantasise about rape. However, it is generally a long way from real-life rape. The woman almost always achieves orgasm and is mentally in control of the situation, even while imagining herself relinquishing control. As Jenny M. Bivona says in her 2008 paper, 'Women's Erotic Rape Fantasies', 'Most rape fantasies are not realistic depictions of actual rape. Instead, they are abstracted, eroticized portrayals that emphasize some aspects of rape and omit or distort other features.' (Kanin, 1982).

Heather, 27, Masters student

'While some of my fantasies include being "topped" or controlled, I do not believe this is more common in the female gender and I would like to see surveys of modern male fantasy to see if they too "want to be tied up". My fantasies and reality are about consent. Rape is not a fantasy. Rape is not consensual. I would like to make sure that women who mention rape as a fantasy differentiate between whether it is consensual and negotiated, or non-consensual. I would hope the research indicates it is consensual in most cases which would really help undermine the stereotype that "women secretly want to be raped". This badly needs addressing!'

Anon, 27, female, I'm studying to be an art therapist/midwife. I'm a big curvy woman with power and affection enough for everyone. One day I'd love to have my own children and husband/wife.

'I have never had a sexual partner but I feel like it only adds to my own sexuality and I have no shame anymore about loving myself. The idea of "virgin priestesses" makes a lot of sense to me now that I'm more connected to my own sexuality.

For a long time I was very attracted to rape but I was also very ashamed of my own sexuality and it was a dark secret that weighed down on me, guilt wise, for a very long time. Now that I've come to terms with wanting to be submissive, and understood that there's nothing wrong with being controlled or that it doesn't exclude love . . . I enjoy "submissive" fantasies, even "rape", but it's changed now to "fake rape" with a loving partner or two who are more sexually aggressive.

Now that my self-image has improved, I love the fantasy of being a desirable goddess . . . being cared for, loved, even being "used" but affectionately . . . to be controlled and loved equally . . . affection and a little safe aggression. Two men as long-term partners at once is also a fantasy of mine.

My fantasies allow me to "love" myself and to feel loved. Although I am bisexual it's men who I have grown up being ashamed of being attracted to. I view the men in my fantasies as my "sacred masculine", an aspect of my own being, and when I was young I was terrified and turned on by them . . . They were aggressive, hurt me, and used me before abandoning me. Now they help me heal my relationship with men in my life. That's why it's so important to have an aspect of love and affection in my fantasies.'

Anon, 30, lawyer

'One of my fantasies is rape. I feel ashamed by it and I do feel (irrationally) that in fantasising about rape I would be tempting fate, so I rarely think about it. I shared this with an ex-partner once because pretending it was rape was the only way I could still get turned on by him and the fantasy, after a while, wasn't enough. We acted it out and he told me he felt awful afterwards. I would not share this with my current partner.'

Anon, 25, bi graduate in a monogamous, long-term relationship with a cis male, had only one sexual partner

'My favourite fantasy is a non-consensual, coercive, "Do what I say or something bad may happen to you"-type thing. The "bad thing" could be threat of violence or humiliation of some sort. I usually play the part of a young, naive girl (13–16) and the aggressor is an older man (sometimes woman) in a position of authority of some sort (teacher, friend's father). Sometimes there are multiple participants. The men always come in me and enjoy making me feel pleasure despite my protests.

Most recently, I fantasised about a partner (not my partner, but another friend I fantasise about) using me as he sees fit, whenever he wants and choosing to share me with a male friend of his, allowing the friend to come in me and they both commenting on how tight I am and how good I look filled with come.'

Anon, 40, single mom of two

'I have always thought that I would never want to be raped. My rape fantasy begins with both my daughter and I being home. Two men break into our house. They are holding my daughter and I tell them they can do anything they want with me if they will let her go so they let her leave. They take turns with me and at one time I have both of them inside of me. The one is doing it doggie style while I have oral with the other one.

At first I just lay there and let them do what they want. At one point the one guy becomes very passionate and sexual and it changes how I feel. I begin to enjoy it and I ask them to do different positions with me. I also enjoy that it isn't just one guy but there are two of them. I enjoy having the one watch while the other one rapes me than having them switch and doing something different with the other guy.

I also fantasised that I would have oral sex with one then the other one. I even allowed them to have anal sex with me. I don't know that I would ever really have sex with two guys but just the thought of it makes me horny. Also in my fantasy I allow them to both have orgasms while inside of me multiple times.'

In allowing two men to do 'anything they want', in exchange for her daughter's freedom, this contributor is being both 'a good mother' and sexually satisfied. The balance of power clearly shifts during the fantasy, as she moves from being victim to being in control. 'I begin to enjoy it and I ask them to do different positions with me.' There is no doubt that she is the one setting the ground rules. 'I even allowed them to have anal sex with me.'

Tina's fantasy is one of the most clearly defined rape fantasies submitted for the book, but even her fantasy shows elements of her retaining power over proceedings: 'I . . . talk to myself like I am the rapist.' Her confession that 'I want to be tied up and to be used', shows her achieving her own desires by mentally ceding control.

Tina, 20, Caucasian college student. Single virgin with brown, curly hair, hazel eyes and glasses

'I have always dreamed of being raped. I think about it all the time. If I am walking home from class, I think about a guy grabbing me and forcing himself on me. Or if I am driving and I break down and a guy rapes me in my car. And my most common is when I am lying in bed and a guy breaks in and rapes me. I even think about a gang rape. I think about it a lot. I even visualise what could happen and talk to myself like I am the rapist. I want to be tied up and to be used.'

Rather than rape fantasies being an indication of women's sexual desire to be raped (an assertion that has been widely and universally disproved), they could reflect the pervasive nature of rape in our culture. Some rape victims find comfort – whether healthily or unhealthily – in rape fantasies, finding it a way to take back control over their sexuality. And many women feel sexually threatened in society, so rape fantasies may be a way of controlling that fear. As Nancy Friday says, 'Through her fantasy a woman turns something fearful into something pleasurable. Her fantasy gives her the sense of control, power and safety she lacks in real life. She turns her fear into a love object. In her fantasy, she gets to tame the beast.' (p.71, *My Secret Garden*)

Emily, extract taken from http://musingsofemilyrose.blogspot.co.uk/ with permission:

'I don't believe we should censor our fantasies. We simply cannot. Ever since I can remember masturbating, before I even knew what masturbating was, I have fantasised about kink. And, being forced by a stranger in a dark alley (actually, it was usually the local park) was a common fantasy. When I came across the kink scene later in my adult life (the internet wasn't around in my formative years) I was relieved to find out that I wasn't the only one, that I wasn't a strange fucked up deviant, but "normal" (at least by the standards of kink. I recognise that if you're anti-kink, you'll still think I'm a fucked up deviant). There is a very common myth, which is part of the rape culture which permeates our society, that women do want to be raped. And, it is a common female fantasy (see Wikipedia). But, rape is not the same as the fantasy.

When I was raped, I felt that I no longer had agency to enjoy those fantasies any more. It was one of the things he took from me. On the boards of Informed Consent (now, sadly, no more), I was vocal in my opposition to "rape play", a term used to describe a scene in which one participant *consensually* cedes the right to consent to what happens, otherwise known as "consensual non-consent". I objected in most part to the term "play" juxtaposed with the act of rape. To me, rape was horrific, it had lost me my job, many friends, my family relationships (now mending), and most of all, my sanity. How could people be seeming to *enjoy* this, how could they call it *play*?

I now practice consensual non-consent (CNC). The very special friend who I have enjoyed (yes, enjoyed) that with has given me back my fantasies; it's probably the biggest, most significant gift anyone has ever given me. In some ways, it's been therapeutic (but I'm not saying I recommend it for rape survivors, that's just a very personal observation). The difference between CNC and actual rape, to me, is the mutual respect. The hugs afterwards. The knowing that what we're doing (what he's doing) is for our *mutual* pleasure. But, during, it is not something I want. It *is* non-consent, but it isn't rape, because it *is* consensual. I expect many of you will be thinking, *oh, that makes him a rapist*. I know he is not. When we talk (and we do talk about this), he is mortified by the idea that he could be. He never could be, he never would, unless he was *absolutely* sure, beyond *all* doubt, that it was something I wanted, craved, needed, desired. Now, I understand why it is often termed "rape play". It is as akin to actual rape as children playing doctors and nurses is as akin to being an actual surgeon.'

Remittance Girl responded to Emily's piece online:

'Any culture in which people are not required to be responsible for their own desire and how they act upon it is with others problematic. We end up back at Aristotle's insistence that people cannot think rationally in the face of sexual desire. This is patently false. Otherwise everyone would rape, if they could; no one would ever think clearly enough to put a condom on; and most children would be victims of sexual abuse, etc. The majority of us can and do think rationally in the midst of desire.

When it comes to the difference between rape and rape fantasy, I believe the issue of agency is paramount. As you pointed out, many women have rape fantasies. A good recent study has put the numbers at about forty per cent. But a person (whether male or female) who has rape fantasies is the agent of the fantasy. The writer, director, casting agent, the editor. It is a little disingenuous to say that rape fantasies never look anything like real rape. There are women who have extremely realistic rape fantasies, with all the brutality and the lack of any sexual arousal that entails. Nonetheless, the woman having that fantasy is still the agent of it. And it is worth adding that many men have rape fantasies too.'

There is no one answer to why women have rape fantasies. As Jenny M Bivona says, 'Contemporary researchers, theorists, and clinicians have created several major theories to explain rape fantasies, and each of these theories was tested in the present investigation. It is unlikely that all women have rape fantasies for the same reason. Instead, a theory may provide a valid explanation for one dimension of rape fantasies, so that various theories would need to be integrated to form a comprehensive understanding.'

The Power of Submissive Fantasies

Once you remove the overly simplistic reading that women who have submissive fantasies are genuinely relinquishing control over their sexuality, much of the outrage (and subsequent column inches) vanishes. Most research into female submissive fantasies tends to point in the same direction: female submission is about being desired as much as it is about being defiled – if not more so. In fantasising about submitting, a woman is actually fantasising about being irresistible.

Cheeky Minx, erotic writer

'My earliest fantasy circulated around domination but one which centred around a powerful and overwhelming male desire for me and my body. Being taken and possessed, allowing my body to relinquish all control and feel pleasure. The male in the fantasy was invariably older and sexually experienced and seasoned.

My earliest sexual fantasy still structures my fantasy life today. But now, they are more complex, varied and nuanced – and the details, sensuality, carnality vary according to my mood. Group sex, lesbian sex and exhibitionism also play a major part in my fantasies now. Older men are still pivotal.

Additionally, oral sex – giving or receiving, involving either men or other women mostly in semi-public spaces – is also another that features heavily.

If I had to pick a favourite it would be a variation on being dominated, one where an older man needs to selfishly play out his own passion but in doing so sates my own desires. Along these lines, the fantasy revolves around being the centre of attention and his passion, being devoured in every possible way and every sense of the term (oral, penetration, anal) and leaving my mark on him – and vice versa – (come, bruises, scratches, clothing to shreds). For the most part, the fantasy doesn't involve restraints but rather his voice, words, hands, body, and inherent power serve as the means of control. Lately, this also involves documenting the sex via photographs, voice recordings and video.'

Anon, 28, professional, heterosexual female. Newly married, no children

'A sexual encounter in the office, either with a co-worker or with my partner. Most often I am in a submissive role, being pleasured but held up as an object of adoration and passion.'

While male submissive fantasies often involve humiliation through taunts about physical appearance (e.g. penis size), it is incredibly rare to see a female sexual fantasy in which she is taunted for being too fat, saggy or otherwise physically lacking. As professional Dominatrix, Mistress Absolute, says, 'Women are used to being judged for the way they look. Perhaps in fantasy, being taunted for being unattractive is too close to reality.'

Instead, the woman's 'failing' tends to be that she is 'too slutty', being punished for inciting other's desires; 'too vulnerable', allowing herself to transcend society's norms by going to, say, a bad neighbourhood or 'dodgy' strip club which clearly demands retribution; or too sexy to be resisted, bringing her punishment on herself by trying to attract men's attention. The woman's desirability tends to be her 'downfall' as this fantasy shows:

Lucy, 32, 'single, and happily so'

'A recurring theme in my fantasies is being in a sleazy biker bar wearing something sexy. I've gone there to pull because I'm bored and lonely and am sitting at the bar alone. A group of bikers is playing pool and take an interest in me. I ignore them at first but that just makes them taunt me more. Soon, they're surrounding me, telling me I'm too sexy to be sitting all alone.

Although I'm scared at first, I soon notice the "lead" guy is seriously sexy – all muscles and stubble. I start to flirt with him and soon, he's buying me shots. The alcohol gives me confidence to tell him I fancy him. He says that he'll fuck me but only if I prove myself first by fucking all his biker friends, telling me it's my own fault for "dressing like a slut".

The idea disgusts and arouses me in equal measure. It feels so taboo but I like the idea of being the centre of attention. I agree to his challenge and fuck all of them. They start off taunting me for being a slut but when they see how far I'll happily go, they start cheering me on instead: nothing they can do is too much for me and I win the respect of the leader. Ironically, by then I've usually got to come so I don't tend to masturbate about fucking the leader who I fancied in the first place!'

Dr Michael Bader, author of *Arousal: The Secret Logic of Sexual Fantasies* (2003), suggested submissive fantasies appease women's feeling of guilt about their sexual power over men. Fantasies about being overwhelmed for being 'too desirable' would certainly fit comfortably within this idea. And of course, the virgin/whore trope has a lot to answer for too.

Compared to forty years ago, the submissive fantasies now shared by women seem considerably less violent and gratuitously fantastical. Forced bestiality, extreme rape and body parts being ripped off feature far less commonly than erotic power games, dressing up, spanking, 'forced' group sex and bondage.

Maybe this is because the guilt women felt for being sexual in 1973 has lessened in 2013. Perhaps women have less anger to release through their fantasies – and as such, less pain to direct inwards. Maybe women are becoming less sexually submissive as they become more sexually empowered. Or it could be that the rise of the internet – and with it, the ability to watch almost any graphic sex act you can imagine – has made women less inclined to conjure up violent fantasies. Now that permission had been granted, many women are making their submissive dreams come true – as the subsequent increase in sales of butt plugs, jiggle balls and bondage equipment clearly demonstrate. And if you're going to make your fantasies come true, you're a lot more likely to imagine things that are feasible in real life.

Despite the hysteria which often accompanies suggestions that women enjoy submissive fantasies, in reality submissive fantasies do not show that women are weak. As Dr Susan Block says on counterpoint.org, 'In love – as opposed to war, politics or business, where "surrender" conjures images of defeat and shame – surrender can be sweet and the ultimate, intimate fulfilment. The ancient Taoist masters said, "In yielding, there is strength." In surrender, there can be power – certainly sexual-fantasy power.'

No matter how or why they exist, submissive fantasies are certainly still incredibly popular with some women – but now women are defining their own boundaries more clearly than ever before, submitting in the way that best suits their needs – and they're happy to admit to their dominant desires too.

Chapter Two:
Dominant Fantasies

'My fantasies seem to be becoming more violent over time. I don't need the violence in them, however. I just enjoy it more."

KOO, 23, SINGLE, STRAIGHT BUT CURIOUS

Domination is the flip side of the coin to submission, but female fantasies of domination are far less studied than female submissive fantasies. This could be because such fantasies run contrary to the norms expected of women, are less common or are more taboo. However, though fewer women shared dominant than submissive fantasies when contributing to *Garden of Desires*, domination was nonetheless an extremely popular theme.

In his study on sexual fantasy, *Who's Been Sleeping in Your Head?*, Brett Kahr found that 29 per cent of people have dominant fantasies. However, the dominant woman is an unpopular figure in society, attracting labels including 'bossy' and 'ball-buster'. In popular media narrative, women are expected to be sexually passive rather than active; and the idea that they could have any desire to dominate is treated as abnormal. This is reflected in the slut-shaming that accompanies any woman who dares to reveal herself as a sexually dominant woman; and in the stereotypes that are associated with the 'Domme'.

The strong, sexual woman has long been seen as emasculating men. In Medieval times, a strong woman who 'wore the trousers' was seen as rendering a man effeminate, while a woman who 'cuckolded' a man drew aspersions about his sexual prowess. Historians Phillips and Reay say, 'Elizabeth Foyster has argued that by basing itself so strongly on control of female sexuality, by being defined essentially in terms of mastery of its "other", pre-modern masculinity was an anxious masculinity, all too easily threatened and undermined by the words of women. Men were continually worried about the potential adultery of their wives and the sexual honour of their daughters.' How different is this from men today being labelled 'pussy whipped' or assuming a paternalistic role in 'protecting' their daughter's virtue by insisting she wears 'appropriate' clothes? The dominatrix confuses this role, her sexuality bringing the male pleasure as her behaviour causes him pain.

Defining the Domme

$\mathcal{T}$he popular image of a dominatrix is a shiny cat-suited, slim, busty cis woman, thighs straddling a whimpering male and making him serve her sexually. She is generally white, slim, dark haired, thigh-booted and whip-wielding; and fits squarely within society's views of what a 'sexy' woman is. There are variations in racial stereotyping of the dominant woman, though all fall within 'accepted' conceptions of beauty. Asian BDSM educator Midori, says there are two prevalent stereotypes of Asian women – 'delicate flowers or dragon ladies' – the latter fitting comfortably within the stereotype of the sexually dominant woman – think Lucy Liu in *Charlie's Angels*.[10] Similarly, should a black woman don 'dominatrix' clothes, she is at risk of incurring the 'jezebel' label – as shown by the way the media has previously treated Rhianna, who has sung openly about enjoying BDSM.

However, this male fantasy of a dominatrix is very different from the dominant fantasies of many women. While certain fetish-scene indicators such as corsets do arise in women's

10 Margot Weiss's BDSM study, *Techniques of Pleasure*

fantasies on occasion, as a general rule, women have creative and individual ways to punish their fantasy lovers, many of which bear little resemblance to the popular image of a 'Domme'. In the confines of her own mind, a woman can be as dominant as she wants in the way that she wants to, without being accused of being 'unladylike' and without risking being objectified in the process.

In her paper, 'Worship Me for the Goddess I Am: Sex, Lies and Self Discovery in the World of Female Dominance', Phillipa Giller suggests that men feel ashamed of their submissive urges, as a result of 'emotional baggage from thousands of years of institutionalised misogyny, not to mention homophobia'. She says that by sexualising the dominatrix, men can distract themselves from their fear of women, removing their insecurity and putting her alongside the spinster, shrew, witch (and arguably the career woman) as 'a target of the same leering ridicule aimed at all women who have demonstrated independence or wielded power'. Giller suggests that many men have the urge to submit to a powerful woman but societal pressures to 'tame the shrews' makes them feel conflicted about their desires. 'Just as the patriarchal psychology forbids women to wield power, it forbids men from aiding and abetting such power, much less being attracted by it.'

Women, on the other hand, have no need for the dominatrix stereotype (unless they are going to choose to work as a dominatrix with male clients, in which case it may be a commercial decision). Within their own fantasies, women can dominate in the way that they want to without having to consider the male gaze. Of course, some women still fantasise about wearing fabulous latex outfits or assuming a stereotypical dominant role but the fantasies submitted to *Garden of Desires* showed much more creativity than the accepted vision of the 'Domme'; penis-in-vagina (piv) sex is rarely at the core of the dominant fantasies submitted to *Garden of Desires*; and the woman's pleasure generally takes a central role. Submissive fantasies and dominant fantasies often sit alongside each other in women's imagination too. Today's woman gives as good as she gets, taking punishment and meting it out in equal measure.

Anon, 25, heterosexual, single, Masters, no children

'I fantasise about being dominant towards a heterosexual man, e.g. bonding, teasing, coming in his face. (I have fantasies about dominance and submission in both directions.) But *without* the whole leather, whip-etc. thing. I've got much more diverse fantasies than the ones commonly shown in porn movies.'

Anon, 34, hetero, Caucasian, single, no children, business owner, completing 3 bachelor degrees, attractive, suffer anxiety and insomnia

'I started fantasising about objectifying men and having them serve me – graphically, a naked man serving his dick up to me on a silver platter, just like a waiter would offer champagne. I liked the idea of a MAN wanting me sexually. My most recent fantasy was about an uber, sexy, alpha man being sexually turned on by another man, often reluctantly. I watch a lot of gay porn, or NC porn. I like to imagine the men in the scenarios. I'm not so much into pain, but I enjoy watching men suffer a bit i.e. vac racks, edging, electro, forced hand jobs.'

Anon, 34, straight, female, Australian

'Having a male sub whom I could make go down on me any time, any place whilst ignoring his presence as a person; and dominating another woman alongside my male partner, pushing consent to its limits, the power play and mind games are as important if not more so than the physical actions. I always wanted to squirt into my partner's mouth or have him go down on me after sex (as he was very scared of his own semen). He was into the squirting but I found another partner to go down on me post unprotected piv sex but shh! that's a well kept secret.'

Anon, 28, bisexual, divorced white woman in a long-term relationship. Undergraduate, no children

'Watching as my boyfriend sucks the dick of a really beefy, strong guy. I'll push bf's head down on that fat cock until he chokes and slobbers all over the place. I'd call him my little bitch and talk dirty while I make out with the beefy guy.'

Mia More, Extract taken from 'Breaking Brad', with permission.

'"Before I accept you as my slave, understand this: Slavery is about total obedience, not occasional submission. I will be no mere Domme, I will be your Mistress. You will be my property, my chattel, and I will own you. You will be denied the option to feel anything akin to jealousy or possession: you are not entitled to me, you belong to me. This is no two-way street, oh no," Liselle tutted, her brown eyes flashing underneath heavy, sensual lids. "Think of it more as an endgame, where you have surrendered all your power and in doing so have become exclusively beholden to your victor – henceforth your owner – whom you must address at all times as 'Mistress'."

Slave kept his head bowed and his eyes downcast. He was becoming uncomfortable kneeling there, Liselle could tell. Perspiration formed on his brow as he concentrated on maintaining his position, fighting the desire to drink in the arresting view of the dominatrix before him. "I will train you to serve me well, and since this is an investment on my time, I expect complete compliance." She moved her foot so that it rested on the flagging beneath his chin, "For example, I will not permit any of that filthy sweat from your forehead to foul my pristine floor. Do you understand?" Slave nodded. Liselle sighed in annoyance. "Yes, Mistress" she prompted.

A look of distress flitted across his face: he'd failed at the first hurdle. "Yes Mistress, I'm sorry Mistress, it won't happen again, Mistress." She smiled at the demonstration of genuine remorse. Already, this novice slave had grasped two of the fundamental principles of their liaison: sincerity and dedication. She felt a frisson of excitement at the journey ahead.

Highly experienced, Liselle kept the smile out of her voice, "Well Slave, good posture is essential, and your . . ." she spat out the words ". . . pathetic posture needs work: it will teach you focus and discipline. I want to be able to 'park' you when necessary, and to do that you'll need to learn to stay still until

I indicate that your services are required. And if you think stone floors are uncomfortable ...." she laughed derisorily "... then you'll never be able to manage any of these." Liselle indicated the various bespoke iron cages in the room, each shaped with a particular purpose in mind, watching carefully to ensure her submissive kept his eyes forward and down. She rewarded him with a perfunctory, "Good," and was gratified to see him respond with an almost imperceptible straightening of the spine.

Such succour was appropriate: Liselle had been deliberately economical with the truth when she'd said their connection would be one-way. Undeniably the relationship between a slave and his Mistress depended just as much on his obedience as on her reading of any given situation: of his likes and dislikes, his fetishes and capabilities. Thus the training process also involved Liselle learning about her slave and tailoring her sessions accordingly, as well as continuously working on the set of skills she'd acquired to keep such men (often, but not always powerful in the outside world) subservient at her feet, here in her live-in dungeon.

She watched as sweat collected on her slave's forehead, droplets threatening to fall towards the floor. She flexed her foot. If she timed it right ... "So, Slave, are you ready to obey? Will you serve and worship me as I command?" A drop trickled down to his chin and hung there for a moment. Mindfulness being part of the tuition practice, Liselle watched as her submissive struggled to remain motionless, hardly daring to breathe. She smiled with sadistic satisfaction. "Answer your Mistress, Slave."

His reply was exhaled through immobile lips, "Yes Mistress, please Mistress." The drop hit her heeled shoe. There was an audible intake of breath as the man quaked before the diminutive dominatrix, awaiting his punishment with nervous yet eager apprehension. Liselle paused for effect, assessing her recruit's innate suitability for the position, her eyes skimming his broad shoulders, tensed thighs and the strong arms straight by his side. He was going to make a good slave, she could tell.

She wasn't too keen on the sissy types, but this man was macho enough to make breaking him in a real pleasure.

Ending his suspense, Liselle roughly wiped her toe clean on her slave's groin, voicelessly challenging him to stay both silent and upright. His jaw tensed and a muscle flickered in his abdomen, but other than that there were no outward signs of her deliberate callousness towards him. Liselle nodded in approval.

"Then your training begins today," she confirmed, noting with some satisfaction that at these words an involuntary tremor passed through her newest pupil. His nipples hardened, his breathing became shallow, and with it her own heart rate picked up pace. She might even allow this slave the privilege of pleasuring her if it all went well, a reward she reserved for the very special few.

Once more Liselle cruelly pointed an imperious foot towards her slave, curious to see whether on this second occasion he would flinch. But although goosebumps bulleted his skin, once more he remained unmoving, bound to her will. Delighted, Mistress Liselle tapped him sharply on the shoulder with a riding crop, whereupon her newly appointed slave bowed deeply to honour the transaction that had passed between them. Revelling in anticipation of the ensuing weeks, Liselle laughed triumphantly: their first training session had been a resounding success.'

What is a Dominant Fantasy?

*A*s with submissive fantasies, a dominant fantasy can vary from simply seducing a partner who's powerless to resist to forcing sex, inflicting pain or humiliation and beyond. Some women incorporate bondage into the dominant fantasies, and several fantasise about wearing a strap-on dildo to penetrate a partner.

A dominant fantasy could entail having sex with someone unwilling (in real life or fantasy), a woman using her sexuality to manipulate someone into doing as they were bid or controlling one or more of the 'submissive's' bodily functions. Some women may want to make their dominant fantasies come true – or already do – while others enjoy dominant fantasies without any desire to experience them in real life.

Anon, mid-twenties, mostly asexual white nerd chick. Knitter, spinner and gamer

'I started having fantasies about 12-ish. I had weird sexual-tinged fantasies as a little kid, but no actual sex. My fantasies were triggered by finding out that yaoi (Free gay porn! On the internet!) was "a thing". The earliest sexual fantasy I remember was an elaborate catboy sex-slave thing: genetically engineered catboys get sold to wealthy people as slaves, and lots of weird bondage sexing happens. My fantasies are still heavy on the gay-slave bondage. Now there's more tentacles. And incest. It's been on and off over the years, but it's an old favourite with lots of variety: gang rape, tentacles, men getting pregnant, bondage, toys – very versatile.

My most recent fantasy was about a guy coming back home and getting somewhere between seduced/coerced/raped by his brother (but he totally wants it). I have no idea why someone who has no desire for sex in real life likes fantasy sex so much, but boy do I! I think what this survey hasn't gotten across is that all my fantasies are very voyeuristic.

I myself am never a part. It's people (usually men, sometimes women) who are not me having sex, and I flit about from observer to what each person is experiencing at will. I've never had a sexual fantasy about myself.'

Why Do We Have Dominant Fantasies?

*M*uch as submissive fantasies are thought to serve multiple functions, dominant fantasies can serve a number of purposes, though there is far less research to draw upon. Therapy, including exorcising anger, and, of course, sexual pleasure are just some of the ways in which women may benefit from their dominant desires. In many ways, dominant fantasies act in similar ways to submissive ones – albeit the flip side of the coin.

Therapy and Catharsis

Nancy Friday suggested dominant fantasies can be a way for a woman to assert control over her sex life – mentally at least. 'It is not about him but her working out her own sexuality.' Many women who answered the survey supported this idea. As one contributor said, 'I fantasise most about domming my boyfriend when I'm feeling insecure.' They can also be a way to exorcise past sexual trauma. One survey respondent said, 'I've lived out almost all of my adult fantasies. Sometimes it's a way of letting go of something damaging, for example confronting feelings of not being safe as an adolescent through age-play. Sometimes it's a matter of just finally feeling like all of me is aligned: sexuality, gender, kink.'

In his book *Arousal* (2003), Dr Michael Bader says, 'The key to understanding this process [of becoming aroused through a dominant fantasy] is to remember that the sadist, master or "top" is inflicting pain on a victim who, in reality, doesn't actually feel victimized – who instead is sexually aroused. Since there is no true victim, there is no true crime. Domination fantasies in which the victim is not only not hurt but sexually aroused powerfully disconfirm our guilty beliefs and as a result free up our sexual excitement.'

Zoltan Dienes of the University of Sussex also supports this theory. He found women with dominant fantasies tended to have a fear of being too sexual. He also found that women who had dominant fantasies were more likely to feel anxious about having a loss of control over their life, so dominant fantasies may help women feel more powerful.

Koo, 23, straight, bi-curious, single, not a fan of the idea of marriage

'My fantasies seem to be becoming more violent over time. I don't need the violence in them however, I just enjoy it more. My favourite fantasy involves a young protester being taken by the opposing side for her outspokenness, being raped, beaten and maybe killed. My fantasies elicit positive emotions but sometimes shame I guess; the idea that I am enjoying in my fantasy something that destroys the lives of so many women.'

Louise

'Although I'm generally submissive, I do have a recurring dominant fantasy which I tend to use most when I'm annoyed at my husband and he wants to make it up to me (and yes, we did make elements of it come true once and both thoroughly enjoyed it). I imagine tying my husband face down on his gym machine so that he can't move. I stand at his head and make him look at my pussy and tell me how much he worships it. He starts off being resistant but I use whips, spanking paddles and canes to beat him into submission and, when he still doesn't please me, use clothes pegs on his nipples and all over his balls.

His whimpers of pain make me wet and I love punishing him for all the minor annoyances he's put me through. I can see his cock get harder as I punish him, the head getting more and more purple and engorged. He's begging for me to let him come but I refuse, instead pulling his head back by his hair and forcing him to lick my pussy. I use him for as long as I want to, which varies depending on how much time I have.

The fantasy ends either with me coming and ejaculating over his face and sometimes pissing over his face too; or with me fucking him up the arse with my strap-on. I'd love to be able to ejaculate inside him but as yet, I haven't figured out a way that's feasible enough for my fantasy mind to let me get away with it.

If I'm really horny, I can extend this fantasy to include another women helping me tie him down and punish him then having sex with me in front of him and denying him the slightest touch of either of us. And sometimes I'll imagine him breaking free of his bonds and punishing me for my behaviour, often with the help of another woman who he forces me to pleasure. Not sure I'd be happy to live that bit out though – I think I'm too jealous.'

A Woman Scorned?

In 1991's *Women on Top*, Nancy Friday identified a surge in anger from women contributing to her studies, saying, 'It is time we admitted some women are as cruel as some men.' She thought the fantasies submitted to *My Secret Garden* were those of women with no control over 'the images that swam into their mind'. By the time she researched the second book, women were seizing control, getting angry – and having more dominant fantasies.

'I had hoped that they reflected society's readiness to explore and accept the full range of woman's character, good to bad,' she said in *Women on Top*. However, within a decade she had already noticed a decline in dominant fantasies, which she contrasted with an increased focus on motherhood. 'My worry is that as women resume their traditional role, the one that more than anything defines their womanliness, their anger will once more be repressed.'

Many people in the BDSM scene would argue that domination has nothing to do with anger. But if the fantasies submitted to *Garden of Desires* are anything to go by, women are certainly prepared to admit their dominant desires once more.

Anon, 48, white female, married for 18 years. I have two children

'I was quite promiscuous and had thirty sexual partners before my husband. He and I were not monogamous in our earlier years and I added more partners after marriage. Frankly I have lost count but I'd say around a dozen more.

Recently, I guess because I am middle-aged, I got interested in the idea of older/younger lesbian sex. You'd think that would mean I'd fantasise about young hotties but strangely I tend to think of older women . . . old enough that most people would not think of them sexually – mid-sixties, say. If I had to say why, I think it's because in my fantasies I want to be the more attractive partner.

Anyway I sometimes think of meeting an older woman at the beach or pool, helping her with her suntan lotion, and then being invited back to her place to have sex. (I think of fingering women more than anything else.) To that fantasy I have added a twist that goes like this: the woman is lying on her back while I finger her, suck her breasts, etc. We hear her husband come in but she says it's OK to continue. Her husband joins us, getting into bed behind me. I never even look at him but I begin to tell her, "Mmm, your husband has a big dick ... Do you know how I know? Because he's fucking me with it right now. *Your* husband's dick is inside *me* ... Look at me, look in my eyes while I get fucked by your husband."

There is a bit of a humiliation aspect in that her husband prefers me to her. Sometimes he tells her how much tighter and better I feel than she does. Sometimes I point out that she's lying there with her legs spread wide open and her pussy wet but her husband still fucks me instead.'

Sexual Pleasure

Almost all fantasies submitted to the survey helped women enhance their sexual pleasure, regardless of their theme. One woman with dominant fantasies said, 'My fantasies serve to turn me on, help me reach orgasm (sometimes I struggle) and they help to broaden my sex life. If something goes through my mind that turned me on, I will generally ask my partner if we can introduce it and many new things have been tried.' Another says she fanta-sises because, 'Neither of my past two relationships have been sexually satisfying. One of my ex-boyfriends was sexually conservative and the other just wasn't very into sex after the first month.' Even if a woman's sex life is experimental, there's no guarantee she won't need her fantasies. 'Sometimes during the wildest experiences I've ever had, I would *still* have to fantasise something else in order to orgasm.'

Anon

'I have dominant fantasies in which my partner is forced to give me oral while chained down or tied up – but he enjoys it in my fantasy (and reality) because he's switch too. I imagine him unable to do anything other than crane his neck up to reach me, and enjoy making him earn my pussy. Sometimes I imagine grinding on his face to a selfish orgasm and other times I like to think about teasing him, making him want my pussy and then denying it and masturbating over his face instead, leaving him hard, horny and desperate for me.

My fantasies generally revolve around things we've done or things that I want to do with him and I often tell him about my fantasies during sex which makes him horny and can get him to come quickly if he's taking his time. I'll often use a fantasy about forcing him to go down on me even when he's performing cunnilingus willingly – it makes it much easier for me to come.'

Laura, literature student, living with boyfriend

'I like to imagine tying and blindfolding my boyfriend. My fantasies are an outlet for sexual ideas, maybe putting an idea into theory before trying it out. It feels good to be able to talk about it with my boyfriend and discover new aspects of our sex life.'

Popular Themes in Dominant Fantasies

Tie You Down

Administering bondage is a popular theme within dominant fantasies. In tying someone down, they become powerless to resist no matter how strong they are – and, as such, are subject to a woman's desires.

Dessica, poly, writer, mother (three children) and seeker

'Most of my fantasies involve BDSM, usually with me as the dominant. Bondage and begging are common. Often I will fantasise about the characters in my stories. They are close to the reality I want, I just don't have anyone to act them out with.'

Lisa, 27, 'has never tried bondage but would like to'

'My boyfriend is very dominant but in fantasy I imagine he's handcuffed to a chair and unable to move (I never imagine any lead up – he just starts off being handcuffed – as in real life he could overpower me and my imagination won't let me fantasise about something so unrealistic). He asks me to unlock the handcuffs but instead I do a slow strip for him, making him horny even though he's angry at my defiance.

I undo his jeans and his cock sticks out. I start to wank him but as soon as he starts to moan I stop and straddle him, rubbing his cock all over my clit. I use his cock to make my clit nice and swollen and then slide his cock between my lips and rub myself up and down against him, grinding against him rather than letting him slide inside me. He's forgotten his anger entirely now and is bucking his hips forwards trying to slide inside me but he can't position himself properly because he's tied up.

By now, I'm really slippery and I love the feeling of him against my pussy. I keep on rocking until I come all over him then leave him tied up and frustrated. I like the idea of him being there hard and horny ready for me to use whenever I want.'

Rape and Control

As with submissive fantasies – and unsurprisingly – control is a popular theme within dominant fantasies. Several women asserted control in fantasy by forcing fantasy lovers to control their bodily emissions. Some women fantasised about torturing a man by holding back his orgasm, and scat and watersports also feature.

There were also several rape fantasies submitted, in which the woman is the rapist. The idea of woman as rapist is so taboo that many governments still define rape as a male-only crime, (absurdly) refusing to count a man being forced to penetrate a woman as rape (even if a man was drugged to render him helpless and give him an erection, current UK Law would only hold the perpetrator liable for sexual assault.) However, in fantasy, some women take on the role of the rapist – whether with a man or woman as their target.

Kalika is an erotic writer in her early twenties, currently doing a postgrad and 'mostly straight'. She blogs at diaryofavirgin-whore.wordpress.com and says, 'I have never had penis-in-vagina sex though I've done BDSM, watersports, anal, blowjobs, knife-play, etc.'

Kalika Gold

'My fantasies include accidental pooping, pee desperation, wetting, mild scat, watersports, torture and they also include public gang rape (of both genders). My favourite fantasy is that an 18-year-old boy gets spanked, caned and paddled a lot throughout a day for wetting/pooing and is given laxatives, put in nappies, dressed as a sissy or baby and then gang raped by girls or boys. Porn is pretty much useless to me because only in my mind can I really feel the humiliation and physical pain of the men or women I fantasise about.'

Anita, 32, queer, bipolar, cis, white, partnered with a man, no children, student

'From the age of six or seven I have had a fantasy when sitting on the toilet of pissing in boys' and men's mouths. I sit there and think, "Whose mouth am I pissing in now?" I find it quite erotic and think about it while masturbating.'

Anon, 26, bisexual artist and graduate in a long-term open relationship (with a man).

'I had a fantasy recently in which I was sitting in my room with a female friend who is younger and less experienced than me and showing her my sex toy collection. As a joke, I put my most insistent vibrator on her clit through her clothes and instead of pushing it off, she has obviously been getting randier and randier looking at my vibrators and this just pushes her instantly over the edge . . . She goes red and kind of inwardly shudders as if she's trying to hide it.'

I imagine that she's wearing something really thin, perhaps just her knickers, so I can see her clit contract and throb through her orgasm. She's sweating and breathless, and ever so embarrassed but I climb on top of her and I position the vibrator on both of our clits, kissing her and undressing her.'

Anon, 22, bisexual chemistry student in a civil partnership with a 26-year-old woman, one five-year-old daughter.

'When I masturbate, I often think about people – usually men – trying to hold off orgasm. In the case of men, it's usually the idea of them physically trying to not ejaculate, or desperately trying to thrust the air because I've instructed them to wait or am withholding sex from them. The idea of desperation turns me on a lot; whether that's people desperate to pee or reach orgasm. I've had the fantasy for nearly as long as I've been masturbating, and I often think about it during sex too, imagining my partner telling me she's desperate to orgasm and can't hold it any longer.'

Anon, 'I'm female, professional, in my thirties, I've only slept with men though I think I'm bi. I'm white, single, no children'

'For the last couple of years, I've fantasised almost exclusively about controlling a man's orgasm, making him desperate to come, dictating when he can, etc. In my fantasies, I have all the power and I am aware of and in control of all of his reactions. In some cases my partner is a much younger man, a virgin, who has not ejaculated in an uncomfortably long time. In some cases he is whoever I am with or wanting to be with in real life.

I've always been interested in the sensation of needing some kind of release, but having to hold back. I'm uncomfortable with this, but I think it goes back to when I was about eight or so and getting dressed after gym class. Another girl had to pee and couldn't do up the buttons on her overalls without help from another girl as she needed her hands to hold the pee in. Not surprisingly, the opening scenes from the film *Buffalo 66* really turn me on. However, I'm not interested in urine, just the holding back, which, I think, is why male arousal is fascinating.'

Hayley, top, dominant sadist, in a sexually monogamous relationship (play open) with my male straight partner of five years

'My most recent fantasy was forced bisexuality involving two of my closest friends. Both are straight. My favourite fantasy is a brutal take down and capture – prolonged confinement and torment. Not to me, to someone else, I might add! I have shared my fantasies, and gotten both positive and negative responses but neither have an effect on my attitude. If these things make me happy then I refuse to let another person's judgement interfere with it.'

Em, 28, bi, 'I wrote this story to turn a lover on. It worked'

'Listen carefully. These are your instructions. You are to be punished for your bad behaviour. If you don't do exactly as you're told, your punishment will be more severe.

First of all, I want you to change into your basque. You know the one. Lace it nice and tightly so I can see your tits bursting out the top of it. Get in the car that is waiting outside. I don't care if anyone sees you. You're my whore and you will do as you're told.

The car will bring you to my playroom. When you get out, you will be led through to me by the chauffeur. You may not make eye contact with me. You are not worthy to look at me after your recent misdemeanours.

You will be blindfolded and tied up, facing the wall, with your arms stretched above your head so you can't touch your pussy. Your arse will be in prime position for a good spanking.

I will get out my paddles and, assuming you've followed orders so far, hit each cheek 10 times, making you count every stroke. You'd better remember to say "Thank you Mistress" after every stroke or your punishment will be more severe.

When your arse is nice and red, I'll plunge my hand between your legs and feel your pussy. I know how wet you'll be by now. I'll force my fingers into your mouth, making you lick your juices from me. My other hand will be busy teasing that tight arsehole of yours. I'll slide one finger up, making you squirm against me. Your clit will be crying out for attention but it won't get any because you've been bad.

Once I hear your breathing start to get heavy, I'll release you from the wall and chain your hands to your ankles so that your breasts and face are easily accessible.

I'll take my crop and flick it over your breasts, making sure to aim for your nipples. The pain will make you cry out and I'll see your juices leaking down your thighs. You like being punished, don't you, slut?

Then, if you're good, I'll let you lick me out. I'll stand above you and force my cunt into your face. You'll still be blindfolded so you'll be led by feel and smell alone. You'd better lick me well or I'll chain you up again and let my friends punish you. But if you're good, I'll reward you with a flood of my juices on your face.

Once I'm done with you, you'll go back to the car, face still wet with my juices and you'll be driven home. If you've followed orders properly, I will permit you to masturbate when you get home.

The car is waiting . . .'

Fuck You

Pegging (penetrating a partner anally using a strap-on dildo) is a sex act that's attracted increased visibility over the last decade, with adult retailers claiming a third of strap-on dildos now sold go to heterosexual couples who want to make their fantasies come true. This is something that's reflected in many of the fantasies submitted to this book. While pegging does not always involve domination, for some women, that's part of the appeal.

Deborah, 48, bisexual, cis, no kids, animal rescuer, slightly short of a BA, varying hair colours, cat person

'My favourite fantasy is currently, hardcore dominating a straight man. Pegging, CBT (Cock-and-Ball Torture), paddling, etc. I have *never* had any rape fantasies or any other types of fantasies in which I was dominated or "forced". I have always desired the dominant role.'

And of course, it's not just heterosexual women who fantasise about penetrating a partner. This anonymous contributor is yet to make her fantasy come true. 'I am in an open relationship and my main partner is a cis male. I have a secondary cis female partner but I don't often have a possibility to see her and we can't afford a strap-on to be honest.'

Anon, Jewish, cis genderqueer, DFAB, pansexual

'At this point my most prominent recurring fantasy is dominating a woman by fucking her with a strap on, making her perform oral sex on me, making her sit on my cock and fucking her until we orgasm multiple times. It comes from a desire to dominate to a certain degree and a fluctuating identity – and also wanting to experience having a penis at times.'

Joy, 27, bisexual and cohabiting with female partner. Masters, about to start a Ph.D

'My most recent fantasy was fucking my partner with a strap-on taking a (uncharacteristic) dominant role. Many of my fantasies in recent years involve fucking machines – particularly my partner, one or two other women and fucking machines.'

All Change

As mentioned before, women with dominant fantasies often tend to have submissive fantasies too – known on the fetish scene as being 'switch'. This allows scope for power games – even if only mental – to suit any mood. Perhaps this reflects the fact that most people yearn both to control and to relinquish control. As Mia More, Editor of Cliterati says about the erotica submitted to the website 'Often you think it's going to be a straightforward submissive story, and then as you progress through it you realise that not only are there are nuances of domination becoming apparent within the submission, but that the characters' power dynamic has evolved throughout the scene and the story's about to end on the flip-side to how you'd imagined it. This is because people's sexuality can be fluid and changeable – even within the same sex session.' However, this is something that may be easier to reconcile in fantasy than in reality.

Anon, Queer cisgendered teen

'I fantasise about beating up my boyfriend during consensual bondage play and getting my face fucked during fellatio, being held down, being grabbed, etc.'

Anon, married, three kids, cis, self-employed graduate, part-time musician

'My husband and I like being both top and bottom, so sometimes I fantasise about pegging him (lots of humiliation and submission) and sometimes I fantasise about being tied up, teased, flogged, with an orgasm from anal sex to finish. Depends on the night.'

The Power of Dominant Fantasies

Submissive and dominant fantasies both give women scope to explore power. The stereotype of the sexless female is shown for the shell it is when women share their desires: women are far from delicate flowers who are scared to be sexual – in fantasy at least. Women crave sexual pleasure, control, acquiescence and domination – and if they can't get it in reality, their fantasy minds will fill in the blanks. In dominant fantasies, a woman can get the satisfaction she needs – sometimes without a phallus in sight.

With submission and domination, women can explore their anger and need for control – and specifically dominant fantasies are just one way that women can explore power roles. Exhibitionist and voyeuristic fantasies open up the opportunity to explore objectification – and the power of the sexually desirable woman. Many women fantasise about controlling a lover through their physical appearance, luring a sexual partner with an exhibitionist display. And while women may be considered less visually aroused than men, more than a few get their kicks at the thought of a voyeuristic peek at something forbidden.

Chapter Three:
Exhibitionist and
Voyeuristic Fantasies

'The things that I think are forbidden to me are the things that turn me on. Once I've pushed the boundaries or fulfilled a fantasy in real life, I've had to push my imagination a bit further to find a new forbidden fruit for my mind.'

HOLLY, 27, STRAIGHT WITH BISEXUAL TENDENCIES, SINGLE

There's no doubt that observing sex or being watched in the act have a strong erotic lure for some women. Exhibitionism and voyeurism have featured in all of Nancy Friday's books, and submissions to Cliterati have featured everything from stripping for a crowd to observing gay men having sex from a hidden location. In his study of sexual fantasy, *Who's Been Sleeping in Your Head?*, Brett Kahr found 19 per cent of people fantasise about being watched during sex and a further five per cent fantasise about stripping in public. He also suggested that many group sex fantasies contain an element of exhibitionism or voyeurism – as reflected in Chapter 6.

I've loosely grouped exhibitionism and voyeurism together as they share many similar traits. Both types of fantasy centre around the visual. Both have been linked to resolving feelings of insecurity surrounding sex. And both show that men are certainly not the only ones capable of enjoying the sexual gaze, whether giving or receiving.

Here's Looking at You

*W*omen are peddled the idea that their worth is in their looks from an early age. Images of semi-naked women are a familiar part of the media landscape. Men's and women's magazines alike feature slim, white, able-bodied, young, semi-clad women, presented as the physical ideal (and indeed, norm). Products from instant noodles to alcohol are sold off the back of 'sexy' images – largely of women. Porn and pole dancing have seen massive increases in popularity over the last decade, fat is still a feminist issue; and the beauty myth is still a long way from being busted. Girls as young as 13 are featured in tabloids alongside leering headlines of, 'All grown up' and even as children, girls are exposed to the unhealthy (and indeed, proven to be biologically impossible) form of Barbie. As a result, it's hardly surprising that many women's fantasies revolve around being looked at and desired.

However, for all the cries of 'pornification', and despite the ubiquity of the 'sexy' image of a woman, relatively few women submitted fantasies about achieving that 'ideal', raising questions about how much these images really affect us deep down. Though a couple of women mentioned wearing traditionally sexy underwear, or having idealised bodies, on the whole, female exhibitionist fantasies revolve around being watched engaging in sexual acts rather than being perceived as a stereotypically 'sexually attractive' woman. (With a few notable exceptions generally revolving around being 'chosen' out of a line up of other women.) They don't just want to *be* sexual but to be *seen* as sexual, revelling in the reaction their sexuality elicits.

And this is not just something that exists in fantasy. As Dr Susan Block says on Counterpoint.org, 'With the advent of reality shows, erotic blogs and obsessive, sexy photo-posting on social networking communities, exhibitionism and voyeurism are busting through the erotic theatre of the mind and into that halfway house between fantasy and reality: the media. More and more, natural exhibitionists are just making and posting their own porn, turning everyone on their "friend list" into voyeurs.'

Erin, 28, straight, Australian, single, never married, no kids, work in transport, Diploma of Psychology

'My most common fantasy involves being with a male sexual partner, and having the crotch of my panties pulled to the side and being admired, touched or penetrated, sometimes whilst remaining partially clothed. The fantasy often involves a passionate desire and deep sense of urgency. My "setting" for this varies from spicing up the mundane laundry tasks, to having passionate sex against large windows. One of my more common fantasies involves being touched and orgasming without the knowledge of others present in the room.'

Anon, mixed Asian-race female, middle aged. Great-looking psychotherapist in an open relationship & happily married

'Creating in my mind two doll-like figures or miniatures out of people, two adults, who are moving toward a sexual encounter – in particular the woman undressing for the man. Essentially "seductive female seduces man", but with variation on an outward theme . . . place, construct, context, appearances. My most recent fantasy was two young women acting very seductively towards an older man and driving him crazy with their antics and erotic energy.'

Kira, 60, female, heterosexual, married, two children, lecturer, Ph.D

'I'm blindfolded and bound in a male club. Several unseen men there caress and undress me slowly before having sex with me, using all of my openings.'

Danielle, 25, have a degree, working in a coffee shop, in a new relationship

'A women walks into a room. The room is full of men in suits drinking, smoking, chatting. She is wearing a short black cocktail dress. In the centre of the room is a wooden table, one of the men takes the woman and bends her over the table with her legs spread. He pushes up her black dress. She has no underwear on underneath. She hears the sound of his zip and then feels the tip of his erection. He pushes against and then grabbing her hips fucks her hard. She feels him come after which he pulls out, the next man comes up to her and fucks her from behind. After this they begin to change position, missionary on the table, against the wall, oral. None of the people have faces; they are always nameless and faceless.'

Michelle, single mother of three, heterosexual
'Having sex in the middle of a nightclub'

Punishing the Sexually Visible Woman

*T*hough porn is widely debated, attention tends to focus on the negative effects that it has on female performers. People rarely consider the idea that some women might enjoy being filmed having sex, and could be appeasing their exhibitionist desires. As a result of the virgin/whore myth, and general judgement of the sexual woman, the idea that a woman could enjoy sex to such a degree that she'd choose to include it as part of her profession is anathema to many people. However, several women I've chatted to in the sex industry not only entered the industry willingly to satisfy their exhibitionist cravings, along with their financial needs, but some also use it as a way to make their wilder (or trickier to organise) fantasies come true.

This attitude ties into the myth that women are less sexual than men, and that a woman who is open about her desires must be in some way damaged. As Gemma Ahearne says in her blog, Plasticdollheads.wordpress.com, 'The idea is that the excessive woman must be stupid, or ill-informed, or a victim of false-consciousness. Or worse still, she is going to contaminate the *"good"*, respectable women, and she must be made an example of and punished. The hyper-visible woman is going to affect all of us. She will make objects of us all. Even by having these images of behaviours in our culture, they will cause us harm.'

Being a pole dancer – or any form of adult performer – is often vilified, frequently by privileged women who have no experience of the adult industry, have never met anyone who works in the industry and have never even thought to ask adult performers about their experiences. Nonetheless, they dictate the sex industry's moral bankruptcy from their ivory towers using populist rhetoric and dubious statistics, labelling all women who work in the sex industry as victims, glossing over the fact that many women enjoy their work, no matter how shocking that might seem, and using the label of 'false consciousness' to describe any *actual* sex worker who dares to disagree with their misinformed vision of reality.

Unfortunately, these ill-informed women are often presented as 'experts' in the field simply because they have the loudest voices, and more importantly, have views that fit with those of the interests of the powers that be. Ironically, they don't seem to realise that labelling sexual women as 'damaged' or treating grown women as if they are incapable of making their own choices about what they do with their own bodies is at least as oppressive as any patriarchy. In applying incorrect labels, slut-shaming performers (in some cases blaming them for rape) and refusing to listen to the women they are claiming to 'save', they are demeaning women in the adult industry far more than the work that sex workers choose to do.

By contrast, exhibitionist fantasies allow women scope to put themselves centre stage, being openly desired and celebrating their sexuality without the fear of being negatively judged. In her fantasies, at least, a woman can be sexually open without being shamed or threatened. While some women do imagine being watched by a Peeping Tom or forcibly stripped in front of a group, many take much more control in their exhibitionist fantasies: whether masturbating willingly for a lover or having sex in front of a lustful audience. Some women imagine being strippers, cheered on by appreciative crowds. Others imagine being watched during sex, whether by a masturbating stranger or room full of fetishists – who might join in at any time.

Sue, 44, married, four kids, stay at home mum, diploma in applied science

> 'I love to think that our neighbours are watching us have sex ... Or I love to fantasise about going to a swingers club by myself. My favourite is to think my neighbors can see me ... and that sometimes they come over and join in ... with the husband watching his wife lick my clitoris. I like to picture him holding me down while she pleasures me. I've told my husband so he vocalises that he can see people watching us. My neighbour's wife has offered her services once after a few drinks if ever I felt like experimenting!'

Anon, polysexual polyamorist

> 'To have aggressive sex via strap-on with a woman while her cuckhold husband hides in the closet.'

However, some exhibitionist fantasies could also be deemed fantasies about submission. Many of the submissive fantasies earlier in this book contain elements of exhibitionism and several of the exhibitionist fantasies contain submissive themes. This is hardly surprising: nudity and sex are both seen as intimate – in allowing someone to observe, the observed is also allowing themselves to be vulnerable.

Frances, 37, married, white female with two young boys

> 'My earliest fantasy was that a boy in my class and I would be the leaders and all the children in the class would follow us at school. There were no teachers and the uniform was only undies. The undies were made of clear, hard see-through plastic. It was like we were children but grown up at the same time. Brett (the boy) and I would touch each other and everyone would look at each other's genitalia. My fantasies have changed over time but mostly still feature some sort of exposure fantasy.

Most recently, I took one of my husband's fantasies and expanded on it. Now I can't stop thinking of it. His fantasy was that all women are made to wear extremely short skirts and no undies so that their bottoms and vaginas are on display. On public transport they would have to sit on men's laps. I branched off and my fantasy was that I would have to travel to work dressed like this but would have to stop and have sex anywhere and with anyone who wanted it, regardless of my feelings.'

While objectification is generally considered to be negative, for some women, the idea of being viewed as a sexual object – and possibly nothing more than that – can be arousing. As one woman says, 'When I was young, I was embarrassed about my large breasts, but as I've grown to be comfortable with the fantasies that my partners share about what they find erotic about me, I'm much more comfortable with my own body. My own fantasies involve me being very confident about using (even flaunting) my breasts and body. This has translated across to real-life lovemaking, which has been liberating for me and my partners.'

The Female Gaze

While voyeuristic fantasies were less common than exhibitionist ones – possibly because women are generally expected to be the observed rather than the observer – some women fantasise about watching other people engaged in sexual acts, whether openly or secretly. It's long been (mis)reported that women are not aroused by visual stimuli. However, studies show that women can be aroused by a wider array of stimuli than men; one piece of research found that gay men are aroused by gay porn and straight men by straight porn, but straight women are aroused by straight, gay and lesbian porn.

Similarly, while men may form the bulk of porn viewers, this is changing as more content is designed with women in mind – and studies have found women get just as physically aroused as men by 'male-made' porn, even if they don't feel – or admit to feeling – aroused. One survey, which involved showing men and women both male- and female-made porn, said, 'Contrary to expectation, genital arousal did not differ between films, although genital response to both films was substantial. Subjective experience of sexual arousal was significantly higher during the woman-made film. The man-made film evoked more feelings of shame, guilt, and aversion.'[11]

As such, assuming women do not enjoy being voyeuristic is a blinkered view. Perhaps the real reason porn is more popular with men is that it's commonly designed with male pleasure in mind. As the alternative-porn market grows, more porn is being designed with women in mind – as shown in the Periodic Table of Feminist Porn (Ms Naughty, FeministPornGuide.com, 2012) – so perhaps the time is finally coming for women to make their voyeuristic dreams come true?

As with exhibitionist fantasies, there's almost always a power dynamic of some kind with voyeuristic fantasies – and usually, it's the woman who's in charge. Mia More notes: 'Power-play is often present in sex even when you think it's not: whether deliberately or subconsciously power shapes our desires.'

Anon, 26-year-old, cisgendered, brunette graduate student

'My fantasies usually involve some sort of equal power dynamic; one person in charge, the other person at their mercy and begging for more. I don't explicitly visualise myself in either role, but I imagine the experience from both points of view. I'm a type-A perfectionist and I think that makes me more interested in this power-dynamic scenario, either imagining being fully in control and all-powerful, or completely letting go and letting someone please me.'

10 'What Kind of Erotic Film Clips Should We Use in Female Sex Research? An Exploratory Study,' Terri L. Woodard MD1, Karen Collins MS, MA1, Mindy Perez BA1, Richard Balon MD2, Manuel E. Tancer MD2, Michael Kruger MS1, Scott Moffat Ph.D3, Michael P. Diamond MD1

What Are Voyeuristic and Exhibitionist Fantasies?

*V*oyeuristic and exhibitionist fantasies cover a multitude of themes, from being forced to watch a lover with another person to starring in a porn film, hiding in a closet to watch people having sex without their knowledge to being naked in public. Exhibitionist and voyeuristic fantasies also commonly include elements of control – though these vary widely between fantasies.

Some women take control over their fantasy lovers by displaying themselves but denying any gratification to the observers – possibly reversing the 'orgasm gap' mentally. Others imagine being displayed in a submissive way, possibly having their body judged or examined – generally before being deemed 'good enough' for sex: perhaps a reflection of the sexual role women are expected to play in society? And many of the voyeuristic fantasies obviously revolve around watching or administering sexual pleasure.

Anon, 30, straight Australian student, living with my partner

'Oral sex given by a porn star-looking female. Or fantasising about just watching people have sex, where the woman is really getting off on it. It comes from watching pornography on the internet. I have never been with a female, and don't think I would like to. I just find it hot to watch, it really turns me on!'

Anon, 27, bisexual, polyamorous, cis woman, Quaker and Pagan

'My most recent fantasy was about a well-known female television presenter feeling unwell and going to a holistic health professional. The health professional examined her and prescribed orgasms, which she proceeded to provide.'

Anon

'My fantasies have varied a lot, but have always involved a lot of "plot" prior to the actual sexy bits, to the point where about 95 per cent of the daydreaming/fantasies are scene-building, and only about five per cent are the actual sex. I think I enjoy the tension, romance, comedy, plot etc. of fantasies more than the actual hot bits (although they are also good). It has always been that way. However it would be fair to say that my fantasies have got more explicit over time, mainly with the development of my own sexual knowledge. Most recently it's been daydreams about me and my current partner moving to a new city and making a new life (I know this doesn't sound hot at all!) but a lot of it is about the voyeurism of our new neighbours and our amazing sex life once we're there.'

Liz, 35, mother of two

'Being on stage fucking the lead singer or other members of the band in a glass ball suspended above the stage. Occasionally the audience get glimpses inside the ball, when it's lit up from inside.'

Anon, 52 (but feel more like 25), two adult children, hetero, graduate, slim and healthy, high sex drive

'A hot gangster kidnaps me, strips me down to my bra and panties and, in front of his men, questions me while slowly removing my underwear. (I saw something like this in a movie and liked it.)'

Why Do Women Have Voyeuristic and Exhibitionist Fantasies?

*A*s with all fantasies, women's exhibitionist and voyeuristic desires can serve a multitude of purposes. However, most readings suggest they are linked to insecurity. In being openly sexual, a woman is validated in a way that she may not be in real life.

Therapy

In *Who's Been Sleeping in Your Head?* Brett Kahr suggests exhibitionist fantasies offer a way to 'be seen' if someone feels invisible – a reinforcement of your attractiveness. This is a common reading of exhibitionist fantasies: they provide the woman fantasising with an ego boost – and some women clearly recognise this.

Given the pressure on women to be physically desirable, it seems only common sense that imagining being admired by adoring potential lovers could act as validation. As one married mother and stepmother in her early forties said, 'I am very self conscious, not at all confident about my body – this is no way my husband's fault, he is immensely complimentary, so I think the fantasy allows me to enjoy the idea of being found attractive and sexual, without feeling embarrassed.'

However, that is not the only role such fantasies can serve. Kahr also posits that exhibitionist fantasies can offer protection against intercourse – keeping a distance from those who may be dangerous. Similarly, he suggests voyeuristic desires allow a level of protection: against intimacy. Some women admitted their fantasies about watching others helped them feel sexually aroused, whereas putting themselves 'in the picture' was something they were unable to do. By being the observer, rather than the observed, you are putting yourself in a position of power; something that you may not feel in your everyday life.

Power is certainly reflected in some of the exhibitionist fantasies submitted to the book – and more so in the voyeuristic ones. Both watching and being watched can offer the fantasiser a form of power: the former from seeing someone in, arguably, their most private and intimate state which gives power over their vulnerability; the latter offering power to seduce, showing a woman's own sexual desirability. Kahr also noticed the link between submission and exhibitionism, and suggests that some exhibitionist fantasies express a masochistic desire to get caught and punished. As with all fantasies, there are multiple motivations for women's exhibitionist or voyeuristic desires – none of which is any more or less normal.

Anon, mostly hetero, low self-esteem, new relationship

'I fantasise about being the most beautiful and wanted person in any situation. It comes from low self-esteem.'

Anon, 26, straight female, manager, engaged, red head, tattooed and pierced

'My most common fantasy is being picked up wearing stockings, suspender, bra and heels wearing only an overcoat. I get picked up from a dark place by a man who wants to take me away and teach me a lesson! I think it comes from a rather promiscuous younger life with men not really appreciating me. It could be realised if my body-consciousness issues didn't get in the way of allowing my partner to see my body in that way.'

Anon, white, British, middle class, self employed, straightish, but with lesbian leanings (and experiences)

'My fantasy is usually exhibitionism. The fantasies always vary, I don't have a favourite, but is nearly always me turning on a group of men or men and women – sometimes just women – and often involves some element of sacrifice or enforcement, though never rape.'

Anon, bisexual, 26, in a long-term open relationship (with a man). Graduate, professional artist, blonde hair and blue eyes

'I don't really have a favourite fantasy as they sort of fall in and out of favour, but one recurring one I have is about being a nurse in a sperm clinic whose job it is to watch the men in the rooms on CCTV. (I know this isn't a real job!) I envisage them having the most fantastic pornography they have ever seen in their lives on a huge overwhelming screen, and some kind of machine that masturbates them, without letting them touch themselves. They are always unable to contain themselves and come quickly, leaving and begging to come again next week.

I watch their faces as the images flash in front of them too fast for them to fend off, sometimes I have the view in which I can see their balls and I watch them twitch and jerk as they come. Other variations of this fantasy are that I *am* the machine, or somehow inside it, like a sort of glory hole, cock after cock dripping wet with anticipation being namelessly put before me.

I love that they are so vulnerable to me behind my screen, they can't see me or what I am going to do, they can't anticipate or control, and become slaves to how good I am making them feel. I also love the idea that I might not even be concentrating, maybe I'm moving position or wiping come off my cheek, and mindlessly masturbating a cock, which starts twitching and ejaculates hot come all over me, unaware that I didn't even mean that to happen. That sounds kind of weird now I write it down . . .'

Anon, cis, bi, female, mid 40s, sex worker

'A man has been kidnapped by a technologically alien species who enjoy both the sexual stimuli humans can observe together with emotional resonance, pheromone scents etc. He has been "broken in" to some degree (medicalised digital penetration in front of a group, gang rape, being sluiced in the semen that has dripped out of his anus during the rape, object penetration, conditioning to train him to display himself or adopt specific positions when ordered) and is now being sold to a long-term owner. In front of an audience both in the room and televised, he is seated in the lap of the "man" who organised his capture – whom he had thought was a friend and to whom he was attracted – he is positioned with his legs raised and arms and legs bound, and penetrated by a fucking machine while his nipples and then cock are played with until he is forced to orgasm. My favourite fantasy is variations on the above. For the last three to five years, my fantasies have exclusively been about male perpetrators and victims of sexual assault; previously male perpetrators and female victims.'

Anon, 34, has not yet stopped to consider whether she wants marriage or children

'In my fantasies I am looking through the eyes of the male perpetrator, and when engaged in sex I am mostly looking through my eyes (although sometimes I shut my eyes and pretend I am a man fucking a woman). Most recently, it was a sleazy photographer abusing models while he photographed them. I am mostly looking through the eyes of the male perpetrator, so I do not feel the negative emotions like fear or anxiety. I feel gratification. But sometimes if my fantasy has gone too far I feel disgust and have to quickly change it.'

Sexual Pleasure

Just as sexual pleasure is key to dominant and submissive fantasies, equally, women with exhibitionist and voyeuristic fantasies say they take a lot of pleasure from their imagination. One woman said, 'I use my fantasies to masturbate about eighty per cent of the time – fantasies help reduce stress, I relax and get to bed after a hard day and I feel satisfied. I do not feel the need for a man as much as want one.'

Anon, bisexual, potentially polyamorous Black female, Christian, life-skills and sexuality researcher and educator

'I started having sexual fantasies at 16, looking at photographs of the various men and women of the world in National Geographic. I remember having an exploration session of my body while looking at the photos.

My most recent fantasy was directing a couple in having sex and having me watch them. My favourite fantasy is teaching a woman in front of her man how to orgasm without intercourse, i.e. toys, clitoral or G-spot stimulation then watching him take over. I feel very positive about my fantasies – it's a healthy release to fantasise, but was raised in a very anti-sex and sex-talk world.'

Anon, female, hetero with bisexual tendencies, editor, married, no children

'Public sex or telling lesbian stories to a man while he is made to sit very still in a straight-backed chair. I fuck him slowly when I'm finished.'

Common Fantasy Themes

Spy on Me

*F*or some women, the idea of being secretly observed is a turn on
– though the observer frequently makes themselves known . . .

*Anon, 34 yrs, white British bisexual female switch currently in
monogamous relationship*

'My earliest fantasies were about being watched by much older
boys peeping into my bedroom as I got undressed and ready
for a bath (though at day time). I dreamed or daydreamed
about being stripped, washed thoroughly and inspected by
others. I also enjoyed the thought of others watching me
undressing (but only in dreams where I had the confidence to
enjoy the positive attention). This evolved into being washed,
inspected intimately and then dressed and left to be further
inspected by older boys or someone older putting me to bed
post-wash and inspection and tucking me into bed safely.

Over time, they got far kinkier and started involving lesbian
fantasies of being taken in by older, more experienced women
that would show me how to please them, by demonstrating on
me first (playing follow my lead). Most of them involve me
being very submissive in nature and having to overcome
embarrassment/ humiliation but feeling so aroused throughout.

Despite being further from real life, I often fantasise about
being abducted, and enduring sensory deprivation and pushed
to my limits in terms of endurance of pain, including many
BDSM elements, even as far as drowning, being urinated on
and coerced into sex acts I'm not comfortable doing in real life.
My early fantasies have evolved in a very medical-fetish
direction: being prepared for surgery, where my skin is cleaned
by abrasive scouring to ensure clean, having cannulas fitted
and anaesthesia administered prior to very invasive acts
carried out on me (sometimes with an audience) to investigate
my responses to sexual stimuli of pleasure, pain, restraint and
psychological fear.'

Anon, 25, straight, single, no children, teaching English in Spain

'My fantasy is that somebody breaks into my apartment though I am filled with intrigue, rather than fear. Who are they? What do they want in my apartment? I lure them into the bedroom and it continues from there. I learn that the burglar has been watching me for a while which turns me on even more.'

Anon, 39, writer

'I often imagine my partner watching me when I masturbate. Sometimes, all I have to imagine is him standing next to the bed looking at me as I masturbate in order to get off. At other times, the fantasy is more elaborate. He might have come home unexpectedly without me hearing him, and be standing in the door looking at me for a while before I realise he's there, his erection getting steadily harder, until he can't resist any more and he joins me on the bed. At other times he might masturbate over me in a more literal sense, coming over my clit as I come. I love watching him stroke his beautiful cock too. I find it such a turn on – it's the sexiest cock I've ever seen.'

Desire Me

Being observed is only one part of the exhibitionist fantasy. In most cases, that observation also leads to being desired and validated. Though penetrative sex may play a part in proceedings, sometimes merely eliciting desire is enough.

Anon

'I haven't told anyone this – not any of my partners. It shocks me and runs counter to various strongly-held views of gender relationships. In my fantasy typology, this is one hundred per cent a never-event. It's not something I explicitly or deliberately fantasise about to get myself aroused; rather, it's an image or scenario that arrives or that I entertain when I'm already intensely aroused.

If it had a name, it would be *Objet D'Art*. In that way, it's a fantasy of perfect objectification. I am in a study, a proper old-fashioned leather-chaired book-lined study with an early nineteenth-century aesthetic. At the centre is a contraption, which I am lying on, face down. You might imagine it as stirrups in reverse, with appropriate support for the rest of my body. A gap allows my breasts to be exposed. Everything is made to the highest standards of workmanship; it's extremely comfortable.

This contraption, and me lying naked and exposed on it, are at the centre of the room. (I was going to write "and strapped" – I can't move, but the straps aren't featured particularly in the fantasy.) The man is sophisticated, gentlemanly, upper class, and he appreciates me as he would a rare first edition, a fine cigar, a superb whisky. I am an object, entirely, but a highly prized one.

What follows varies. It invariably involves stimulating me and making me come: sometimes with a dildo, which is sometimes manually operated and sometimes by pressing buttons; less often, with actual sex. My response to stimulation is much admired. Most often, he has a friend with him, to whom he is exhibiting me and my sexual responsiveness, just the way you'd show any especially rare and prized thing.

More recently, the uses and sexual stimulation to which I'm put involves actual people, rather than dildos etc. (Previously, I was sometimes even under glass.) And most unusually, the central gentleman has been played by someone I actually know. (I've never invited anyone I know into that fantasy before.) That included the usual "admiring friend" character and a very handsome manservant who was called in to complete the scenario. (The two men were taking me in the pussy and the arse simultaneously; he was required for me to fellate. He approached this a bit in the sense of taking on a duty – nothing he was loath to do, but as a part of his job.) They varied their positioning, but the main male character spent the least time actually inside me – his detachment seems to be as much a feature of this fantasy as his admiration.'

Anon, 39, building a coaching practice

'My most recent fantasy was being on my hands and knees with someone I am interested in, and having them give me an orgasm while they used a dildo on me. I was watching their face and and they were talking to me. I love it when people talk dirty to me during sex so it's usually a factor in all of my fantasies. It hasn't been something I've had in my sex life until recently. I also imagined masturbating with a water bottle in my friend's car while he was driving, mainly because I would like to see the look on his face. I want to watch his expressions.

Right now my favourite fantasy is the one with the water bottle. We're driving to the beach, it's a nice car, the sunroof is open and the windows are down. We both have cold water bottles, I pull my dress up, take my panties off, and pour water over myself while he's driving before using the bottle to help me masturbate, rubbing it between my legs. The whole time I'm watching his face and looking down periodically to see the water all over me with the sun reflecting off of it, and he starts touching me and talking, encouraging me. He's trying to avoid passing vehicles where someone might be able to see into the car. I orgasm several times on the way ... That's most of it. Most of my fantasies involve water, either being in it or being sprayed with it or having it poured on me.'

Holly, 27, brunette, straight with bisexual tendencies, single

'I think my most frequent fantasy I have when I pleasure myself, is to have sex with a man in front of a group of other guys, while tied up. On the contrary to the assumption that when tied up, I should be in submission, I am not. I am always the person in complete control of the situation, nothing can happen that I don't want, but the feeling of having my hands restricted turns me on. Sometimes I know the guys who are watching, but often they can morph into another person during the fantasy; the same for the person I have sex with, sometimes they morph too, but they are often faceless or a stranger.

Often I find I get many flickering images so my fantasies change often even during the build up to my most common fantasy. One minute I'll be myself, and a guy will be pleasuring me, and the next minute, it switches to me being in the perspective of the person giving oral sex to a woman, and it can change just as quickly to me becoming a man, receiving oral sex from a woman.

I think I've fantasised about being with multiple partners at once for at least the last ten years, maybe even since my early teens. But I don't think I would ever actually have sex with multiple partners at once, as I find sex to be a very intimate thing between two people. In reality I would feel very uncomfortable with more than one person. But the things that I think are forbidden to me are the things that turn me on. And once I've pushed the boundaries each time, or fulfilled a fantasy in real life, I've had to push my imagination a bit further to find new ways to find a new forbidden fruit for my mind.'

Anon, 39, single, straight white cis female, no children, depression, working on creative writing Ph.D

'I was probably about six to seven years old when I started fantasising. I vaguely remember some TV that I was probably too young to be watching but it was along the lines of *Coronation Street* not porn. I must have been about seven or eight when I had the first fantasy I can remember. I worked as a serving girl in a castle, and the prince lined up all the serving girls to choose one to be his princess, and we had to show him our breasts – note I didn't have any breasts at eight and still don't to speak of, but in my fantasy they were like a page three girl – and he chose me because my breasts were the nicest, and that's where the fantasy ended, we lived happily ever after. Bit like real life really. Ha ha ha. Over time, I would say they have changed from being about finding an amazing relationship to just having dirty no-strings sex. My most recent fantasy was a co-worker/friend taking advantage of me at work out of sight of CCTV.'

Maggie, 39, hetero, in a relationship, one child, teacher, ex traveller

'My most common fantasy is that a group of men are watching my boyfriend and I get it on and they are wanking wishing they could be my boyfriend. I also have a fantasy about only my fanny and arse being visible to a group of men examining me anonymously – they do not know who I am but are intrigued and touch me and look at me very closely – that turns me on just as much as the other fantasy.'

Anon, 48, tall, toned, dark blonde hair, highly educated, work in the arts, ride an old Moto Guzzi

'I walk into a dark tunnel. Men are in the dark. I don't know how many. I can't see who the men are. I am naked. Two men come to do oral sex to me. I am standing up, they are both on the knees, one in front, the other one at the back. I feel their penises on my feet.'

Marie Rebelle, 46, married, submissive to my husband, bisexual, redhead, erotic writer, my blog: rebelsnotes.com

'My earliest fantasy was being told what to do. I used to fantasise about being a minor royal and being told what to do by the king and queen. Much of that included that I had to expose or touch myself. My fantasies matured, but it's still mostly about being told what to do. Just like in real life, in my fantasies too I do not like to take the lead in a sexual setting. My favourite fantasy is being dominated and used by two men. Other than exciting me, it calms me. I frequently fantasise in bed and it calms me so much that I fall asleep and dream about sex.'

Perform for Me

While it's long been accepted that many men find the idea of seeing two women engaged in sexual acts arousing, the idea that women might find man-on-man sex play arousing is much more taboo. However, many women – including lesbians – fantasise about seeing men engaged in gay sex, sometimes with dominant themes: the woman enjoys watching one man force another to perform oral sex. Other women simply fantasise about enjoying the spectacle of two male bodies together.

Samantha, 47, single mother of four, biker chick

'I was about 25 years old when I started having fantasies – I watched a porn movie and it went from there. My fantasy is mainly about watching homosexual sex. It is more so the energy and animalistic passion rather than the act itself. I can have hetersosexual as well, and lesbian fantasies. My favourite fantasy involves three men having sex – spit roast – the giver is new to anal sex and he is on a high as it is such a tight sensation. The more he gets aroused the more the other guys get aroused and it gets more and more heated.'

Teri, 26, pansexual, single, works in publishing

'Two gay males.'

Anon, 23, cis, English, feminist, fangirl

'The one consistent thing about my fantasies is that they have almost always been in the third person. I rarely fantasise about myself having sex, although I have done slightly more so since my late teens/early twenties. Most recently, I featured characters from the History Channel-scripted drama *Vikings*. Specifically I fantasised about the monk Athelstan, who has been taken as a slave by a Viking called Ragnar Lothbrok, having sexualised feelings of submission towards Ragnar and struggling to reconcile those feelings with how he thinks he should be feeling. I enjoy the eroticisation of guilt and inner turmoil.'

Jess, 30, queer/bisexual, white, mental health issues, cis female, in a long-term partnership, no children

'I had primarily heterosexual fantasies for a long time, despite being a lesbian, and these days it's more homosexual men. What hasn't changed is that I'm almost always outside of the action (so to speak), and that I tend to think about scenes of extreme receptivity, one partner consuming the other or others.

My most recent fantasy was a blow job scene between two men, where they traded off control over the blow job, one holding the other's head, then the other pinning his hands to the bed. My favourite fantasy is – oh god, this one's embarrassing – a grey, amorphous, devouring entity. I feel like a very odd duck when I think about that one.

I love how much my fantasies are based on consuming, because I think that's different, and I like that I think about sex in a strange way. I think it's very yonic of me, if I can be that ridiculous. I don't like that a lot of them involve an element of rape fantasy or dominance – it feels like I'm subjugating myself. I sometimes think that I ought to work on making my fantasies more diverse, or less injurious to myself/my identity, but it's difficult. A lot of my fantasies are about a man being in heat or being in a subservient position. In writing, I enjoy connecting characterisation to sex, where the zing of the scene is in the developing relationship between two characters.

I think some of my internalised homophobia and misogyny shows up in my fantasies, and I suspect that the fantasies in turn continue those phenomena in me. I fantasise about male homosexuals because it allows me to think about dominance and submission without feeling like one partner is "weak" for submitting, for example. I suspect that it's had a real effect on my sex life. I frequently imagine myself as male while I'm having sex these days, which I previously did not do; before that, I didn't really feel present during sex very much, and thought about myself as being there largely to give the other person pleasure. It's made me much more present in the sexual moment, so to speak.

My real life doesn't influence my fantasies much. I don't like to think about myself or imagine myself present in my sexual fantasies. If I try to fantasise about myself or about scenes involving me I get turned off. My work as a professor and student has made me much more aware of the social prejudices that are reflected in my fantasies, which can contribute both to my pleasure in analysis but also my guilt about fantasising.

I largely use fantasies to get myself off, either alone or, sometimes, with a partner. In writing, I use them to connect with other people. I write fanfiction, and producing fic is part of how I support the community where I'm a reader. Thinking about it again, the amount of male/male fanfiction I've read, from a relatively young age, has heavily influenced my fantasies about male/male sex.'

Anon, 32, blonde virgin

'I fantasise about being forced to watch while my lover has sex with a girl half my age and then being savagely forced to deep throat him while they gently caress each other, I've had the fantasy since I was 24 and use it for masturbation.'

Anon, 39, straight, married, one child

'Making my husband watch me with several other men at once.'

Anon, 41, single, straight-ish, graduate, two kids

'Man or woman desperate to pee in public place – i.e. railway station or top deck of bus, etc. – letting it all go, possibly being seen by other people.'

Jenny, well educated, gainfully employed, happily married, flirty forty

'I have this recurrent fantasy about watching my husband have sex with another woman – or even another man. My husband also fantasises about watching me fucking other people, and we often share these stories during sex.

This has led to us exploring swinging in real life, but contrary to what you might think, the biggest part of our enjoyment isn't because after twenty years of marriage we're having sex with new people, it's actually from watching each other fuck different people. For me it's a mixture of how sexy my husband looks in action and genuine pride in how good a lover he is – it almost makes me fancy him more. It's not a jealousy thing, it's more a reminder or even a confirmation of how attractive my husband is (and he's far from a chiselled male model-type).

I love it when we're both fucking someone else (or even the same person) and catch each other's eye – he looks so super-hot when he's having sex. At the sex parties we go to I also like to watch him having sex with someone else while I sit there with a glass of wine in hand, taking in the view. And yes, I do inevitably end up with my remaining hand buried in my ... ahem. Unfortunately, although my husband's open-minded he's mostly straight, so I've only had the pleasure of seeing him with another man once – but it's been stored in the wank bank for posterity!

I can't imagine not fancying my husband (despite marrying young we have always maintained a great sexual rapport), and I'm sure some of that's because we both react quite visually to the other. A simple wriggle of my bum makes him want me, and when he shoots a certain look in my direction – it doesn't matter where we are – I'm his. I just have to glance at his broad shoulders and I go weak at the knees. Visual stimulation is very important for us, and we do watch porn together occasionally, but it's not a regular part of our sex life – which is weird since we're both into voyeurism. I guess it's because nothing compares to seeing the real deal when we go to saunas or sex parties ...'

Much as sub/dom fantasies are intertwined with power, exhibitionist and voyeuristic fantasies reflect the sexual gaze. In accepting that some women fantasise about watching sex, or being watched, it casts doubt on the idea that women aren't sexual – or indeed, visually inspired.

However, unlike the real world, in fantasy a woman can be adored sexually without feeling insecure or threatened. If a woman displays herself 'too' sexually in reality, she is liable to be slut-shamed – or worse, blamed for any violence she may face. Similarly, the lecherous woman is a figure of fun: think Dorian from *Birds of a Feather* or Peggy in *Married with Children*. And a woman who admits to enjoying porn films or looking at naked pictures is likely to be slut-shamed in the same way as her exhibitionist sister. It is still not deemed normal for a women to be overtly interested in sex. Perhaps these fantasies offer women a chance to flaunt their sexuality and watch others' without shame.

Without the stigma that accompanies female sexuality, would these women want their fantasies to come true? While many women said no, several said they'd already explored their exhibitionist and voyeuristic desires to some level. And in many ways, group sex fantasies allow both desires to be sated without even being explicitly expressed. As Mia More, editor of Cliterati says, 'Don't be fooled into thinking the common fantasy scenario of a woman surrounded by men is for their pleasure alone: it's just as likely she's the one calling the shots.'

Chapter Four:
Group-Sex Fantasies

'I like the idea of being over-stimulated . . . I guess it's also the idea of sex without emotional attachment. It's just sex without the complication of emotion.'

ANON, THIRTY, IN LONG-TERM RELATIONSHIP,
WORKS IN MARKETING

Next to submissive fantasies, group-sex fantasies were one of the most popular categories submitted for this book. This is hardly surprising, as they can contain numerous fantasy elements. Group-sex fantasies allow you to be the observer or the observed. They offer scope for new sex acts, and exploring sexuality. They can contain elements of dominance, submission or both. And of course, they offer excess: a multitude of partners to enjoy.

Mia More says, 'There's a certain degree of anonymity in group sex, and for some it's that uncertainty of who's touching who, and where, that's a big part of the attraction. Add to that the base physical functions that are fulfilled in such a scene – not to mention the sheer volume of sexual stimulation – and you have a potent fantasy. It's not for nothing that Roman orgies are mentioned with something approaching a combination of awe and envy.'

In *Who's Been Sleeping in Your Head?*, Brett Kahr found that twenty per cent of people fantasised about orgies; 15 per cent of people fantasised about sex with a man and a woman at the same time; 18 per cent fantasised about sex with two or more men; and 35 per cent fantasised about sex with two or more women.

As with the submissive and dominant fantasies, some women who replied to the survey had made their fantasies come true. While it was a pleasurable experience for some – and sometimes a part of women's regular sex lives – group sex was far from universally seen as a positive. The reality of a threesome (or more) can be very different from fantasy: something several women bemoaned.

What is a Group-Sex Fantasy?

*G*roup-sex fantasies involve three or more people but can vary wildly in scope. Some women fantasise about a threesome with their lover – sometimes the same gender, sometimes different. Some women imagine orgies; some imagine elaborate events in which they are the starring attraction; and some fantasise about more submissive group activities.

For some, group-sex fantasies represent their sexual reality: Terri Conley and Bjarne M. Holmes have been studying non-monogamous relationships in the US and estimate around 5 per cent of people have some form of polysexual relationship. However, the vast majority of women with group-sex fantasies do not want it to be a regular part of their sex lives: it simply offers erotic stimulation.

Anon, 29, bisexual writer, married with no children

'I fantasise about group sex, usually with just three or four women, occasionally with one man but not always a participant, more as a voyeur. There is some kind of BDSM element or role-play involved and plenty of toys, particular double-enders and strap-ons. I think it comes from the fact that I identify myself as bisexual but my experiences with women have been very limited in comparison to my experiences with men. The lesbian sex I have had, although limited, has always been so memorable and exciting, in stark contrast to my experiences with men which have for the most part been very disappointing or unmemorable. I think my fantasy in a way is trying to recapture those feelings of excitement that I doubt I'll ever experience again. They are close to experiences I've had in the past but not my current situation.'

Anon, 40, married

'My crazy, favourite fantasy is that there's a college fraternity having its initiation rites. There's a "house father" who presides over the initiation. All pledges are assigned a house member or mentor. The initiation rite involves bringing out the "slave woman" (me). The pledge fucks me vaginally, the mentor fucks me anally, and the house father fucks me orally. In order for the pledge to be accepted to the house, all have to finish. I get to be kept as a slave until all pledges have gone through the ceremony.'

Why Do People Have Group-Sex Fantasies?

*R*ather than seeing group sex as a purely physically desirable fantasy, Brett Kahr suggests group fantasies can serve other unconscious purposes: healing a hurt ego after rejection by attracting multiple lovers to reinforce your own attractiveness; disguising concerns about your body – e.g., if you're insecure about small breasts, you may imagine a threesome involving a large-breasted woman; a way to escape intimacy; a way to explore suppressed homosexual urges (or heterosexual urges in lesbians); or even a way to recreate the comforting memory of being 'snuggled between your parents in bed as a child'.

Group-sex fantasies also allow scope for diverse stimulation: more hands, tongues and bodies to explore. For some women, group-sex fantasies give an opportunity to indulge in lesbian or heterosexual fantasies – sometimes using their lover's presence in a fantasy to confirm that they're simply playing with the new sexuality rather than seeing it as anything significant. However, there is no reason to assume that the people we fantasise about are a reflection of our sexuality: straight women fantasise about women; lesbians fantasise about men; and our imaginations generally let us explore alternative realities if we so wish.

X-Rated Inspiration?

Some might argue that female group-sex fantasies are inspired by porn, and there are certainly some women whose fantasies bear more than a mild resemblance to the group-sex porn acts: being ejaculated on, insulted or forced to perform. However, these fantasies have shown up in almost every investigation into female fantasy, long before group-sex porn was commonly available. As such, this reading is lacking – and perhaps influenced by the erroneous idea that women don't like sex.

That so many women fantasise about group sex, in almost every configuration, suggests that they do not always need romance to enjoy erotic pleasure. Though some women enjoy romantic fantasies and many women do fantasise about their partners, more than a few add at least one other person into the mix.

Mia More says, 'Erotic stories involving threesomes or two couples are sent in to Cliterati more often than those involving group sex, but that's likely due to the challenge in writing a group-sex scene successfully, rather than because it's less popular. Certainly from speaking to sex writers and those who read erotica it does seem that group sex is a particularly popular fantasy – albeit one that's perhaps most socially acceptable as a threesome.'

Group-sex fantasies are not confined to any gender, sexuality or even number of participants – though threesomes certainly cropped up more frequently than mass orgies. This does raise the question of whether it's because, as Mia suggests, threesomes are more socially acceptable – or perhaps it could be because we are more likely to fantasise about a scenario if it at least fits within the realm of feasibility?

Anon, early 30s, anglo, uni-educated, single, just out of LTR

'Being in a F/F/M threesome and tied up by the other woman . . . Both of the others having their way with me, but the leader of the group being the female.'

Lucy Felthouse, 27, straight, long-term relationship, no children, writer, degree, lucyfelthouse.co.uk.

'My most common fantasy is having a threesome with two men. I think it comes from the idea of having twice the amount of focus on me, two mouths, four hands, two cocks, etc.'

Anon, Dutch female queer sociologist, MSc in sexuality, girlfriend, working in education

'My fantasies have changed over time from heterosexual to homosexual to heterosexual, to interracial, to fantasies in which I am the man, fantasies of men having sex and so on. Right now my favourite fantasy is that of a car with four men in it and me on the back seat. I start with the men not driving in the front and the story ends with the driver stopping the car and fucking me hard because all the other men went before him.'

Common Fantasy Themes

Twice the Fun

*F*or some women, group-sex fantasies are simply about enjoying an extra lover. It's about satisfying a physical desire. As one woman says, 'I guess it's also the idea of sex without emotional attachment, it's just sex without the complication of emotion.'

Anon, 38, straight, married woman with 3 children. Physically very active. I work part time

'Double penetration with a friend of mine and his mate. We start out having drinks, then my friend and I try to slip away to have secret sex, but we get caught in the act and his mate joins in.'

Anon, 40, straight female. Divorced, one child. Tall, slim, dark, very attractive

'Sex with two men. I have only been in that situation once (it happened in the previous 12 months). I asked a boyfriend I was seeing recently if he would indulge me, he said no – even if I said I'd reciprocate with him and another woman, which is not my thing. I like men a lot and have never had an attraction to females.'

Mel, 30, cis-gendered female, not straight, single, child-free, social worker

'Having a threesome with both a male and female. Starting to have sex with the male and he inviting the female in as he knows it is something I like and want.'

Anon, heterosexual, co-habiting in committed relationship. Business owner. Dog lover, child-free

'Having sex, serially and simultaneously with two to three men. I am the only female.'

Lisa, 37, straight, single for far too long

'Double penetration with two men. Not in a rough-sex way, but as part of a mutual threesome. I'd also like the men to be comfortable with each other and touching/sucking each other. I want to be the main attraction/centre of attention though!'

Anon, straight white woman, married but also recently polyamorous. College dropout but smart as hell

'I'll usually be with a man I already know, naked and both horny, touching each other but not yet fucking. Another man (who I also already know in real life) appears in the doorway of the room (this is usually a large house party or a sex club), and helps to restrain me at the wrists while the first man makes me come in as many ways as he pleases and then fucks me hard. Sometimes I am also giving head to the second man, sometimes they switch places. We all enjoy ourselves immensely and collapse in a joyful heap. My experience of group sex and restraint is quite limited but it's always been something I wanted to explore.'

Deborah, 25, ethical slut

'Seducing/being seduced by a hetero couple. It usually starts in a bar and moves on to their place. The idea of participating in other people's existing sexual dynamics is exciting! I've come pretty close and I wouldn't be averse to trying it out.'

Anon, 40s, white British graduate, living with partner but never married, no children

'My favourite fantasy is some kind of happenstance threeway with tradesmen, generally in my kitchen, so de rigueur, but it works! I'm in a flimsy dressing gown and they are in overalls with large, rough, work hardened hands . . . mmm . . . and I have the most amazing breasts over which they spend inordinate amounts of time.'

Anon, 30, in a long-term relationship. I work in marketing and I am interested in being creative and expressive

'Having sex with two men at once. I like the idea of being over-stimulated – lots of things going on at once and also it seems a bit naughty. It's not something I think I'd actually do. I guess it's also the idea of sex without emotional attachment, it's just sex without the complication of emotion.'

Anon, 43, graduate, four kids, happily married for almost twenty years

'I'm basically straight, but I love playing with beautiful women too. My fantasy is me, alone in a bar, meeting a married and beautiful blonde younger lady. She is there with her husband and they are vanilla (monogamous). After a bit of chatting/flirting, we all end up in a wild threesome.'

Mia More, Editor of Cliterati.co.uk (extract taken from 'Why Cava Would Never Be The Same Again')

'. . . As if by some secret signal they both dipped down to suckle my breasts in stereo. This may not have been entirely expected, but that's not to say it wasn't welcome: I'd had fantasises about this kind of thing, but never in my wildest dreams had I thought it would be so easy to engineer – or feel so natural. It was neither awkward nor intimidating, and I genuinely couldn't believe my luck: I couldn't have imagined my threesome any better. And to think the real fun hadn't even begun . . .

I turned so that I was facing Sebastian and had my back to Mario, and writhing and rubbing myself against both of them laughed out loud as we stumbled: "¡Bocadillo!" I whooped. It was one of the few Spanish words I'd learned, and it meant sandwich. Well, what can I say: it seemed appropriate at the time.

"¡A comer!" Sebastian responded. Let's eat!

And eat they did: Sebastian leaned to lick and suck my nipples, whilst Mario bit and kissed me from my neck down to the base of my spine. When he got to the bottom he reached for some cava, and tipped the fluid so that it dripped from the small of my back down the cleft of my buttocks. With a command from Mario, clearly the more experienced of the two, Sebastian also took a cup, spilled it between my breasts, and, dropping to his knees, he met Mario's mouth under my pussy.

I genuinely couldn't quite get a grasp on the incredibly horny thing was happening to me: granted I was slightly tipsy, but to have two men out of the blue playing with me, licking me, one from the front and one from behind, so that their fingers – and tongues – touched at the entrance to my pussy, was more than I could bear. It was so unbelievably hot, and I felt so . . . edible . . . oh! . . . so ripe . . . fecund . . . so – desired! . . . that it didn't take long before I reached climax, gasping and shuddering in waves of pure joy.

My two lovers stood, and as I reached down to take a cock in each hand, as if by tacit agreement the boys batted me away and instead lay me down on one of the benches, Sebastian by my head and chest, and Mario – ah! – Mario had his face buried in my pussy again, and I found myself moving involuntarily against him, my body seeking out the bursts of pleasure he was blessing me with, his tongue licking and caressing, his stubble sandpapering my post-orgasmic sensitivity in a shower of sparks. And sexy Sebastian was kissing me, his tongue exploring, probing, his teeth biting, whilst his hands traced sensual circles around my breasts, making my nipples erect and giving me goose-pimples.

I felt as though I might pop: I had one of those rare orgasms building, one that starts in the belly – almost in the womb – as a hot, burning ache of desire, muscles clenched in tension like a coiled spring. The heat spread to my cervix, to my G-Spot which Mario was ably massaging with his fingers, out to my clit, hot and hard in Mario's mouth, and up again to the outside of my stomach.

I was a complete circle of sensation, and there was nothing for it but to go with the flow, ride the waves and let my body convulse as I came, forcefully, almost painfully, as if I was pulling my tummy muscles in the process. The burst of pleasure-pain dynamic was so great that I heard myself cry out in a voice I'd never heard before: deep, guttural, raw, it was desperate for release and relief and came from deep within.

Serving me first, the guys poured some more drinks as I got my breath back, and as Sebastian locked the carriage door we all had a chuckle at the fact that thus far it'd been open to all and sundry. It could've been a close one – although Mario commented that since the conductor was such a fuckhead no doubt he'd have been joining us in no time. It tickled all three of us that a joke would make sense in our respective cultures, and we had a laugh exchanging imaginative swearwords and names for our various intimate body parts. Ah, the international language of extravagant insults and hot sex: so much fun to be had.

Drinks downed, I beckoned the boys over: it was their turn now. Sitting on the bench I manoeuvred them in front of me, so that I could alternately take a cock in my mouth and in my hand, switching from one to the other as I pumped and licked. Mario was bigger than Sebastian, and they both had the most gorgeous dicks: I couldn't get enough of them on my tongue or in my mouth. From the looks on their faces they couldn't either . . .

Sebastian indicated that I should get on all fours, and after a mimed discussion about condoms, I turned to face the back of the bench, my bum tipped skyward, ready for action. I turned my head to face the window so that I watch our reflections. Dark countryside sped by as Sebastian's rubber was rolled on, and ready first, he placed his cock at the entrance to my pouting pussy. Sometimes, this was my favourite part of sex: the anticipation, the feeling of waiting to be penetrated and filled, the wanting. I relished the pause Sebastian took, touching his tip to my hole and using the rhythm of the train to tease me. I also enjoyed watching Mario masturbate as he took in the scene.

In the end it was I who initiated the inevitable: I just couldn't stand the suspense any longer, and when a particularly forceful jolt from the train threw us together I took advantage and speared myself onto Sebastian. My, was he hard, and boy did he feel good. As he thrust away I marvelled at how completely at ease my likeness looked in the window. I was being fucked by one man while another watched and wanked, and I was loving every goddamn last minute of it.

Suddenly Sebastian pulled out and Mario took his place, pumping hard. As my pussy embraced his cock I could feel a familiar flush spreading. It began at my chest, travelling upwards. When it hit my cheeks I knew I was on the edge. I turned my head towards the door to cool my other cheek on the back of the seat. But it wasn't Mario who made me come. Or at least I don't think it was, as suddenly he pulled his cock out and it was Sebastian's turn again. Once Sebastian had fucked me for a while it was back to Mario. And so on and so forth, until I wasn't sure who was inside me, and I was genuinely loving not knowing: it was so filthy, so depraved, so utterly low down and dirty. This was something I would never have felt entirely comfortable doing in my own country, but since I wasn't going to be seeing these gorgeous men ever again it seemed the perfect opportunity to celebrate my inner slut then and there. And celebrate I did – with aplomb.'

Watching Gay Men Play

The idea that men enjoy watching lesbians together is so accepted that a heterosexual man is almost doubted or mocked if he admits to finding the idea unappealing. However, the idea that women could become aroused watching men together is much more taboo. Hazel Cushion, founder of Xcite Books says, 'We found that sixty per cent of our gay MM fiction was bought by female readers.' Some women are as happy to observe as to join in.

Elle, 28, pansexual, tomboyish at times, single but in love with a sailor, first-class medical student, no kids

'My most recent fantasy was getting double penetration with my sailor and his mate (who I've invented) in a hotel, with others around us also having sex. My favourite fantasy changes depending on my mood! Often orgies at the moment.'

Anon, 46, lesbian, cisgendered, in a relationship

'My earliest fantasies were triggered by Mirror-Spock putting his hand against McCoy's face to read his mind in "Mirror, Mirror". I then fantasised about Vila and Avon from "Blake's 7" fucking. I bought my first "slash" fanzine ("Blake's 7") and was really overcome by the idea that I could write my fantasies down because there were other people who felt the same way. "Slash" is the fannish term for erotic fanfiction written about two men or two women characters, usually film or TV, often characters who aren't openly presented as LGBT. Obviously it can be more than two, but it's always same-sex. Obviously. I now like House/Wilson: Greg House tied up, naked, totally helpless: James Wilson, in suit and tie, fucking him. But I still like reading, fantasising and masturbating to stories about men fucking each other. I have the feeling that the actors who play the characters I've fantasised about probably wouldn't want the job of starring in my own private porn movie. (We'd do safe sex! Honest!)'

Anon, 52, queer straight/girlfag, married, polyamorous researcher with two male partners, one daughter

'Scenes with two or more men, watching them together, all of us playing together, me anally fucking them, they both sharing me, lots of oral on me, piss-play where they drink my pee, comeplay where they come in me and they eat it together, prostate play, etc. Me their mistress in BDSM. I've always felt a strong affiliation and arousal with gay men and boy-on-boy action.'

Orgies and Excess

Other women conjure more Bacchanalian images of group sex, with an abundance of playmates in their fantasies. While this fantasy may offer women nothing more than indulgent and carnal inspiration, it may also represent a desire to be sexually free: something often scorned by society. As Gemma Ahearne says on her blog, 'Sexual excess, vulgarity and lack of self-control have long been associated with the working-class woman, and the media loves to feature grotesque and shameless bodies as symbolic of chav values.'

Nice girls don't want group sex. But away from the judgemental eye of society, plenty of women do – at least in fantasy.

At the extreme end of this spectrum lies the gang-bang. Though it's often cited as a sign of the misogyny in porn, for some women at least, the fantasy of a gang-bang offers hedonistic delight.

Sally, 47, straight, causasian, divorced postgraduate, no children, carer for my mother, business degree and Masters

'I've been made part of a harem unwillingly and the other ladies of the harem prepare me for having sex with the owner of the harem by washing me, massaging me with scented oil, doing my hair and making me otherwise ready for sex, including kissing me all over and performing cunnilingus. Then they hold me down when the owner comes to have sex with me, as I'm still resistant. However, he turns out to be an excellent lover, we sleep together and I find myself happy to be a member of the harem after a night of magnificent sex.'

Anon, 18, pretty, brown hair, student, single

'An orgy in a chocolate bath.'

Vicky, 36, bisexual, married to a man

'Group sex with several people, male and female.'

Heather, 33, heterosexual, bi-curious, fabulously single, research scientist, curvy, atheist, daydreamer, feminist

'I'm tied to a table, blindfolded, legs spread, sex exposed. Another woman (no one in particular) is bent over, face close enough to lick my clit, has her arms bound behind her back and is suspended so just her toes touch the ground. A man (no one in particular) is behind her, teasing her – sometimes penetrating her so she is swung slightly off balance while she is licking me. I'm being penetrated by a 'fucking machine' and there is another man (sometimes two or three) masturbating while watching me being extremely pleasured. The man/men ejaculate on my clit and the dildo penetrating me while the woman is licking me. I have an incredible orgasm! The specifics change often, but the general theme is either myself orally pleasuring another woman while being penetrated, or she is pleasuring me while I'm being penetrated.'

Anon, 33, wife with two children in a failing marriage

'Tasting myself off many penises. There would be about ten men of all races, set up in a circle around me. A curtain would be concealing them all except their penises would be protruding through holes, into the circle so that there would be ten penises in various states of excitement, all blindly waiting to be exercised. I like to put them inside me then pull them out and put them in my mouth. I like the changing taste of myself after the sex has gone on for a while. Finally, I would have them, one by one and silently, ejaculate in my mouth. Then I would carry that semen to the next penis and perform oral sex on it without the owner knowing what I know about the "lubricant".'

Hannah, 21, from New Zealand, bisexual, long-term straight relationship, short red hair, busty

'I want to be in a gangbang with ten men fighting to fuck me and have all my holes filled then get covered in come.'

Emma, 26, straight, white, not married, no children, work in an office, no qualifications, blonde, quite heavy

'My fantasy is to have a group of men enter the room while I am having sex with my boyfriend. They pull him off of me and rough him up. Then they begin to tie me up, gagging my mouth. Then one by one they have their way with me. All the time my BF is watching but can't do anything.

The men are huge and muscly with very large penises. They take me in every position, slapping me, biting me, even using me two at a time. They then go on to have extremely hard anal sex with me. I do not actually like anal sex but the thought of it being forced on me is very appealing in a strange way.

After some time the men have used every hole I have and begin to come one by one, some in my vagina, some on my face or in my anus. At the end I am literally covered in semen. As I stand up, more pours out of my vagina and anus which they make me lick up off the ground. The whole time my boyfriend can only watch. I make eye contact with him throughout the whole experience which turns me on even more.'

Lydia, 30-something escort based in London

'My most recent fantasy was being fucked by a group of men in a pub.'

Anon, 36, project director, straight, divorced, in an open relationship

'Group sex in which I get fucked by a lot of strange men of all ages.'

Michelle, 28, UK female, size-ten brunette, office-worker, graduate with no children

> 'Being shared by three men, I always picture myself dressed up in a school or nurse uniform or perhaps lingerie and the men have sex with me together triple penetration.'

Rose, 78, bisexual, divorced, two grown children and grandchildren, retired but active in the Lions

> 'Most recently, it has been gang bangs.'

Anon, twenties, cis straight woman, kinky (sub), feminist

> 'A gang bang or MMF threesome where I'm fucked by several guys at once, e.g in the arse and cunt, while someone else comes on my face. I've had this fantasy for a couple of years; it's kinda my go-to for jerking off. I've always been interested in kinky stuff but in the last few years I've begun to feel like that's okay, and I have "permission" to mentally (and really!) explore the kinda stuff that turns me on. Meeting other kinky people was kinda the trigger for that, even though I was shocked at first . . .'

Anon, 39, mother of one, bisexual, married for 15 years

> 'My earliest fantasy was flying to a white planet accompanied by a nameless male where 49 women and fifty men awaited me to complete their number. All nude. My fantasies change all the time. Most recently it was a threesome where my husband and I share a male lover. My favourite fantasy is changeable but usually a threesome with either myself with a m/f couple or myself with teenage boyfriend and his best friend (which actually happened, but goes further in the fantasy).'

Sharing the Love

Several women incorporated their partner into their group sex fantasy. Some said that they felt their fantasies were cheating if they didn't include their partner in the mix. Others liked the idea of imagining a twist on their existing sex life and for some women, the fantasy was something they wanted to come true.

Summer, 35, bisexual female, in an open marriage to a man, poly-amorous, homeschooling mom to four children

'I often fantasise that I am tied up and being forced to accept pleasure until I am dripping wet. I sometimes also fantasize about my husband having sex with another man. Most recently, I fantasised that my husband had me by my hair and was forcing me to suck the cock of another man, taking it deep in my throat.'

Anon, in my forties, straight, son entering his teens. Work in print media

'Donning a snug fitting strap-on to pleasure a very erotic, sensuous and horny woman as she sucks my partner's cock.'

Anon, 28, white, bisexual, childless, in long term relationship

'My boyfriend and myself sharing a pre-op transsexual.'

Tracey, 48, married 22 years, together 27, three kids

'My husband and I with another woman. It came from going to a full nude strip club with hubby, getting turned on and wanting to touch the dancers. My fantasy came true in the past week! We had our first threesome!'

Anon, 28, caucasian post-graduate, hetero-flexible!

'I have a boyfriend, but we are in an open relationship, child-free and do not want any in the near future, if at all. I most often fantasise about being in a sexual situation with multiple males. It involves oral sex and vaginal and anal penetration. I am the centre of attention and the only female, surrounded by aroused men. Often the men are strangers and we have no connection other than sexual. Sometimes my partner is there encouraging me.

I very much enjoy the male body and love to explore men. I also like the idea of being the only woman, of having those men to myself. I love to give oral sex to a man, and having the opportunity to give it to more than one penis at a time is exciting. I also find I am left wanting more penetration after my partner has ejaculated, so it excites me to think of having several men to service that need.'

Annette, 48, married mother of two, self-employed, nothing outstanding in appearance or outlook on life

'Having sex with my husband and his friends or work colleagues. These friends are completely fictional though and are usually younger than husband and myself. They are also usually inexperienced, so I have to teach them the joys of sex.'

Nicola, 32, heterosexual, financial administrator, soon to be married

'My most recent fantasy was about my fiance, masturbating, watching me fuck another man. After the other man leaves my fiance fucks me hard and deep.'

Anon, bisexual performance artist, mostly monogamous

'A threesome with my boyfriend and an Amazonian woman with lots of tattoos. I'm fucked by him as she sits on my face.'

Charlie, 25, straight, single, white

'Being with my partner and two other guys. Essentially the centre of attention.'

Ali, 23, hetero graduate, work in a call centre, unmarried, no children, review sex toys on my blog

'My most common fantasy at the moment is to have a threesome with my boyfriend and a close male friend. I have had this fantasy for about half a year. I think part of what triggered it was using a suction cup dildo whilst performing oral on my partner. I feel quite conflicted about having this fantasy because I have strong monogamous beliefs.'

Megan, 59 (40 in my head), heterosexual, Australian, divorced, deliberately haven't had sex or relationship for 21 years

'Having sex with an ex-partner's ex-wife while he watches and then participates, with both of us having sex/stimulating the ex-wife and then both of them with me. Gets me every time, within about three minutes! It never happened and it wasn't my fantasy when he and I were together. I think they would have been up for the experience, having previously swapped partners for an evening. He left her for me, so she hated me. Also about having sex with a woman. I seem to be particularly impressed with large breasts and oral sex.'

Anon, 41, bisexual cis female. I am married to a man and have two children

'My most common fantasy is a threesome involving me, my husband and either another man or another woman (it tends to alternate). With another woman, I am going down on her while my husband takes me from behind. With another man, my husband and I are doing it missionary style and the other man takes my husband from behind. This gives my husband an incredible orgasm, which I really get off on. I think my fantasy comes from my bisexuality. I've known for 20 years that I'm bisexual but I've only recently admitted it to myself and my husband. I fantasise during masturbation and sex but my fantasies are far from reality right now. My husband and I have a good dialogue going that I hope will bring us to a place where we could explore these fantasies.'

Group-sex fantasies can satisfy a multitude of needs. They can allow women scope to explore their attitudes towards monogamy and sexual experiences outside their usual preference. They offer excess: a guarantee of satisfaction even if one person is not enough to satisfy a woman's needs. For some, they also form a way to test boundaries mentally, particularly those women who are curious about making their fantasies come true. And of course, not everyone is monogamous. As such, some women are simply fantasising about experiences they've enjoyed in the past or wish to try in the future.

In fantasy, a woman can safely explore group sex designed purely with her pleasure in mind. She can be the centre of attention being both sexually desired and satisfied. In reality, while some people enjoy happy non-monogamous lifestyles, many people reject the reality of group sex over the ease of the fantasy. And indeed, many women prefer the idea of sex with just one partner – though that doesn't make their fantasies any less complex.

Chapter Five:
Partner -Sex Fantasies

'It would be nice to have good sex . . . so I fantasise instead.'

ANON, CIS FEMALE, MARRIED, NO KIDS

*M*ost surveys into sexual fantasy report that fantasies about one's partner are among the most common, particularly for women. In *Who's Been Sleeping in Your Head?*, Brett Kahr reported that 58 per cent of women have fantasised about their partner at some point, and 37 per cent of people have had romantic fantasies. Mia More, Editor of Cliterati confirms, 'We receive many erotic stories featuring two strangers in all sorts of sexual situations, and it's not unusual for the tale to end with a twist: the two people concerned are actually a very happy couple, and the experience explored was a mutual fantasy – it's like a guaranteed happy ending. We get lots of these submissions, but the beauty of it is that from the beginning to the end the journey is always completely different. It's still a surprise when it turns out that the couple haven't randomly just met on a train and had sex in a station, but instead have been married forty years.'

While women's partners frequently made appearances in fantasies across the different fantasy categories, traditional romantic fantasies were far fewer on the ground than previous research has found in submissions to *Garden of Desires*. Far more fantasies included a partner and domination; a partner and exhibitionism; or a partner engaging in something else beyond the 'normal'

190

representations of sex. Sometimes these fantasies are inspired by reality; and at other times, fantasies that would never come true – whether because of the woman, her partner or both.

Some women commented that they didn't fantasise during sex because they considered it to be cheating. Perhaps in fantasising about a partner, women appease any guilt they may feel for being sexual on their own terms? Or maybe, they really have found the partner of their dreams?

Of course, partner-sex fantasies don't always involve a real life lover – by partner I mean sexual partner, not necessarily a husband or wife or long-term love. Many people imagine a fantasy partner, whether they are in a relationship or not. Some women focus on a particular celebrity, while others recall teenage crushes or previous relationships. In fantasy, women can imagine their partner to be whoever they want, no matter how forbidden or distant they may seem.

Helen, very happily married with grown-up son who has left home. I work in a theatre and feel sexy

'Having sex with David Bowie circa Thin White Duke.'

Fiona, 53, married with two kids, now a farmer, husband commutes to the city and doesn't get enough sex. Have been having relationship counselling and my homework is to have ten sexy thoughts a day. I find this hard, I have to get into the mood which means taking time out from a busy day to have some thinking time.

'I have often thought about being out in the open country, walking along through a pretty paddock and coming upon a tree with a swing in it. The man I am with who is not my husband runs over to the swing and sits on the swing. He has taken his shirt off and his muscles are rippling as he starts to swing backwards and forwards.

I notice that his jeans are hiding the bulge of his erection. He sees me looking at it, and beckons me over to sit facing him on the swing. Somehow we manage to fit without too much trouble, and then he pushes off and starts swinging. I feel his erection under me, and start to grind against it as we move back and forth. He indicates to me to pull myself up off him so he can release his cock. Up it springs, and as I lower myself down carefully, I am able to manipulate his cock through the side of my undies and it slides up into my wet pussy.

It is really hard to get into an easy flow of movement, but I can feel myself starting to come, my face feels hot and I can hear my partner groaning and we jiggle as best we can to come together. I have no energy left to lift myself up off him and so we just stay there, floating backwards and forwards in the breeze for some time.

I often have this as a dream, I wake up feeling aroused and hopefully I can use it to move into making love with my husband. It makes me feel great at the time, but afterwards, I feel sadness that I am no longer slim or strong enough to be able to engage in such an activity. I think maybe this fantasy was triggered by my having sex in the water with my first boyfriend. We didn't actually have penetration, but I could surely feel that erection pushing up against my swimmers and that surely felt good.'

Anon, 30, university student

'Arriving at my boyfriend's house in a bra, Santa mini skirt, and high heels underneath an overcoat. Walking into his house, taking off the coat and telling him that Santa had sent me to punish him for being naughty.'

Anon, 35, single mum of two, primary-school teacher, have been seeing a man for nearly two years

'My most recent fantasy was being with my boyfriend, at his house with *no kids around*! In his kitchen I approached him wearing a long coat with nothing underneath but lingerie and grabbed him and told him what he would do, which then proceeded to sex, with me calling all the shots such as telling him to go down on me.'

Anon, 26, white, uni-educated female, lefty, single but not celibate

'Dirty talk from my partner, or if more extreme, rough sex.'

What is a Partner-Sex Fantasy?

*T*hough partner sex is commonly used to describe fantasies about sex with an existing lover, of course they aren't always about one's own partner. While some women like to imagine their loved one engaging in all manner of sex acts, others use their fantasies to explore sex with other people. Sometimes this is a genuine sign of desire but many women said they wouldn't want to have sex with their fantasy figure in real life – more evidence that fantasy and reality are not the same thing. However, in her imagination, a woman can have as many partners as she sees fit without any fear of judgement – or risk to her relationship.

Amber

'The girls I masturbate about are always gorgeous: curvy, big, fecund girls who I could lose myself in. Mmmmm . . . I like my women to be womanly and my men to be big strong men. Although I'd also happily sleep with a ladyboy or trans M-F or F-M. Believe it or not, I'm picky in real life, but extremely open-minded with it. If someone has something attractive about them – and I'm not one for classically good-looking – then that works for me. There has to be some sexual connection, and that can be hard to find – except in my fantasies. With regards to girl-on-girl fantasies, for me these tend to be a whole lot sweeter and more nurturing than my stories involving men. Generally I'm "making love" with women and "fucking" men – but there are always exceptions.

My female fantasies are also seen in much closer detail than those with men, which are usually part of a bigger picture. In my mental dalliances with women I can take nipples in my mouth, kiss gentle lips, trace my fingers down curves of soft skin. It's heavenly rather than devilish like my male used-and-abused dreams, and soft-focussed and romantic – as if I'm exploring a Rubens painting in my head – a gentle yearning rather than a full-on fuckfest.

Meanwhile during my fantasies with men I'm often watching myself and the proceedings from above: objectifying myself as

I'm being objectified by the men. I don't see faces or cocks, and I don't look to: I just see male shapes and hear their vocal commentaries as they joke about my sluttiness with each other. Likewise even when I'm watching two gay men fuck in my fantasies I don't see the details, I just get a more general feeling about the scene as a whole.

In reality I've enjoyed naughty nights with women and also very loving relationships with men, so thinking about it now it's interesting how much my fantasies with men and women differ – in content, approach and perspective. I wonder if this radically different experience is also the case for other bisexual women and their various fantasies. Food for thought . . . Interestingly I have never – even as a teenager – fantasised about real-life film stars or any other famous people who are perceived as being sexy . . . Perhaps because my real life – my relationships – have usually been pretty sexually fulfilling, so I've never needed the boyfriend/ girlfriend fantasy experience.'

Why Do People Have Partner-Sex Fantasies?

*A*s an issue, this has barely been considered for research. This demonstrates the way in which certain types of sex are normalised by society. In investigating submissive or dominant fantasies, it marks them as 'outside the norm'. However, the motivations that women gave for having fantasies about their partner varied widely, suggesting that it's an area which would be worthy of study.

Mia More speculates, 'Perhaps women often include their partners in their fantasies because they're their current go-to for sexual relief and are therefore mentally closest to hand (excuse the mixed metaphor), or it might be because incorporating their other halves is a way of making their fantasy more acceptable to the relationship – especially if it's an activity that's particularly transgressive. Or it could be a case of simply showing their love for their partner: "I like being with you and I want you to come with me to fantasy-land.

Plus you're a fantastic fuck and I'm sure the rest of the room could learn from your extensive sexual skills." Or something!'

At its simplest, a partner-sex fantasy can represent wish-fulfilment – making an erotic idea come 'true'. In fantasy, a lover may be far more devoted than reality, taking time to ensure the woman is satisfied: something that can be used to reconcile dissatisfaction with reality. A partner-sex fantasy can also be used to self-comfort – if your lover is away or emotionally absent; and/or be used to reinforce your feelings of love. It can also be used to mentally 'try on' a sexual experience you're curious about experiencing with a lover.

Emily, 20, heterosexual, single, Christian, student, bachelor of marketing, Melbourne

'I am now a Christian so now my fantasies are more about love making than sex. My favourite fantasy is the perfect wedding night in a luxury penthouse hotel suite.'

Anon, mid-50s, middle class, caucasian, two adult children, post-graduate, long divorced

'I'm working with a very attractive Indian man (tall, dark and handsome, funnily enough), and I seduce him in his office when we are working late at night. We have sex in his office, on the desk and sitting on the chair, illuminated by the night time city view. The tall, dark Indian man referred to is a REAL individual, and we did have sex (albeit not in his office). I know many fantasies are disappointing when they are acted out in real life, but this one was amazing; the gent in question turned out to be the most *incredible, stupendously skilled* lover – the real life experience was actually beyond my fantasies, and it made me feel great about myself.'

Anon

'Vanilla sex with my fave actor.'

Sam, 35, hetero, Anglo Australian, married no children, blonde, digital production

'I fantasise about my husband's boss. We accidentally meet up when my husband is away and end up at a hotel room. The sex is fast, passionate, aggressive until we both climax. This fantasy does not make me orgasm. I don't masturbate during this fantasy, but I love being "fucked" aggressively. I'm not even that attracted to him real life, but there's something about his alpha-maleness that turns me on in my fantasies.'

Foreplay

Some women enjoy writing fantasies for their partner, either as erotic inspiration or as a form of foreplay – possibly both. This fantasy was submitted by a woman who wrote it for her partner and posted it on an erotic website to seduce him and let him know how she felt: a sensual love letter.

Anon

'I want him. It's a deep ache that ambles between my gut and my chest, making me crave his smell and desperate for his touch. I want my hand tangling in his chest hair. I want my lips around his cock. I want the smell of his come in my nose and the taste of his balls in my mouth. I want my pussy wrapped tight around him as he looks into my eyes and kisses me deeply. I want his cock in my arse as he strokes my hair from my eyes and kisses me softly. He is not here and I want him.

Less than 24 hours ago, he had his cock in my pussy, in my arse. It goes against all the rules but anal sex is all about feeling him come inside me. We've been tested but it still feels taboo. And it's the most intimate love making we ever share.

I love feeling him push his way slowly into me, moaning as he feels me opening to him. We usually pile on the lube but sometimes, when I'm feeling really relaxed – usually after a glass of wine or two – I love to slide him inside me with the help of nothing other than my spit.

He never forces the pace, just lets my arse slowly open up to take him inside. I love feeling my body acquiesce to him: allowing him to enter me in the most intimate way, feeling his flesh against mine, the warmth of his cock inside my tightly stretched hole. I love it when he spits on his finger and runs it around my arsehole, loosening me up, trying to make me as comfortable as possible as he throbs inside me, making me flinch at his girth.

I love the feeling of conquering my own body: of persuading it to let my lover inside me even though there might be a little pain. He's gentle – until he doesn't need to be gentle any more – but my arse is still relatively unused to sex. He is the one who has brought my arse to life: made me crave him inside me.

Last night, when I managed to wriggle back onto him, high enough to use saliva alone, I felt such a sense of achievement. And when his dick lubricated my arsehole with its own juices, and he slid deeper inside me, I wanted him as far as he could go. I pushed into him, grinding back, taking him deeper – and felt my pussy getting wetter with every passing second. Knowing he was lubricating my arsehole with his own juices made me feel hot as fuck.

And when he realised that his arse-fucking was making me wet, his reaction made me all the wetter.

Our anal sex is not the carnal, violent act of porn films – though there are some porn star moments. It's loving; sharing; closer than close as my heart tells my body to relax and allow my lover in. I want to feel him shoot inside me; I want to feel the warmth filling me, his seed flooding me, his juices trickling out of my arsehole afterwards, soothing my aching muscles. I want him to own my body. I want to give my body to him.

My arse gives up the fight too early. Pain outweighs pleasure. I have to move and feel bitter disappointment: I've come so near to what I want – to giving him what I want to give him. And now my body has let me down. It is a traitor.

Luckily, it's a traitor with multiple facets. One condom later and he's buried inside me, fucking me hard, pile-driving into my cunt as I hook my ankles around his waist and dig my heels into his lower back, pushing him deeper inside me. I lean back, tilting my pelvis to give him access to every part of my body I can. We breathe each other's kisses, suck each other's lips, grip each other's shoulders, paw each other's bodies. My pussy is getting wetter with every "slap, slap, slap". I can feel my orgasm building, ejaculation looming.

He pushes so far inside me that I have no idea where I end and he begins but it doesn't matter and we are one and we are breathing and we are biting and we are silently screaming and he pulses in me as I pulse around him and we clutch and hold and breathe and love and sweat and breathe and kiss.

And we separate.

I wish I had his come inside me as a physical memory. But all I have is my muscles, clasping at air, and his body next to me; his chest hairs drawing me to stroke them; his chest calling me to lie on it; his cock wilting slowly under the condom.

I peel it off, cup his cock with my hand and drift to sleep, arsehole still aching in a poignant reminder of what could have been.

I want him.'

Joy also uses her fantasies in this way. She says, 'I normally write stories for my partner of my fantasies and then over time, when she is comfortable with the ideas we try them out. She is less experienced at sex than I am and where I have very clear ideas of things I like she does not. I use the stories to show her that those ideas are not that scary. She keeps the stories by the bed.' She kindly sent one of her stories in for this book.

Joy, this first chapter was written in October 2010 while she was living in South Africa and I was in the UK. It was in anticipation of her coming home in December

'I start thinking about what we'll be doing the next night, smoking and chilling and fucking. The thoughts keep me warm on the cool night, I pass the spliff into my other warm hand and slip my cold fingers into my panties and feel my hot flesh. I feel myself wet and swollen. I start to play and smoke lazily.

My excitement is building and my mind keeps drifting to the box in my car. I keep thinking about how we're going to play with it tomorrow night. I can't concentrate even on what I am doing, I can't wait another day. I am aching. I decide I might as well set up the machine so we don't have to do it tomorrow since I am worried about scaring you. I go out in my dressing gown and grab the necessary box and scurry back to the house.

Having braced myself to having to do quite a bit of work it is remarkably easy to set up and I have it in position within a few minutes. I was very close when I decided to stop to set it up my pleasure has subsided but I am definitely getting wetter and more swollen. I get onto my bed and start playing again. My eyes are drawn to it sitting there in front of the covered mirror. It is smooth and shiny. I can't seem to play despite how wet my hand is even after a few seconds gently probing. I want something more intense than my hand can provide.

After a bit of thought I think it is important to try out the machine so at least I can show you what to do. I uncover the mirror so I can see what's happening. So with a little ginger manoeuvring I am on top of it just lowering myself into position and I turn the dial a little, the sound instantly makes me gush and I feel a tremor down my spine and straight to my clit. I lean forward pushing onto the vibrating pad as I get myself into position over the small dildo.

Just as I am about to lean back onto the shaft and force it home I hear a knock on the door. I think "Fuck" but shout "I'm coming" grumbling to myself about not being close enough for that and throw on my dressing gown. Coming down the stairs I can't see anyone outside and am instantly put on edge. I grab an umbrella, just in case and unlock the door.

There's a bag on the doorstep a big, army bag, my heart gives a leap even before I step forward to see you trying to shout up to the window. I run to you trying not to scream and wake the whole island. I throw myself into your arms and we hug. I pull away enough to sweep your mouth into a deep hard kiss. Your gaze catches my thigh as you push me up against the garage and you realise that I am naked underneath and you groan and push me hard. Your hand slides up my thigh and feel how wet I am by the time you reach a few inches above my knee and I can hear how much you like it.

You start to drag me inside. We each grab a bag, stagger into the house and drop them. We bundle upstairs stopping to kiss and remove clothing. Mine falls away quickly since I am not wearing much. You are dressed in a few layers, you're probably feeling it after the summer heat. I am pulling clothes from you as fast as I can. I bare your top half and marvel, even as you are marvelling, over each other's bodies. Both familiar yet strange. Both tauter and firmer yet feeling softer. I kiss your breasts as though greeting old friends. You run your finger over my tree. I shudder. I am negotiating your jeans when we reach the hall when I suddenly realise that I have left the machine set up in my room, still glistening with my juices. I try to fight you into the sitting room but you're determined about your destination. I pull away from you, trying to think of an excuse and say something when you see into my room.

"Looks like I turned up just in time." I look a little sheepish and try to think of something to say.

"So how does this work?" You step forward and run your finger over the dial, then over the vibrating bit and I see you roll your eyes as you feel my wetness on it then your finger traces a path up to the tip of the shaft also wet from only a few seconds ago. You look me in the eye and slip your finger into your mouth. I the pleasure of the familiar taste evident on your face.

You take my hand and draw me back to where I was only a few moments before. I am not sure but you encourage me to sit back. Your hand reaches over to the dial, I am hovering over the apparatus but as you begin to turn it. The exciting humming draws me nearer my knees soften and my clit once more comes into contact with the vibrator. I sigh and push down onto it harder. I move and you pull me into position over the up-standing latex. You look me in the eyes again and say "Is this how it goes? I love you," the last as you see me nod a little and you push on my hips so I am invaded suddenly even as my clit swells against the vibrator.

You look into the mirror and see me from a different angle, my tattoo as I arch with my stomach firm and my breasts pointing skyward. You climb onto the bed and kiss me from behind as I face the mirror. Your kisses fall onto my shoulder and neck. You wrap your hand round my waist and add to the excitement of the machine on my clit with your fingers gliding over it. You catch my eye in the mirror and hold the dial up to me and turn it slowly but steadily up while you hear me calling out and grinding, arching then falling forward while pushing down.

The sighing, gasping and moaning grow until I am screaming and riding the machine that is doing your bidding. You hear that I am reaching the final straight when you pull my head back by my hair and kiss me on my mouth. I start to shudder and buck against it and you push me down, forcing me to keep going. After a few minutes you think I can't take any more and you pull me up and quickly turn it and me round and push me back down onto it. You have your legs on my shoulders to make sure I don't get up and you lie back onto the bed and I smell your glorious wetness. Not waiting to be asked I plunge into your inviting pussy. My fingers spearing straight into you as my tongue immediately gets to work. This first taste in so long has me delirious with pleasure. I taste and lap at your clit and lips. Quickly my tongue is flicking back and forth and my fingers seem to remember just how to curl up into you to make you arch. Quickly this time you start to build to orgasm. I feel it building inside you and fuck you all the harder realising my rocking for that is only improving my ride. You gasp something and I watch your eyes roll back as the first wave of orgasm breaks over you. You buck and writhe as you come, squeezing my fingers harder and harder with every contraction. That alone pushes me over the edge and I come again just from knowing you are.

Eventually your spasming dies down and you let go of my head. I lie on your thigh just panting for a few seconds. I look at you, you look sated but I know you can take more. While you lie with your eyes closed I quickly bring it onto the bed. While your eyes are still shut I pull your hand up over my still soaked and engorged lips, I know you are stirring but put a musky hand over your eyes. I run your hand over the machine and trusting you to keep your eyes closed reach for the controls. I give it a little flicker and feel you tighten beneath me. I know you want to play too. I guide you upright with kisses and embraces. Your eyes still firmly shut I get you to swing one leg over the machine. You settle down onto the dildo and pad very easily, possibly the familiar feeling of something between your thighs or the eagerness to experience what I just have. I let you rock a little on the dildo and my fingers to get you accustomed to the situation. Then I do it.

I turn it on enough to give a faint rumbling. You start at first then give yourself up into the glory of the sensation. The warmth tingles through your clit into the rest of your body. I look at your face to be sure you want more. You look keen so I crank it up a small amount. You look startled for a second as the excitement increases you accept it. You watch me reach again for the control and will me on. Again a small increase, you're expecting it this time so you don't look surprised and just wriggle further onto your saddle.

A few small increments later you are beginning to be frustrated and I know it. I am giving you another small increase when you snatch it from my fingers and crank it full way in one motion. You moan and begin to ride. You rock and bounce on it crying out. I deftly grab a vibrator from my drawers and press it onto my clit. I am almost sore but I keep it firmly pressed against me with one hand while I stroke your breasts and stomach, pulled tight by leaning backwards with your hand on the wall. You are pounding against the machine and I straddle it from the front. I lean into you and kiss you. Rough, possessive kisses, ones that have waited six months.

You make your final arch then slam down one last time onto the machine. You shake and cry out and kiss me harder and harder. With every peak it is all you can take and yet somehow you keep taking one more. Slowly the kisses become leisurely then gentle and almost lazy.

We slide onto the bed in each other's arms. We push the machine carefully off the bed and I tweak the drape over the mirror again. I sigh loudly as our bodies slot together. I start to kiss your neck and back and finally stop to say, "Hi." You giggle your response then pull me on top of you. You squeeze your hand between my legs to feel how wet I still am and then pull me up your body til I am right above your face. Your tongue reaches out for a second. The moment you taste me you grab me and pull me closer. I fall forward, off-balance. I smell sweet pussy and automatically draw my tongue over your abused clit. You move against me, a final shimmer of the orgasm you had. As you lick me and I lick you.

You and I are almost competing now to make the other come first. The more furiously your tongue moves the closer I get the more determined I am to win the harder I lick. We build, again quickly but both reach a plateau which keeps us near but not too much to allow us to enjoy the sensations of each other's bodies. As we realise this is not going to end sticky we begin to try different techniques, swirling round to flicking up and down, different hand and head angles and finger movements. We start to build again together. You want me to come first but I don't want it. I kick my leg over you and turn round so I can lick you. I have one hand buried in you while my tongue goes to town on your most sensitive regions. My other hand has grabbed the vibrator again.

With an attitude of "Oh no you don't," you push me over and get on the floor. Kneeling to lick me you are not riding the machine but it is providing a useful bum-rest. You grind a little against the still warm cover. I sit up and show you the remote asking with my eyes. You get my drift and precisely resume your seat. I start to use the dial to show you what my favourite things you are doing. As the vibration only seems to increase and the intensity is becoming less a background feeling more a desperate urge to come you know I must be close. I can't believe how long I am holding off against your tongue but I am enjoying seeing your corresponding increases.

Together we come. Crashing down together. We both take more than we would to try and keep going longer. We both eventually slump and I haul you back onto the bed and under the covers.

Since I no longer have an early start tomorrow we might as well have a smoke. So we smoke, we chat, we make love slowly and affectionately. Much later that night we play again with the machine, testing it and ourselves. Eventually we fall asleep in each other's arms and wake up sore, sated, warm, content and above all, wet.

By the way I came while writing this. Will come again now before bed.

Love you very much x'

Common Fantasy Themes

Romance and Seduction

*T*he common stereotype is that women require romance to be aroused. Indeed, romance novels are often the first place that women read about sexual exploration. The success and longevity of Mills and Boon and its ilk shows that for some women, the idea of a tall, dark, rescuing stranger is highly alluring. However, more graphic submissive fantasies were far more common for this book than pure romance. That said, ideas such as the roaring log fire, sensual boudoir and caring but firm lover are still apparent. Similarly, sexy lingerie and seductive routines also play a part in some women's fantasies.

Anon, 28, bisexual caucasian female in LA, graduate, internet writer, corsetière, pin-up, and sexual submissive

'I had a crush on a family friend, and I used to imagine being trapped with him in a house in a snow storm. He was timid and questioning, but gently forceful. It was heavily influenced by Disney archetypes of femininity; and I was the blushing virgin.'

Anon, 18, single straight Asian student, my curvy body-type is unusual for an Asian girl, with size DD breasts, wide hips and a rather curvy butt. My stomach is essentially flat and my legs are muscular, toned and somewhat lean (unfortunately, not long and lean yet). In another 10 lbs (which will happen in the next several months), I would have the figure akin to Beyoncé, Kim Kardashian, and other curvy celebrities

'My favourite fantasy involves a marathon sex session starting in the living room on a sunny Saturday afternoon with me doing burlesque in black lacy lingerie (black bra, lacy panties, garters) and red 5-inch heels. The curtains are open, but we are in a house with a yard and a fence, so no one will see us. I lap dance for him, and then proceed to slowly striptease him, removing each article of clothing and keeping eye contact with him. He is staring, wide-eyed, obviously wanting to touch me, but he can't. Haha.

I start with the garters, then the bra, leaving my breasts bared to him. He is practically salivating, and then I proceed to take off my underwear, gyrating my hips as I do. I walk confidently and slowly, lithe as a snake towards him, still in the heels.

I smile slyly and smugly, knowing that I'm torturing him with need. His cock is at attention as he reclines on the couch. "No touching with your hands," I say, still smiling. He blinks and nods. I stroke his face and then bring my chest to his face. He kisses me, and then I quickly move back. I straddle him, my knees on either side of his legs, take his face into my hands and give him a long, sensual smooch. "Now you can touch me," I whisper, smiling wickedly.

He pulls me to, hard, and kisses me with such fervor that I'm momentarily stunned. I regain my equanimity and rub the back of his neck with my right hand. The other hand explores, stroking his face and neck, running through his hair, down his shoulders, his back, his chest. Then both hands are just touching him all over as we kiss passionately. He touches me all over my back, grabbing my breasts, my face, my upper arms and shoulders.

I am so turned on at this point and I just want to move on to the next part. I firmly hold his face in my hands and give him a long kiss. I pull back, staring deeply into his eyes.

"I love you," I say.

"I love you too," he replies, smiling.

Then he suddenly dumps me off his lap onto the couch so that I'm lying down. I blink, shocked, but love how he's taking control. He proceeds to put his head between my legs and give me oral sex. I gasp and moan as he finds my clitoris and lavishes it with his tongue. He keeps on going as I am climbing higher and higher to the peak of ecstasy. I am moaning so loudly at this point, interspersing "Oh yes" with his name. I reach the point of no return and I climax, my head going back and to the side, my hips vibrating.

He kisses up my stomach slowly, his mouth working towards my breasts. He sucks each of them and then gently bites them. He moves up and kisses all over my neck. He pauses, smiles at me and then kisses my lips. We just make out for a bit. He lets go, playfully kisses my cheek and rudely flips me onto my front. I gasp in surprise and before I could get my bearings, he quickly plunges his member into me. He starts going at it and I urge him to go harder. He complies, and pumps harder and faster. With each thrust, I feel myself ready to come again. Soon, he reached his peak, and does one last hard shove into me. I scream, coming all over again, even more intensely this time. He comes too, and I feel the aftershocks inside me.

He then pulls out, lies on the couch and puts me against him in a spooning position. He nuzzles me, kissing the back of my neck and wraps his arms around me. It's my favourite place to be, in his arms. His arms are really muscular and when they're around me, I feel so safe and protected. We lie there, replete, and doze off together for an afternoon nap.'

Laura Jane, 22, straight and engaged to the man of her dreams

'Having my partner arrive home after a long day, to find me preparing his favourite meal in nothing more than black lacy underwear with garter belt, stockings and Doc Martens (these are significant to us). Allowing him to eat, but not touch as I cater to almost every need. Once this is done, I lead him upstairs where he is quickly tied to the rails of the bed and blindfolded. Then I slowly start to tease before ensuring that absolutely every need has been met.'

Nicole, 30, heterosexual, unhappily married, no children, public service, bachelor degree, brown hair

'I am in love with a person, but because of the current circumstances we cannot be together at the moment so I think about us being together sexually in many different ways. Although my fantasies at the moment are about being with this man, in the past I would also fantasise about other people, sometimes famous people, sometimes women, sometimes no one in particular. I found that it would help me reach climax. I also do not watch porn (something my husband is supposedly not into) given that I would feel embarrassed but I think I might actually like it. But we have never discussed it and I would find it to be more enjoyable if I watched it by myself anyway.'

Anon, 25, single, heterosexual

'A particular man who I fell for and who lives overseas comes to where I live to see me, although in reality it's been a long time since we saw each other. He knocks on my door and I stare at him in shock. He tells me he can't stop thinking about me, as much as he's tried to put me out of his mind, and takes me out to dinner. After dinner we are walking through the city and when we're alone he kisses me. It becomes passionate and he pushes me back against the wall, kissing and touching me with unrestrained passion but an odd gentleness at the same time. He reaches under my dress, fingers me as I unzip his jeans and he makes love to me up against the wall, holding me up with my legs wrapped around his waist. Then . . . you know, we fall in love and live happily ever after and all that.'

Exploring Sexuality

Many straight women admitted to having fantasies about lesbian experiences. Similarly, many lesbians admitted to having fantasies about heterosexual – or gay male – experiences. It has long been asserted that sexual fantasies about someone of the same gender in no way make you gay; and vice versa. However, the fact that so many women fantasise about a sexuality different from their own suggests that perhaps sexuality itself may be more fluid than we think.

As one woman says, 'I don't really like men. They are okay (and dateable, apparently), but I rarely see one I like. I like yaoi (like, the bear-man kind of it [bara]) but I would not want them for myself. Many men scare/confuse me and apply their little rules on how a women should be to me. I hate that. I have a lot of male friends, like motorcycles and cats but I would NOT describe myself as a lesbian (Oh, the cliché!).' Given her attitude to men, her fantasy below is unsurprising.

Anon, 20, shy to strangers, loud with friends, monogamous, small, chubby, messy

'Having sex with a girl I don't (yet?) know. I always know, I know her, but never, who she is. She is soft and nice and smells really tasty.'

Ana, married for 16 years, 3 children, business owner, university educated

'Lesbian, two-timing my husband.'

Anon, young college professor, gold-star lesbian

'Usually in an historic time period, mostly the Victorian period (I like the cumbersome clothing). An aristocratic man introduces me to the varied joys of heterosexual sex and incorporates bondage, orgies, young housemaids, etc. in an attempt to convert me from my lesbian proclivities. In real life I'm a hardcore lesbian and I've only been with women and am fully committed to my wife of many years.'

Nancy, 33, heterosexual, anglo saxon, married, three children, writer, dyed black hair

'I fantasise about having sex with men and women. I think I may be bisexual.'

Michelle, heterosexual single mother of 3

'Each time I was pregnant I fantasised about sleeping with a woman, not that I want to carry that out, but I think that was hormonal.'

Anon, 28, heterosexual, in a relationship with no children, sufferer of severe anxiety, degree in social sciences

'My fantasy is having an exploratory liaison with a curvy female. I've wondered a lot about where it comes from; I've never had a relationship with a member of the same gender beyond a drunken kiss. I do find females attractive but on an admiration level, rather than sexual, although I have felt turned on by certain women. That said, I love the sight of big breasts. I will often watch lesbian pornographic videos whilst masturbating, too.'

Ally, 21, straight, single, language student

'I've been fantasising about going alone to a lesbian bar or club, and standing at the bar getting slowly tipsy whilst making eye contact with another woman. It's clear to her that it is my first time in the bar, and she takes me home to give me my first lesbian experience. The build up/kissing is the best; in a taxi, or in the hallway to her flat.'

Anon, 30, single female (although with a fuck-buddy or two)

'Lesbian sex. Being with another woman. From gentle kissing and frottage to oral and fucking her with a strap-on. I've kissed a girl but there's never even been a hint of anything else.'

Carolin, female, married with children, bachelors degree and professional career

'I fantasise about a woman smelling me through my pantyhose and loving it. So much so it inspires her to masturbate and offer me her pussy to smell and taste.'

Zoe, 19, straight, blue eyes, dark brown hair and currently in a relationship

'My most common fantasy has to be a sexual encounter with another woman. I am straight. However, I think most women will come across this fantasy of sex with someone the same gender as you are. It's more accepted by male society than a male/male relationship and I think I'm just curious if it could be as amazing as people think it is.

I don't think that this fantasy would happen any time soon. As I am in a relationship currently, I don't fancy just bringing a woman into bed with us to see what it feels like.'

Matilda, 18, straight, 5ft 11, white British, student, in a relationship

'Having sex with a woman. I think that's due to lesbian porn being sensual and almost beautiful in a way. I fantasise about having sex with a woman but don't ever feel attracted to women or have had the urge to have sex with a woman.'

Being Rescued

The 'man as saviour' is a familiar theme in romance novels. From the 'knight on a white charger' to a bad boy on a motorbike, racing off into the sunset with the heroine holding on tight, the desire to let someone else take over and solve all our problems can be intoxicating.

Rita, 57, female, Caucasian, married, 4 children, business owner, A Level (UK), naturally blonde, blue eyes

'A civil war had broken out in the country where I was working. I was taken hostage by one side and my captor became attracted to me. He would show me kindness by wiping my face with a clean damp cloth and making sure my restraints were not hurting and feeding me. He went away for five days leaving me with the other renegades to keep an eye on me. They never touched me but I could see it in their eyes they wanted to.

My chief captor returned and he took me away from that place as he said it was becoming unsafe. We had to go further into the jungle. We went ahead of the others and soon nightfall came. He untied my restraints and ordered me to take my clothes off and then indicated that I get into the single sleeping bag he had brought with him. I slid down into the sleeping bag, my eyes focused on him at all times.

He began to undress himself and he revealed his slight but muscular and fit body to me. He slid down and nudged me further over into the now tight space and zipped the bag up. We were in a cocoon. With his hands he turned me to face away from him. He moved his head slowly and I could feel his breath on the back of my neck. I was trembling inside and then my whole being began to tremble. I could not lay still.

He wrapped his arms around me tightly pulling me further into him. He whispered in my ear that the renegades were warned not to lay a finger on me. I was his and then he began to pleasure me and it felt wonderful.'

Anon, I'm married, I teach high school, and am 52. I'm heterosexual and WASP

'I have been kidnapped, by some unknown, and then a huge search ensues by all of my male friends. The one who succeeds in rescuing me nurses me back to health and falls hopelessly in love with me. We then have wild sex, many times a day!'

Anon, 25, heterosexual, New Zealander, single, no children, medical student

'A doctor colleague (imaginary) and I are stuck in a situation where we're in a place we shouldn't be. He's very attractive and finds me to be the same. We hear someone (the police) coming and will get arrested if we're caught and to avoid looking suspicious, I pull him close to me and we start kissing. The idea is to pretend we are a couple of horny idiots making out in what is "accidentally" an out-of-bounds place and the police believe the scenario, but we find after we've kissed that it wasn't all that fictional and then have lots of hot sex with each other. Repeatedly. It's pure sex though, with no romantic intentions.'

Specific Sex Acts

Though some women's fantasies involve complex narratives and fantasy lovers, for others, partner-sex fantasies are focussed simply on a specific sex act. In some cases this is a familiar favourite, indulged in regularly with a lover. In others, it provides the woman with a way to 'experience' desires that are not being fulfilled in real life, through the medium of fantasy.

In fantasy, a woman's orgasm is central to proceedings. Fingering, oral and other sex acts are just as common as penis-in-vagina sex, if not more so.

Anon, Cis-gendered female, adult, married, no kids, apparently very straight, well educated, not sexually adventurous

'Being given oral sex, followed by fantastic PIV (penis-in-vagina) sex with one of the fantasy men in my head. It would be nice to have good sex . . . so I fantasise instead.'

Ellen, 24, mostly heterosexual, Australian, uni student and environmentalist, living in rural Australia, boyfriend of 2 years

'Being anywhere, in a dress or skirt, and having the person I'm with caress me all over, then finger me while they bend me over or lie me flat on my stomach, bringing me to climax.'

Anon, 32, married to my second husband, no children yet, living long distance for work

'I had a one night stand with a guy I work with. He was absolutely amazing in bed, but since it was only a one off, we didn't get to do all sorts of things. My most recent fantasy was finding myself naked in bed with him, and persuading him to fill in all of the gaps – most notably, anal sex, which he's just the right size and shape for!'

Ali, 24, lesbian, single, sport graduate

'I fantasise about the person I am with mostly if I'm in a relationship. My most common fantasy is to be licked out whilst driving along near a beach somewhere hot at night in an open top car. Males are often shown receiving oral sex whilst driving in movies and song etc. This may have placed the idea in my head, but also the thrill and danger of being in control of a fast moving car and climaxing is just my idea of heaven.'

Anon, single, 33, straight, British, Caucasian, MSc

'Pretty romantic – slow build up sex. Started with flirting and then kissing, and moved onto foreplay and finally sex with the guy who I fancy at the moment.'

Anon, 25, bi, in a monogamous long-term relationship with a cis male, has had only one sexual partner, no children

'"One last fuck before we die" scenarios, high-adrenaline sex after a dire situation.'

Anon, retired lecturer, 64, married with 2 adult children

'Oral sex with my partner having my clitoris licked gently.'

Kim, 44, bi-curious, Caucasian, engaged/defacto, 1 child, manager, diploma, blonde

'Rubbing my clitoris against the clitoris of another – tribbing!'

Anon, work in marketing, have a boyfriend, dark brown hair, am kinda short, but in pretty good shape

'Lying back and having a yummy looking man fill me up and go hard into me.'

Anon, 30, female, straight, blusher-loving lawyer

'Pretending to be asleep and having my boyfriend start to have sex with me, me trying not to respond.'

Specific Locations

And then there are women who imagine a fantasy location. From a desert island fringed with palms to an opulent hotel room with four-poster and sensual furnishings, the imagination allows you to go anywhere you want. Unlike previous studies, relatively few women were specific about their fantasy location, however. Perhaps as women become more confident about asking for what they want to do, they care less about exactly where they do it?

Anon, 17, straight, Lebanese, in a relationship, at school, brunette, goody 2 shoes, not a day of school ever missed (during the past 2 years anyway)

'On the hood of a Ford GT XY, in a public carpark, at night, with the car on (screw the price for petrol). I picture my boyfriend pushing me down onto the car and feeling it vibrate and hearing its sounds, feeling intoxicated by the smell of petrol, and knowing there may be someone watching. What triggered it? A picture online of a couple making out on the hood of a car. Why the GT? It's just my favourite car, so masculine.'

Liz, artist, 35, mother of two daughters, in a defacto relationship of 11 years

'In my fantasy I dreamt of opening an art gallery with a special pleasuring room out the back, where I seduce my buyers. In this particular fantasy, the buyer was my very wealthy neighbour, and he tied me up and pleasured me and fucked me and told me he would come back tomorrow and the next day and that he means to buy all my art.'

Jane, 21, straight, Caucasian, single, no children, student

'A trip to the Bahamas full of sex and relaxation.'

Anon, 23, straight, in sales, no kids, blonde, blue eyes and new to this

'Sex on a car hood in a full moon while it's pouring raining.'

Anon, 39, building a coaching practice learning Equine Facilitated Coaching

'Right now I am in an office and it's my first office job, so there have been a few fantasies regarding my desk and a co-worker from another department. I also fantasise about someone taking off all of the clothes I wear to the stables, and having sex with me while I'm dirty and smell like hay and horses. I think that one's pretty normal for most horsewomen though. The smell of the leather, grass, and the horses, the feel of wearing boots and tight jeans, it does something to your imagination unless you're just dead.'

Anon, 24, Australian born with a Punjabi ethnicity. Single, hetero-sexual, 5'11", Bachelor of Law and Bachelor of Business

'My most common fantasy involves me in a sky high apartment that overlooks the city at night. I normally "meet" the male (he has always been one guy who I am best friends with) in my fantasy in a random encounter whilst I'm out (either with friends for dinner, shopping etc.) and he invites me back to his apartment to have a quick catch up.

He ends up revealing some personal things and I decide to seduce him, and we end up spending the whole weekend together locked up in the apartment testing out different surfaces. I'm not a person who tends to tell someone that I am interested in them, so I guess my fantasy shows my inner self in doing something that I've wanted to do for the last four years or so to the male in my fantasy.'

Anon, 28, black/colourful hair, average build, height on the short side, straight, single but prefers long term relationships; no children. Causasian

'There's music playing loud and with a strong bass line. I'm in a hallway of some kind that is lit indirectly by lights from nearby, but the lights in the hall itself are off. It's out of the way and there isn't anybody around, but there's people nearby – likely out listening to the music as a band plays. There's someone with me, who is tall and has nice shoulders, and we're kissing, grasping at each other.

My arms go up around his shoulders and he holds me against him. He kisses down the side of my neck and pushes me up against the wall, lifts me, and holds me there. He grinds into me and trails his lips downwards, moving my shirt as he does. I run my hands over his strong back, moving one arm down and grasping his bum, squeezing the rounded muscle, and pressing him tight against me. I wrap my legs around him as I kiss him back, moving up his jawline to his ear.

We continue holding, and kissing, and grinding, getting more and more intense. I undo his shirt buttons and tug at his belt. He moves his hands down my body and reaches to lift my skirt, pulling away slightly to give space to pull my underwear aside. I take the opportunity to undo his belt, button and fly and reach my hand down his pants to grasp him, pulling him free. I arch to rub myself against him whilst holding him there with my hand. He pushes me back against the wall, strong but not rough, and kisses me deep and long as he presses his hips against mine. I use my hands to guide him to me, and as he presses again he moves inside of me.

I lift my legs back around him and squeeze him tight in between them. I slip my hands back around him, wandering, feeling his muscle, teasing, scratching a little, and hanging on to him and his hands press against the wall either side of me, holding me up, keeping me from moving or falling, whilst he explores as much as he can with his lips, urgent and fevered. We pause as we think we hear someone pass nearby, but don't stop. Once they've passed without finding us, we focus again, even more impassioned, breath catching and silenced gasps, until we come, intensely.

I lean against him, spent, as he holds me against the wall, leaning fully into me now, panting heavily in my ear as the last quakes rack through his body and leave him, his weight against mine to keep me from falling as we hang together.'

Eva, 32, white British, married, two children, pediatric surgeon

'My most common fantasy is having my man on top of me whilst we gaze in each others eyes; on the cool grass of a local wood.'

Jillian Boyd, 22, queer/bi, able-bodied, cis, in a relationship, no children, erotica writer, fast and furious redhead

'My earliest fantasy was shagging by the fireplace. I still fantasise about that! I think I have less concrete fantasies these days. I fantasise about places I want my boyfriend to fuck me in, mostly. My favourite fantasy is sex in a ski chalet, by the fire, on a nice faux-fur rug.'

Partner-sex fantasies offer romantic escapism and sexual experimentation, help preserve erotic memories or inspire sensual adventures. Fantasising about one partner offers monogamous women a chance to explore sex with different (fantasy) partners, whether with a celebrity crush, an ex, a current lover or someone you would never have sex with in real life who nonetheless ticks the fantasy box. They can offer a mental escape route from a relationship – imaginary cheating – and help you explore different aspects of your sexual self.

Monogamy is far from a natural state – humans are one of the few species that prioritise it and even then, around half of men and women cheat on their partner. Perhaps fantasies about different lovers are what keeps the other half faithful?

Anon, 28, BA, based in LA

'I've come to the realisation that my fantasising about women during sex with men was an attempt to access intense sexual feelings where there were none. During the last three years I have been celibate by choice in an effort to discover my true nature. Now that I have come to a realisation about what and who I am, I hope to be able to pursue sexual relationships in the future that allow me to be truly present.'

While partner-sex fantasies allow us to explore different facets of our personality, some women feel a need for even more difference. Much as some women fantasise about being a different sexuality to the one they usually define themselves by, for others, it is gender they choose to explore.

Chapter Six:
Gender Fluidity

*'I really like thinking about myself as male during sex,
probably in part because of the way my thinking about male
sexuality is shaped by society.'*

JESS, BISEXUAL, 30

*W*hile society has finally started to accept that sexuality can be fluid, the idea of gender fluidity is still considered taboo. The ideas of 'man' and 'woman' are deeply ingrained into society, to such a degree that trans and intersex people are often massively stigmatised. However, in the privacy of her own mind, a woman can be anything that she wants to be – including a man – and she can have the body of her dreams – including a penis.

Most of the women fantasising about having a penis expressed no desire to be a man – excluding two transmen who filled in surveys (I include them not because they are female fantasies, but because the transmen submitted their surveys for the book and offer an interesting contrast with women's phallic fantasies). Instead, the penis offers them the opportunity to try a different sexual role. Strap-on dildos and vibrators are becoming increasingly popular, and not just in the queer community. More heterosexual couples than ever before are experimenting with strap-on sex, with industry experts reporting that a third of strap-ons sold in the UK go to straight couples. It helps that many online sex shops now feature 'How To' guides to pegging and strap-on sex, and that even the official *Fifty Shades Of Grey* collection includes anal beads and a butt plug.

Some women see having a penis as giving them freedom to be carnal or demanding. Some see it as a way to dominate a partner. And some fantasise about using a penis to have sex that would not be possible with their current body: for example, several lesbians imagined being gay men penetrating a lover anally and feeling the sensation on their shaft.

It is Better to Give Than to Receive?

*W*hether a woman is curious about taking a dominant role, wants to be a man, likes the idea of being the penetrator rather than the penetrated or something else entirely is something that only the woman fantasising can know. But for the first time, a woman can give as good as she takes when it comes to penetration: and if sales of strap-ons to heterosexual couples through Ann Summers, Lovehoney, Sextoys.co.uk and a host of other retailers are anything to go by, many women are strapping on a cock to experience controlling a phallus, using it to pleasure a lover – or simply themselves – as they see fit.

Of course, not all strap-on fantasies involve gender fluidity. Assuming the penis makes the man and the vagina makes the woman is outdated and limiting: there are men in bodies with vaginas and women in bodies with a penis (commonly referred to as transmen and transwomen accordingly). Many women fantasise about using a strap-on without imagining it's a penis, but instead using it as a tool to make their partner writhe beneath them. Others imagine using it for sex acts they couldn't otherwise do, without their self-perceived gender identity changing at all. And some women imagine changing gender without a strap-on in sight. In fantasy, anything is possible after all.

The fluidity and non-binary nature of gender is something that is only just beginning to be explored, but in women's fantasies, more and more are admitting that what they want is a penis.

Maybe women fantasising about having a penis are subconsciously trying to gain all the advantages that come with having one; or perhaps some women are bored of being the sexual recipient and want to be the giver instead. Now, the increasing commercialisation of sex has given more and more women the opportunity to buy their own penis – available in any size and shape that they desire.

What is a Gender-Fluid Fantasy?

*G*ender-fluid fantasies can involve a woman using a strap-on or growing a penis. She may be a version of herself in male form, or a man who is very different from herself. She may imagine assuming multiple gender, age and societal roles or simply imagine being one constant 'man' in her fantasies. A woman may also imagine herself as intersex – with elements of both 'male' and 'female' genitalia; or simply focus on sensation without picturing specific body parts at all, instead taking pleasure from a 'masculine' or 'feminine' energy. After all, as Mia More, Editor of Cliterati, notes, 'Since many fantasies specify details such as location, situation or set-up, it's surprising how often the participants are described as "faceless", or not even physically described at all. This can make the fantasy all the more fluid with regards to gender or sexuality: it's more about the feel and flow of a fantasy rather than the pigeonholing of the people involved.'

Transmen may imagine being their true selves. However, their gender exploration is not a fantasy but a reality, limited by transphobic views about gender. While a cisgender woman may imagine being a man as a way to enjoy a different sexual role, a transman's feelings may be very different, as shown below:

Anon, 32, designer

'As a transgendered man (female to male) I don't know what it's like to have a phallus (yet). I come to the conclusion that everyone has both male and female aspects. My "junk" is currently female, since I haven't had lower surgery yet, although it has altered with the effects of testosterone which has given me loads more sensation and much fuller orgasms. Presently, I feel I currently reside somewhere between male and female. I see sexuality and gender as being a movable spectrum that people traverse throughout life

I identified as genderqueer for a really long time (pre-medically transitioning), and for the sake of simplicity I label myself as a FTM transman. However, I do question the binary and like to play with gender. It's a privilege to pass as male.

I wouldn't say my fantasies have changed since starting to take testosterone. However, I would say I am more visually stimulated now (like most cis men). As a trans-person, pre-lower surgery, I do fantasise about having a penis. However, if I had that apparatus, I wouldn't want that fantasy to go away. So perhaps that's not a fantasy? I would say my sexual fantasies are more like the mapping out of my physical mind-set.

Also, I think it's really important to note that the way I view sex has changed. I remember hearing about how much a sexual appetite you get once you start taking testosterone – and that urge does present itself during a few days in my three month cycle of hormones. However, this urge is dampened by the fact that I don't have the apparatus I feel I should have (a penis).

After chatting with more spiritually minded people, I have started to question the entire sex industry, the highly sexualised western world we live in, and what orgasm actually means. According to some, when people orgasm, the energy (the kundalini) goes straight up through the body and is lost (through the head). This is a powerful energy and can be harvested somehow. I have heard about how it's possible to make love so that every cell in you is affected by an orgasm which can rush through your body and rather than leave through your head, can loop around and head back down through you, and is not lost. The ankh symbol is supposed to represent that. That is how I would like to make love, although

I am currently on a break with my partner, and I have very little sexual appetite.'

Anon, I'm nearly 25 and originally from another EU country, but live in the UK now. I don't have any children. I'm a Ph.D student

'I have a female body, but I'm not a woman. I am very attracted to the idea of male-on-male relationships, and it variably bothers, hurts or affects me that this is not something I will ever be able to have. I would place myself on the spectrum of trans and/or genderqueer and genderfluid. Most of the time, I don't feel like my gender matters to me, but because it is so important in how people relate to each other, I am forced to engage with it. I resent that.

I guess my favourite fantasy could be described as a D/s (domination and submission) gagging/blow job scene, but that doesn't really capture it. It involves two male-bodied male-identified people. In my head, I can be either participant, most often my perspective switches throughout the scene. It involves a ring gag and face-fucking (leading up to anal penetration), the gentleness/roughness can change within the scene or stay the same. The dominant person drags the tip of their cock over the other's face. This is important. It conveys a very difficult emotion that includes ownership, gentleness, a feeling of privilege, love and affection on both persons' parts.

There can be little storylines around this, where it happens or who the people are. But the submission aspect plays a big role, as well as the unquestioned loyalty and respect of the participants for each other. It is always a secure established relationship or one that is heading in that direction.

I haven't had sex with anyone but myself since I was 19 (I am now almost 25). My sexual experience with others is extremely limited and was hindered by very poor communication and lack of knowledge especially about my own wants and needs. In my fantasies, it is always a given that I want (and actively desire) what is happening. In my sexual experience, I got turned off very quickly or only physically turned on and not mentally/emotionally. Sex was mostly very boring.

I would like to put some fantasies into practice, but I assume that is going to be very hard. I think that by now I have identified that in order to be relaxed and trusting enough to enjoy sex with somebody else, I need them to fully acknowledge and see me as a male participant in sex. The rest of the time, it doesn't even matter as much. But being read as a woman in sex is akin to degradation and shame. I don't know why.'

However, a transman's fantasies are very different from a woman imagining that she is male. Most of the women fantasising about having a penis identify happily as women. The gender – or indeed, body – fluidity simply allows them to explore different sexual roles and acts.

Jess, 30, bisexual

'I really like thinking about myself as male during sex, probably in part because of the way my thinking about male sexuality is shaped by society (I imagine "male sexuality" as involving being in control, subverting norms by being receptive, more likely to orgasm). I've told my partner about my fantasies, although largely a general statement of thinking of myself as male. I don't like to share particulars, because I worry he would think I was mentally cheating. He's been pretty great about it! The language he uses during sex has changed a little bit, and instead of just using a strap-on to fuck him, we've also done some stuff where I wear a strap-on during PIV sex. Strap-on sex in general is one of his major fantasies, and it's been fantastic. I really love doing it, for a lot of reasons.'

Why Do People Have Gender-Fluid Fantasies?

Although gender fluidity has not been academically explored as a fantasy theme – outside the realms of some work on transgender experiences – the idea of masculine and feminine being less static than we currently treat them is something that's long been espoused by myriad people. The Intersex Association of America reports that not only are one in one hundred people born with bodies that differ from standard male and female, but one in one thousand are born with XXY chromosomes and and one or two in one thousand people has surgery to 'normalise' genital appearance. Many feminists argue that gender is a construct created by society; and trans activists are finally starting to be being listened to when they say gender is not as simple as being based on the body parts that you have. In Sydney, a person called simply Norrie recently won the legal right to be identified as gender neutral. Norrie's solicitor, Emily Christie said, 'This is the first time that we've had any court of law in Australia saying that sex could potentially mean something other than male or female. We're hoping that this decision will then be taken on in a broader context both for courts of law – and also for government agencies.'

Fantasy researchers have also discovered that, though there are gender differences in fantasy between men and women in some cases, 'There were indications of a convergence of male and female fantasies towards middle-age, which might be interpreted as resulting from a liberation from the effects of testosterone and oestrogen respectively.'[12] This offers more evidence that gender may be more fluid than we think. Once we are 'liberated' from our sex hormones, why should we expect our gender experience to remain the same?

As Dr Susan Block says on counterpoint.org, 'Our society tends to make things black or white, good or bad, male or female, heterosexual or homosexual. But the human sexual imagination is most definitely bisexual, even what you might call omnisexual . . . Men are not from Mars, and women are not from Venus. We're all from the same beautiful, wild, sexual planet Earth, and we're far more alike than we are different.'

While I use the term gender fluidity to cover fantasies that

11 'Gender differences in sexual fantasy: An evolutionary analysis', *Personality and Individual Differences*, Glenn D. Wilson, 1997

involve any kind of change in gender, it technically means someone who experiences a fluctuating idea of gender, sometimes including being agender, like Norrie. However, many people believe their gender to be static but to fall outside the 'gender binary' (the idea that people are either one hundred per cent female or one hundred per cent male rather than having traits along a masculine/feminine scale, both biologically and socially).

Many sex educators are working on defining the new sexual world that reflects the non-binary nature of gender and sexuality. The Genderbread Person (http://itspronouncedmetrosexual.com/2012/01/the-genderbread-person/) demonstrates the fluidity of sex and gender, suggesting that rather than being disparate camps of 'men' and 'women', in reality, our sexuality is a continuum, taking in gender expression, gender presentation, biological sex and who we are attracted to.

Gender in History

Gemma Ahearne says, 'The presumption of a human being male or female is commonplace, and to subvert gender or transcend it is revolutionary.' However, while it may sound radical, again, it has historical precedent. Phillips and Reay say, 'Before the late eighteenth century, a woman was portrayed in medical texts as a man with sex organs inverted: the vagina was an interior penis, the ovaries were testicles. The . . . correlation between male and female as different genitals, was not part of the pre-modern mindset.'

Procreation required both the man and the woman to 'ejaculate' in order to create a baby (this meant female orgasm was considered as important as male orgasm). As such, in some ways, our ancestors had a more mutually beneficial and forward thinking definition of sex than we have.

Similarly, there are many cases of men dressing as women and women dressing as men throughout history, some secretly, some overtly. And people have long had the accoutrements to take this gender experimentation from fantasy into reality. The first documented case of a woman using a strap-on was Bertolina, in 1295, something that was recorded because she was accused of committing sodomy (*Sex Before Sexuality*), so it's safe to say that women's interest in assuming a penetrative role in sex long predates the current surge in sales of strap-ons.

Gender and Maternity

So why is it that we still cling on to the ideas of man and woman so strongly? While some might argue that it is about procreation, now that contraception and IVF allow many women to control their fertility, the idea of woman as baby-carrier and man as sperm provider is outdated. As Daniel Bergner, author of *What Women Want: Adventures in the Science of Human Desire*, told salon.com, 'we've managed to convince ourselves that one gender is all about reproduction and the other is all about sex. That is, women are all about reproduction and men are all about sex. A complete distortion.'

Modern technology means that people of all genders can have children in numerous ways – and some people don't want children at all. One study found that 20 per cent of women in the UK aged 45 didn't have children – and a third of female graduates were child-free. Another found that Germany had the highest proportion of child-free women at 30 per cent – or forty per cent for graduates.

This does not mean that mothers should be negated or marginalised, but to assume that being a woman and being a mother are one and the same is inaccurate – and reinforces the virgin/whore stigma at a fundamental level. By treating motherhood as an essential part of the female condition, we are categorising all women as breeders or breeders-to-be: childless rather than child-free. We are also excluding transwomen from the equation, pretending a group does not exist because it doesn't sit within our comfortable theory. However, maintaining a binary approach makes it easy for us to be marketed to. Do you want to be a real woman? This is what a real woman is. Buy our product and you can be one too. It allows for easy social control because everything fits into place.

Biological sex is socially constructed. The idea may seem alien but it has repeatedly been demonstrated both culturally and historically. And it has chilling consequences. Maria Lugones explores this – and more – eloquently in her paper, 'Heterosexualism and the Modern/Colonial System' (2007). While we may assume that 'man' and 'woman' are disparate categories that have been there throughout history, in reality, gender has long been understood to be more fluid than that by other – arguably more evolved – cultures. She says, 'This understanding of gender views gender as a colonial concept. It views the gender system as composed of a "light" and a "dark" side. The "light" side is constituted by sexual dimorphism (male/female), the gender binary (man/woman), heterosexuality and the patriarchal distribution of power. The "dark side" reduced ... to non-human beasts ... depicted as hermaphroditic monstrosities, non-gendered animals.'

Though this may seem challenging, the idea of gender binary helps reinforce sexism, racism and the status quo in general, damaging all who fall outside its strict rules. If we could lose the gender binary, perhaps the war of the sexes could finally be resolved.

The Power of the Penis

Of course, there is another reading of why women are increasingly fantasising about having a penis. We live in a society that worships the cock and as such, are driven to desire it. 31-year-old lesbian photographer Bex says, 'Quite a common fantasy/comment from lesbians is that they desire to sleep with cisgendered men, not always just for the purpose of penetration of varying kinds, but for the sole act of making a man have an erection. By getting a man hard they take on a position of control and can visually appreciate the undeniable fact that the man is turned on. In comparison, it is difficult to "'see" the wetness which normally determines if a woman is turned on. Therefore, for a cis female who ordinarily has sex with other cis females the possibility of that level of control of a penis can often be perceived as exciting, empowering and adds an extra element of eroticism.'

Interestingly, the stereotype that women want a lover who is hung like a horse was barely represented in female fantasy. Relatively few women submitted fantasies about wanting to be penetrated by a penis of a particularly specified size. By far the most notable fantasy cocks are the ones women are imagining springing from between their own legs. Perhaps this is a replacement for the 'knight in shining armour': rather than being saved by a man, the modern woman can become one. Being in control of a penis is more tempting than being controlled by one.

bell hooks said, 'Many sexist men fear that their bodies lose meaning if we value penises for the sacredness of their being rather than their capacity to perform . . . When women and men can celebrate the beauty and power of the phallus in ways that do not uphold male domination, our erotic lives are enhanced.' And how better to celebrate the penis without upholding male domination than by wearing a cock of one's own?

Common Fantasy Themes

*T*he gender-fluid fantasies submitted to Garden of Desires fitted into two main categories: having a penis and changing roles. For some women, the penis represents nothing more than a physical difference – a chance to experience sex in a different way. For others, it is more tied in to assuming a different sex role: that of the penetrator rather than the penetrated – or simply enjoying the act of pegging.

Having a Penis

Freud speculated that women suffer from penis envy and indeed, could take a generous helping of blame for the amount of attention the penis gets in psychoanalytic theory. However, regardless of the psychoanalytic arguments, it is certainly true to say that some women do fantasise about having a penis: 'I imagine it's more sensitive than a clitoris as it's more accessible on all sides.'

For some women, it's about curiosity or fascination with the penis; for some about a genuine desire to have a penis; and for others, it's a tool to get sex they're unable to ask for without a phallus, whether physically or mentally.

Anon, cis, queer, 25, feminist

'My most recent fantasy is that I am a bear male and my (cis male partner) is my fag. I enjoy spooning my cis male partner whilst I masturbate him, feelings of his penis is my penis etc.'

Anon, straight, switch, college student, cisfemale, though I've been pondering lately if genderqueer or something similar may be a more appropriate label. (The jury's still out on that one)

'I've frequently imagined myself as male. Having a penis was a very regular part of my early fantasies. In addition to having sex with my boyfriend, my main dominant fantasy involves pegging him, mostly going back to that early desire and fantasy of having a penis. I also occasionally fantasise about having my boyfriend wear female clothing or feminine underwear.'

Anon, 48, bi-poly, have three partners (one husband, one girlfriend who lives with us part-time, one boyfriend), self-employed web developer and farmer, 1 adult child, BA degree and other further schooling

'During sex I fantasise that I've got a penis (as I imagine it's more sensitive than a clitoris as it's more accessible on all sides). I enjoy gender-bending stuff in others as well as myself. It helps me orgasm when I have trouble, whether masturbating or having sex. I think my experiences with witnessing how sensitive a man's penis is triggered it. Also, my bi-ness helps me feel fine about imagining having sex with a woman or her doing oral sex on my penis, even though I wouldn't really want a penis at other times.

After I shared this fantasy with my husband, although hetero, he's found that he likes to imagine I have a penis at times when he's sexually excited too, so we sometimes pretend his penis is mine while I jack him off while he's on my chest or I'm sitting on him . . . and that he's having anal sex with me (something he likes to imagine but I do not enjoy actually doing). This is after I've already had an orgasm or more from other activities or when I don't want one at the time. He often does oral sex with me in a way to enhance my imagining that I have a penis too, which is fun. So, although he didn't trigger it, he's engaging in it with me at times and we're both enjoying it.'

Changing Roles

Many women have a curiosity about what it would feel like to have sex as a man, trying on different sexual roles. In addition to enjoying the idea of watching men have sex (see Chapter 3, Exhibitionism and Voyeurism) some women take things further in fantasy, by imagining being a gay man. This was a fantasy shared by women across the sexuality spectrum. And some women fantasised about being a number of different types of people, depending on their mood.

Lea, 31, bi but in a long-term heterosexual relationship, civil servant

'The first fantasy I remember I was recreating the storyline of a soft core porn film I'd seen on TV about a guy who sleeps his way to good grades, then with all sorts of women around a fancy castle. I was a man in that fantasy, and I am in fact a man in my fantasies more often than not (but I identify as female).

I have had two recurring ones recently: one based on a comic book strip I read where as a powerful businessman I get a woman to go down on me in a swanky office in exchange for money; the other is inspired by a scene in True Blood – as a male vampire, I am penetrating a woman from behind as her hands are tied to the ceiling; as I ejaculate I bite down on her neck and suck her blood.'

Anon, 40, lesbian, single, researcher, Ph.D

'Being a man, picking up a woman, and having unprotected sex in a park. Another one about being a woman, picking up a 17-year-old lad and having sex in a car, before getting caught by a policeman and being forced to have sex with him. Another one about having sex with an old man, which disgusts me and turns me on at the same time.'

Anna, 38, marketing director

'I read an erotic story about a woman growing a penis and it got me thinking. The idea had never appealed but when I thought about what it would feel like to have a penis growing out of my body, it made me feel hot. I masturbated imagining what it would be like to grow a cock and fuck my husband with it. I came hard but felt a bit embarrassed at first.

After a couple of weeks of toying with the fantasy without sharing it, imagining masturbating it, peeing through it, feeling it grow and making women suck it, as well as fucking my husband up the arse with it, I told him what I'd been thinking about. He was really good about it and even suggested that we try strap-on sex.

That was a year or so ago. Since then, we've had lots of strap-on sex and he's sucked my strap-on too. I wish I could get one that would let him go down on me and lick my pussy as my cock was in his throat. It's odd – when I'm wearing the strap-on, my whole sexual persona is different and I become much more aggressive, demanding and sexually selfish – even though my partner isn't like that at all.

More recently, the fantasy has been evolving. I noticed that when I use my magic wand vibrator, the vibrations are powerful enough that I can imagine it's actually growing into me – my body fusing with the toy then turning into a massive cock, kind of like something out of David Lynch's *Videodrome*. I imagine it's a huge, heavy, spunk filled cock and I can wank it hard until I explode with loads of come everywhere. I imagine coming over my lover's face and making him deep throat me, imagining the head of the toy is actually the head of my cock. Sometimes I imagine him being helped by other women.

When I'm feeling really close to my partner during sex, I sometimes take this further. I love the idea of growing a cock to penetrate him with, and him growing a pussy so we can fuck and be connected as man and woman all at once, his cock in me as mine is in him. I think it comes from an idea I heard about Plato's 'split aparts' – that couples were originally individuals who were split into two parts by lightening after angering the gods. I don't buy into that kind of romantic 'the one' idea but the idea appeals in fantasy: I am my man and he is me but neither of us is man or woman – we are just one combined fucking animal. Of course, we come together – at which point the world sometimes explodes. I think I mixed an ancient myth I heard about lovers who created the world through sex and will destroy it if they ever have sex again. I get my fantasies from some strange places!'

A penis is no longer something that is the sole domain of the man: women can buy their own, to penetrate with or be penetrated by, and as such, we can explore gender roles more than ever before.

If the idea of gender fluidity is new to grasp, it is just one more step towards a true appreciation of the diversity of sexuality. Others see even this as too limiting.

Anon, female, 3 children, 40, long term cohabiting with male partner, academic, queer sexuality

'My favourite fantasy is being outside, preferably in the woods, where the trees and plants come alive and join in the sex I am having with a human who changes gender during sex. I totally come alive in the outdoors – senses heightened, body alert, sexuality/eroticism is ripe in the wild. I think sexuality is so narrowly defined and we need to open up and think about our sexualities that extend beyond the human.'

Not only does this woman see gender as malleable but also extends her sexuality across nature. While this may seem unusual, many pagan religions incorporate elements of sexuality and nature into their celebrations. Indeed, many fantasies that may seem unusual at first glance have strong roots in history. In the garden of desires, the esoteric blooms offer the rarest insights of all.

Chapter Seven:
Esoteric Fantasies

*'I'm always into fantasies where the sexual appetite is so great
that that one time destroys my life.'*

ANON, STRAIGHTISH 30-ISH FEMALE

It may be tempting to think that women's sexual fantasies fit neatly within the categories that are so often repeated in women's magazines: sex in a new location; sex with a stranger; dressing up; mild bondage; or spanking. However, while these fantasies do certainly reflect those of some women, there are many women whose fantasies fall outside these parameters.

Around a fifth of the fantasies submitted to *Garden of Desires* didn't fit into the major fantasy categories that emerged from the research. Some themes had cropped up in previous studies into sexual fantasy while others were entirely new – at least to me (having read thousands of fantasies submitted to Cliterati and *Scarlet* over the last 14 years, this is a rare occurrence).

This shows just how diverse female sexuality is. While some women's fantasies are inspired by *Sex and the City*, porn films or *Fifty Shades of Grey*, others have a sexual imagination that is far more unique.

Anon, Cisfemale, pansexual, 22, RN, single and not remotely looking, taller, broader-shouldered, and heavier than most women, bi-polar type 2, creative writer, all of which add up to my preferring fantasy and a good sex toy collection to attempting any sort of connection with someone else. It's easier that way

'I remember having a bit of an omorashi/watersports fetish since before I even knew what sexual excitement was. My first overtly sexual fantasy was of a character from one of the books I read when I was that age having sex with a semi-ridiculous self-insert character of mine.

These days, my fantasies don't even have to involve myself, at all. They're largely fictionally oriented, though. I have three. In ascending order of strangeness: Being pleasured by a robot/artificial intelligence much larger than myself, suspended by cables and being pleasured from multiple points. Meeting a female reptilian/humanoid alien (think Madame Vastra from *Doctor Who*) and making love to her. Making love to my (imagined) twin sister. (I don't have a twin in real life, and the business of real-life incest repulses me.)'

What is an Esoteric Fantasy?

*A*n esoteric fantasy can be anything that sits outside the norm – although we're beginning to realise that there is no 'norm' in sexual fantasies. While most fantasies tend to focus on people and relatively common sex acts, some people have a more creative sexual imagination. Some may draw erotic inspiration from items as diverse as balloons, shoes, custard, furry animal costumes or mythical creatures. Some may enjoy imagining animals, plants, aliens or ghosts engaging in sex. And some may imagine acts that other people would not deem sexual, including urination and defecation.

Annabel, the last person on earth you'd expect to enjoy watersports. No, the other kind . . . !

'I'd never understood the whole "watersports" thing 'til I met my boyfriend. Up until that point being peed on or peeing on someone just seemed . . . weird. Not gross, just a bit pointless. But now I've been introduced to it it's all I fantasise about. I love the hot pee on my face, my breasts, and when we play SM games I love being commanded to piss on my boyfriend whilst we're having sex (try it – it's actually quite a challenge!).

However, scat is definitely not our thing. No chance! I understand a lot of people use shit or piss in SM situations (and like I said, we do occasionally), but for us it's the heat of the pee itself and the raw body necessity of having to urinate that's sexy. It's like letting go of all your inhibitions – it's both liberating and relaxing. It's also filthy (happily in the naughtiness sense of the word), and taboo, and that forbidden pleasure is in itself arousing for us.

Although it's not exclusively what we're into (otherwise we're surprisingly quite traditional in bed), after a good few years exploring watersports together it's got to the stage where if I'm in the shower having a good lather, and he's in the mood for some nookie, he'll sneak his cock behind the shower curtain and piss on me because he knows I find it such a turn-on I won't be able to refuse him. Especially when there's no clearing up necessary (nothing sexier than a self-cleaning sex scene – definitely the way to my heart)!'

Why Do People Have Esoteric Fantasies?

*W*hile some may consider these fantasies unusual, it suggests that not everyone is as open to societal representations of 'what is sexy' as we may assume. Some people have an erotic imagination untainted by ideas of what is 'normal' and instead revel in their uniquely tailored desires.

As with all the fantasies, it is important to remember that fantasy and reality are two very different things. Incest, bestiality and torture may all be taboo, but in the imagination, people can indulge their darkest desires without fear of the consequences. Our fantasies allow us to accept ourselves – if we let ourselves indulge without guilt.

In rejecting the norms of sexuality, people with esoteric fantasies are making their own rules, unafraid to accept even their most unique desires and explore their sexuality no matter what form their desires take, refusing to let potential judgement stifle their expression. Some may not even include sex as it is currently defined.

Anon, 27, bisexual polyamorous cis woman, with several invisible illnesses including vulvodyina. Dating, no children, studying for a Ph.D, Quaker and a Pagan

'The fantasy I have most often, which is not always sexual, is about two people who are equals – often men, often characters from a book, film, or TV show comforting or helping each other, often with emotional problems. I am confused by my fantasies. They do not seem to relate to my sexual, physical, desires, but to be about emotional content. Sometimes I use them to excite me during masturbation but not sex. At other times, the same characters and story lines feature in non-sexual fantasies.'

Anon

'Male models. I want to own one.'

Common Fantasy Themes

While all the fantasies in this chapter contain less common desires and acts than those within other chapters, there are still several themes that crop up in multiple fantasies. Paranormal fantasies were popular – hardly surprising given the increasing popularity of paranormal erotica over the last decade. Watersports, incest and bestiality all featured, though less frequently than in fantasies submitted in 1973 for *My Secret Garden*. However, of all the esoteric fantasy themes, by far the most popular was expansion, pregnancy and motherhood.

Growth and Maternity

Given the pressure on women to be maternal – and thin – it is perhaps unsurprising that the theme of growth was relatively common. Women are pressured to desire motherhood from an early age, first through dolls and later through magazines, novels and even media campaigns. However, motherhood is strictly constrained by societal rules. While they vary between cultures, many expect women to have children between certain age brackets. Too young is transgressive – as Gemma Ahearne says, 'The working-class single mother, especially the teenage mother, has long been a body of disgust onto which cultural anxieties about decline and decay are projected. This figure also serves as a warning to all women; that improperly performed femininity deserves punishment.' However, having children 'too old' is also deemed to be inappropriate, with advertising campaigns focussing on the increased risks that older mothers may face.

A recent UK campaign directing women 'not to leave it too late', was funded by a leading pregnancy testing company which does make one wonder about the extent to which the numbers of women deciding against motherhood may be affecting the bottom line for those involved in the business of maternity. Similarly, motherhood has often be used as a tool to drive women 'back into the kitchen' when they've become too outspoken.

There are also acceptable parameters of size: fat is negative aside from pregnancy. Women are encouraged to morph seamlessly between two states: thin sexual woman to assexual pregnant woman and back again.

Some fantasies present the female expansion as desirable in itself and others have more of a sense of peril. Some involve assuming a maternal role and others focus more on pregnancy.

Some women enjoy the idea of fattening a male partner up, assuming a sense of power over their partner while others see their expansion and feeder fantasies as a way of indulging hunger they would never satisfy in real life. As one woman said, 'I am too scared/pressured by society to stay slim [for me] to gain weight even if I wanted to.' In indulging fantasies of growth and expansion, a woman can satisfy her hunger, whether for food, motherhood, freedom or all three.

Anon, straight 30ish female

'My earliest fantasies were inspired by pregnancies, on telly and in magazines. The earliest "erotic" stories I remember reading were those awful ones in trashy magazines. "I skipped the school prom to give birth to my dad's baby alone in my wardrobe" – you know the kind. Then I started buying *Bizarre* magazine with my friends and became interested by an article about vaginal stretching, fisting and DP, which featured heavily in fantasies but only slightly in reality. I'm always into fantasies where the sexual appetite is so great that that one time destroys my life.

The first fantasy I remember was that I was dancing at a ball and was pregnant, someone had put some magic moth balls in my shoes which made me grow fatter and fatter. After that but before I knew the mechanics of sex, fantasies involved rolling around on the floor with boys at school discos. Then a really good one was this house where myself and my two best friends each had a room, and men would queue to be able to come in and see us. A teacher brought her entire class of boys to me so they could learn sex.'

Matilda, 18, straight, 5ft 11, white British, student, in a relationship

'I think my earliest fantasy was the idea of giving birth which sounds so weird to write down but I feel that's what set it off, it seemed to me like it was a pleasurable thing? I still find pregnant women attractive though, even though I'm straight and feel like I'm excited to be pregnant and sexual.'

Ann, 53, bisexual female in a relationship (polyamorous) I currently just have one partner. No children of my own but my partner does have one. Psychotherapist. Post graduate diploma in psychotherapy. MBA. Purple hair!

'Being mummy to a grown up baby and him playing with wooden bricks while I watched television. Putting on a nappy and rubbing cream into his bottom.'

Anon, 25, single white female from New Zealand, no children

'I fantasise about expansion; my breasts enlarging as I am being aroused by a man, becoming too big for the clothes I am wearing and busting out of my top.'

Anon, 26, female (but in my mind I consider myself genderless or at least don't think about my own gender). White Brit, living with long term male partner, mostly straight, have had polyamorous relationships in past

'When playing make believe with toys with my sister, all my toy-characters would be greedy/love food/be fat. My fantasies haven't changed over time. Weight gain is what turns me on most. But they've deepened. I enjoy male/female bodies of all shapes, and have an interest in animalistic/furry sex. I certainly prefer weight gain on males than females; most females I've fancied have been of a similar build to me.

My favourite fantasy is any weight gain on a guy, I like thinking about my partner, but it can be a faceless guy, it's the weight gain that turns me on not the person. I like it if they're slightly embarrassed/inconvenienced by it, but not so much that it really upsets them/impacts their life. I like it if they can't help themselves around food.

Weight gain is a tricky fantasy to put into real life. It is my partner's choice whether he gains weight. I am not really turned on by myself gaining weight, and I am too scared/pressured by society to stay slim to gain weight even if I wanted to. Plus I like exercise and want to remain healthy, so wouldn't want to gain too much anyway.'

Anon, Cis hetero female, white single student

'I've had male weight gain and male pregnancy fetishes since my late childhood/early adolescence. Thinking about it recently I think what I like most about both is the sense of inherent male vulnerability as well as the tenderness it can require from the partner regardless of gender. In every fantasy I have these are the two common elements regardless of fetish content. I need to know that people can care about each other and recognise and respect vulnerability as opposed to taking advantage of those things. Generally I still feel ashamed of what turns me on and I don't like to share it with anyone, though I do masturbate/ become aroused to both with significant frequency.'

Anon, cis student

'My most common fantasies (there are two which I feel are interrelated) are male pregnancy and male weight gain.'

Anon, single white student

'My absolute earliest fantasy revolved around a male entity growing fatter and fatter without limitations. This was largely reinforced by certain tropes in children's media/cartoons. Most recently, I have fantasised about gay male relationships where either weight gain or pregnancy are prominent themes. There is also a heavy emphasis on tenderness, care, and understanding in these scenarios, and the relationship is never purely physical or emotional but a strong mix of both. The fantasy most guaranteed to make me orgasm is of a hetero, cis relationship where extreme weight gain is the erotic focus to the point of the male party's immobility and almost helplessness.'

Anon, cis, married, 2 kids

'Imagining women as feedees, wanting to become fat.'

Paranormal Fantasies

Paranormal fantasies were once deemed to be unusual, if not taboo, but recent years have seen their popularity soar. The underlying metaphors within *Dracula* may give a clue to the eternal popularity of the vampire but over time, more supernatural characters have started to enter women's fantasies.

Paranormal fantasies offer clear evidence of the way in which societal attitudes to sex move on. Popular adult fairytale themed shows and films from *Buffy* to *True Blood* and *Charmed* to

Teenwolf have opened women's eyes to the charms of demons and werewolves, minotaurs and monsters, and it is no longer deemed 'odd' to have a fantasy about a vampire. As Mia More says 'When a hugely successful TV and film franchise such as *Twilight* makes rich celebrities of stars Kristen Stewart and Robert Pattinson – who've been a couple in real life as well as on screen – vampires don't only become acceptable and normalised, they also become aspirational. This is bound to filter down into our deepest desires: vampires such as Dracula may have long been sexually charged, but the latest trends in TV cannot but fail to have an impact on us at home in the bedroom. No doubt the popularity of historically themed fantasy series such as *Spartacus* and *Game Of Thrones* has led to fantasies involving "wenches", men in Greek loincloths, Roman togas or medieval doublets, and maybe even a dragon or two.'

In women's fantasies, there can truly be a fairytale with a happy ending guaranteed – though some of these fantasies contain more than a hint of Grimms' tales.

Karla, 29, hetero, Caucasian, married for two years (together for seven), no children, English teacher, Masters, brunette, medium build

'It has the setting of some movie where there is a girl dancing in a black dress with a giant black ruff. And I have sex with a devil who has a giant cock the size of a school bus. And there are two demons that feed from my breasts as I am being fucked, but not torn apart, just full up with juggling large breasts.'

Anon, opera singer, Masters, hetero (but have dabbled either way), brown hair, passionate for creativity, insatiable in the bedroom

'I've always fantasised of being a vampire's victim! There's something so damn sexy about being bitten on the neck, by a handsome stranger (especially when you're just about to orgasm!) I've thought about this ever since I was a teenager. I think the insatiable passion they have for the taste of blood and sucking the life force out of you, amounts to the insatiable passion I have for multiple of multiple orgasms. This also feels like the life force is being fucked out of me – hehehe! When a guy kisses my neck, I find it very difficult to control my reaction in public. It always sends shivers through my body, and if I could I'd take them into the nearest closet and shag their brains out. It's a good thing most people don't know about this!'

Joan, 46, unemployed college grad, married 23 years, mother of 1, severe arthritis

'I've always had a thing for vampires since seeing the 1979 version of *Dracula*. My fantasy is a man in a cape with hypnotic blue eyes, I am powerless to resist him, he is staring at me, I can't move, he swoops in, wraps me in the cape so I am pressed against his body, his lips travel all over my face with light, feather like kisses, down my neck, one hand holding my head so I don't move, the other busily unfastening my shirt buttons . . . how we're still wrapped in the cape, I don't know but we are . . . my hands now are unfrozen and I begin to undo his shirt buttons, untucking his shirt, running my hands through his chest hair, he's pressed up against me, I can feel how hard he is. He's got my bra off, he's cupping my breast with his one hand, his lips leave my neck to nuzzle my breast, now his hand has unfastened my pants, he's tearing at my underwear, his fingers work their way inside me to find that I am already wet. I have undone his pants in the meantime and have been caressing his erection. He pushes me against a wall, I wrap one leg around him, leaving the other on the ground for balance. As he enters me, he bites down hard on the pulse point of my neck causing me to cry out . . .'

Ruth, bisexual, polyamorous consensual sadomasochist aged in her late fifties

'Quite a few of my fantasies are about characters in books, TV shows and movies, most recently a Harry Potter future, auror school.'

Trace, 29, straight. Mixed race – half Chinese, half European. Single, no children. Artist. Brown hair, hazel eyes, average size

'Sneaking off with a guy that I know or one that I just met. The other fantasy would have the element of the supernatural. I love the idea of a mate, like the vampires and werewolves that have been written about.'

Anon, I'm genderqueer (androgyne), currently struggling to transition. 26, attracted to those who are not my gender (namely, binary gender presentation). More attracted to women; also attracted to men who look like my current partner. I'm a masochistic sub who likes BDSM up to far more extreme fetishes like gore and snuff. I'm a computer programmer. I have PTSD. I'm introverted

'When I first started to think about sex my fantasies were about men; once I admitted to myself that I was attracted to women, they involved women a lot more; when I was single they were relatively tame; and now I have a chance to experiment more in the bedroom, they are becoming more and more intricate, extreme and unusual. My most recent fantasy was being shrunk, becoming just 6 inches or so tall; my partner grabbing my tiny body and crushing me against his penis, holding me and it in one hand and masturbating with me until he comes.

My favourite fantasy is being gored, eaten, and fucked by minotaurs. I keep coming back to this one, lingering on different parts – the bull head snorting hot, wet air on my face, the sensation of horns piercing my skin, being pinned in place by them, or thrown into the air; fantasising about fleeing one minotaur or being attacked by many; them ripping and twisting my limbs from their sockets or taking bites straight from my flesh; being fucked, the feeling of enormous cocks filling me up, breaking me. No real narrative to anything I dream up, just sensations and emotions; fear, adrenaline, pain. Can you tell I'm a masochist?'

Watersports Fantasies

Though the act is still deemed taboo by society, some women are drawn to watersports fantasies – namely, imagining urinating on or in front of someone or watching/being urinated on themselves. Though being urinated on may seem degrading to some women (which can sometimes be the point) to others, it shows acceptance: taking all a partner can offer. Many women use a water faucet to aid masturbation – some watersports fantasies simply get a woman's partner more integrally involved in the process.

Conversely, some women enjoy the idea of urinating on a lover, whether as a form of punishment, expression of sharing or simply physical release; or they like the idea of having their own urination controlled. Mia More notes: 'Full bladders can be used in D/s situations where the submissive might be ordered to repress their need to urinate during sex despite – or because of – potential discomfort and difficulty. Likewise they can be commanded to pee on demand. It's a power challenge where the most base of human needs is controlled, making it an attractive proposition to many.'

Watersports can be a simple physical fantasy – holding onto urine will obviously increase the size of the bladder which can stimulate the G-spot, but can also lead to kidney infections – and the physical sensation of flowing urine over a body appeals to some women. However, it can also signify vulnerability, release or acceptance. In allowing someone access to what is usually a private function, it shows trust and intimacy.

Anon, 23, pan sexual, New Zealander, single, student, blonde

'When in the shower I imagine someone outside the shower door telling me exactly what to wash and for how long then telling me to piss on my hands then masturbate but only being allowed to orgasm when I am told to. At the time I am completely absorbed in my fantasy but afterwards I often get worried that there is something wrong with me.'

Jaq, 24, single, partway though a Ph.D, straight, but had two passionate crushes on other women as a teenager but never said a word, and one fling with an undergraduate a year older than me

'I fantasise about weeing – there, that's an odd one! – not about "watersports" and being pissed on and humiliated, just . . .

Weeing. I wet myself as a kid, but only ever do that deliberately as an adult. I like peeing hard, and like the thought of other people – men and women – doing it. I like doing it on the ground, I like just letting it trickle down my legs, I do it in my swimsuit all the time, I pee in my shorts for the heat of it if I can find a place in private to do it.

The biggest fantasy that I've acted out is wearing shiny latex leggings out to a club and weeing myself in full sight, and nobody knowing: that got me a bit hot (read: a lot! As in flushed, short of breath, dilated pupils) and my friends tried to set me up with the bloke they thought had turned me on! I have no idea where it came from – and I keep it quiet, I'd have no friends and the men who are into this are not at all nice.'

Anon, 33, wife with two children

'I really like to fantasise about the exchange of bodily fluids during sex. Everything excepting blood and feces. I imagine urinating in my husbands mouth and having him drink it, then watching and feeling him, by choice or force, perform oral sex on me. Finally he ejaculates as deep as possible inside me then cleans it all out with his long tongue and rubbery lips whilst I release my erupting ejaculation into him through his mouth. He cleans his sperm and my orgasm completely out of me, leaving me clean just before I fall asleep.'

The Taboo

Though 'extreme' fantasies are relatively rare, there is no doubt that women's fantasies can be just as subversive as men's. That transgression does not always involve violence: however, it does shine a spotlight on the way in which society deems certain kinds of sex to be acceptable and others taboo. Several women commented that our current definition of sex is too limiting: and indeed, one woman suggested that we have 'too humanocentric' an approach to sex. The darkest sexual taboos can often shine the most light on society.

Anon, 40, two children, married 18 years

'My husband had a sexual fling with a woman a couple of years ago. I have a lot of mixed emotions about her. Supposedly she was molested by her father when she was a child, yet at age forty she still lives in a house with her parents, which made me wonder. So I have a couple of different fantasies of her fucking her dad. Her mom goes to the grocery store and her dad calls her to the room and demands sex. She refuses and he tells her, "Fine," he will put her belongings on the street. He's an old fat guy sitting in a recliner and he makes her give him head to get him hard and then climb on top of him and fuck him in the living room. The whole time he's telling her there's no pussy in the world as good as your own daughter's pussy and he tells her he'll stick his finger up her ass to get her off. She tells him he's a sick bastard to make her come on her own father's dick but it feels so fucking good she can't help it.

I have another fantasy about her where she is getting ready to go out for a night in a hotel with my husband. She was known to never wear panties so I fantasise of her dad (he's not fat in this one but has grey hair) coming into her bedroom where she's packing and tells her he doesn't see why her married boyfriend should be the only one who gets to fuck her, and he knows it's no accident she goes around the house in no underwear all the time. She has on a short denim skirt and he fucks her doggy-style on her bed, again telling her how the best pussy in the world is your own daughter's, and how he's so glad she's at no risk of getting pregnant anymore so he can shoot his come all up inside her.

At times I also have him invite a very undesirable, ignorant-seeming uncle or friend to watch him fuck her. She has no choice but to let him, but the really humiliating part is how she always winds up having an orgasm in spite of herself.'

Anon, 55, born female, still female, straight, mum of one, living with my male sadist lover

'When I was 15 or 16 there was a movie where a man was being bull whipped. The sound both terrified me and aroused me. I imagined being in an audience and watching men and women flogged, whipped. I'm not one to think about sexual penetration, I like bloodied welts. If I fantasise when I masturbate, I'll find a torture video and fast forward through the annoying sex parts and get to the real money shots: blood dripping or raised welts.'

Anon, female, Caucasian, student, blonde, 6 foot tall, athlete

Having sex with attractive twins (boy and girl) separately. Both in love with me rather than casual hook ups, but I can't choose between them.

Anon, 36, straight, white writer born in South Africa

'At the moment I'm suffering very, very badly from stress so my fantasies are at their mildest and least threatening. (At the moment, any loud noise, demand, or overstimulation counts as "threatening".) So my most recent fantasy, last night, was an extremely mild one of a particular friend (we both fancy each other and are both in relationships) going down on me. The story-fantasy preceding this was a bit naughtier. It featured the same chap. We have a strong family resemblance, though no family connection, and have joked that we might be related. Being a story fantasy, it had to whisk through the usual essential set-up to get us into a position with sufficient privacy, opportunity, etc (I won't go into detail there because that will give away identity).

In this fantasy, he already knew that his "father" wasn't his biological father (I didn't want the fantasy to be dealing with emotional fall-out so he had to know that already) and on meeting me, his mother, on her way out, warned him that my father was his father. This made us half-siblings. He came back and told me this – so there was significant shock in that way BUT nothing too severe.

Slightly overwhelmed to discover that our massive attraction *was* a factor of being related after all, I hugged him and the proximity led to kissing and to very intense sex. The question of incest intrigues and bothers me. I've always found it titillating (Virginia Andrews has much to answer for!), but if I put it in the context of my own family members, disgusting and unattractive. I've heard research about the incest taboo being a function of being brought up together which overrides an otherwise intense attraction, and use this explanation to justify an attraction which I find otherwise appalling. I think this particular story is a phase!'

Anon, poly, two grown kids, two still at home

'Being lovingly "prepared" as a participant in "corn god" ritual.'

Anon, married, 3 kids, cis, self-employed and account manager for software company.

'Bjork referenced *The Story of the Eye* in a magazine article when I was 13 or 14. I ended up finding the book somewhere and it turned me on instantly. I knew I didn't want romantic vanilla sex even before that, though.'

Anon, largely cisgendered 20 year old homosexual, studying in London. White, unemployed and no children. I have brown hair if that helps!

'Orchard-related crazy stuff.'

Anon, straight 30ish female

'My husband is the ruler of the land. He's angry with me for not having given him a child, and knows that the only way to get me to conceive is through the ancient ritual, which involves washing the womb with the fresh come from a white bull. (It's probably he who's infertile anyway and he's just a bit sadistic.) I'm terrified for obvious reasons, so decide to begin training – with the help of my maid servants.

We source a variety of objects of increasing length and girth until gradually I can take and enjoy a fisting from the one with the most delicate and slender arms. The day of the ritual of the White Bull arrives. I am prepared by my girls in ceremonial dress, and smeared with cow pheremones. I lie face down over an altar specially constructed for the purpose.

All the court is gathered as witness. One maid removes the dildo I have inserted for stretching purposes, and the bull is led toward the altar. Servants help him to get his front legs up on the altar and the maids masturbate him and guide his cock toward its destination between my legs. It's quite a slow progress, so that I can feel it keenly, and I come a couple of times. (The maids are soothing me, mopping my brow and caressing me. My husband is enjoying the fact that I'm ashamed from taking pleasure in the act.) Then obviously the bull fucks me to injury, his never-ending come splashing down over my clit and onto the stone floor like a waterfall. The stench of it is great.

Once he's done, he is led away to a grand bed but I can't move from exhaustion. My husband fucks me but I can feel very little now. So he puts his cock, slimy with his and the bull's come, in my arse and fucks. That's about it really.'

The women who were brave enough to share their more esoteric fantasies are particularly important in helping build sexual acceptance. In sharing their desires, they show that female sexuality does not fit between clearly defined, societally acceptable parameters. They show women's violent, base, crass, crude, messy, dirty or simply creative drives. And until we accept that women have just as many animal desires as men, how can both genders truly be considered equal?

Conclusion:
What Do Women Want?

Women's fantasies show how much more diverse their needs and desires are than the 'normal' version of sex that's presented by the media, suggesting – thankfully – that we may be less affected by media representations of sex than some people claim. Some women are asexual and others sexually voracious. Some enjoy sharing their sexual fantasies or experiences and others see it as something to keep private. Some want slow and sensual touch and others want a harsh beating. Some want all of the above at different times depending on their mood.

There is no such thing as 'normal' (and all of these points can equally apply to men). Presenting a singular ideal of 'what women want' helps no one other than the advertising industry. To group all women together regardless of their experiences, opportunities and environment is to deny the diversity of existence. However, there are certain themes that emerge from women's fantasies that may give a clue in answering Freud's eternal question, what do women want?

Power

Submissive and dominant fantasies combined form at least a third of female fantasies in almost every sexual fantasy survey, including this one. Many women with submissive fantasies also have dominant ones and vice versa. This suggests that, if such fantasies do relate to a woman's real life status, that's something that fluctuates over time for the switch woman. However, sub/dom fantasies also – obviously – give women the opportunity to explore themes of power.

In real life women are discouraged from engaging with their sexual power. Society serves to limit women's sexual power by deeming female displays of sexuality as 'degrading', 'unladylike' or 'slutty'. While men are pressured to be well hung, virile and hard of erection in order to show his sexual power, with terms such as 'big swinging dick' used to describe a high status man, women are pressured to be passive and receptive, with obvious sexual behaviour being frowned on and terms including pussy and cunt being far from complimentary. The pill gave women the power to say yes to sex without fear of pregnancy. However, we are still learning and negotiating how best to say no.

Real sexual confidence is as much about saying no as saying yes: who's more confident – the woman who grudgingly acquiesces to anal sex or the one who says, "I don't fancy that. How about we try something else instead?" It is only when women feel as comfortable saying no – and indeed, feel confident enough to articulate and share their own desires with a lover – that we will really have the power that we crave: the power to get the sex that we really want.

Desire

Unsurprisingly, desire was a central factor in many women's fantasies. Recent research, from academics includings Marta Meana, suggests that desire is central to female arousal and this is certainly reflected in women's fantasies. Submissive, exhibitionist and romantic fantasies all show the power that being desired has to arouse a woman.

While some people paint the growing pole dancing, burlesque and alternative pornography scene as objectifying women and perpetuating patriarchal agendas, there is another reading. Many women who display their bodies publicly do so because they want to. They enjoy being looked at and appreciated – and not necessarily in a sexual way.

Pole dancer Louisa Allen says, 'I would think it inevitable that some do have exhibitionist fantasies – though most who I've spoken to fantasise about being able to manage a complex move more than arousing people.'

Perhaps the rise of pole dancing – and other ways for women to display themselves – explains the comparatively low number of exhibitionist fantasies compared to both previous studies and other fantasy categories. Now, women with a desire to be watched have any number of ways to do so that are approved of – or at least accepted by – society. Pole fitness (as opposed to pole dancing in a club), 'boudoir' photoshoots, burlesque and cybersex are just a few ways that women can put themselves in a position of being desired.

In seeing a woman engaged in some form of sexual display as nothing more than an objectified image, it is denying her agency. While some women may wish to keep their sexual side hidden, others genuinely enjoy being desired. Limiting women's opportunity to explore this aspect of their sexuality, under the guise of slut-shaming or censorship, infantilises women. In objecting to women choosing to display their bodies for public approval, it sends the message that women cannot be trusted to make choices about what to do with their own bodies, demeaning them and, ironically, reducing them to nothing more than their body.

Women are encouraged to control desire throughout their lives: being desired 'too much' has dangerous consequences, or so say the slut-shaming hordes. In a woman's fantasies, she can be desired without any form of moral or physical price to pay.

Pleasure

Orgasm is by far the main reason that women fantasise, and pleasure is central to all fantasies – even if delivered through exploration of pain. Research has found women tend to focus on their own orgasm during fantasy whereas men are more likely to picture their partner's pleasure to spur their climax. In fantasy, women can be sexually selfish, with no regard for anyone's pleasure but their own. Group sex fantasies, in particular, show women's thirst for pleasure: she is pleasured in multiple ways by many people because one person is not enough.

While popular evolutionary theories suggest that women are less promiscuous than men because men need to spread their seed and women need to nurture their eggs, modern analysis is discovering a different side to animal sexuality. In 'What Do Women Want? Adventures in the Science of Female Desire', Daniel Bergner explains that experiments on female rats and monkeys have demonstrated that they enjoy sex for pleasure, even when procreation is not an option. He also says research on monkeys suggests that, rather than being a sign of female lack of pleasure, the real reason it takes females longer to climax is so that they can enjoy sex with multiple partners. Female monkeys have been observed having sex with multiple partners rapidly after mating. This is thought to help ensure that their progeny is a product of the strongest sperm and elicit plenty of potential fathers to protect and provide for the infant upon its birth. As such, from an evolutionary perspective, being a 'slut' is a sound life choice if you're a monkey.

Assuming women want any less pleasure than men is foolish. Women's fantasies show that they want more extended pleasure without guilt; they want orgasms; and they want a lot more than simply penis-in-vagina sex. Fantasy offers a route to sexual pleasure.

Diversity

If I was to list every sex act included in the women's fantasies in this book, it would fill pages, as even a brief glance at the glossary shows. While media representations of sex tend to focus on penis-in-vagina activity, perhaps with a little oral thrown in, the erotic worlds within women's imaginations are much more diverse. Spanking, massage, being splashed with water, being observed, being bound, being desired, using toys on a partner, and being held are just a few of the fantasies women had that did not involve the penis at all.

In 1976, Shere Hite suggested that women would benefit from a wider definition of sex that included increased sensuality and touch; less emphasis on penis-in-vagina activity; a repositioning of foreplay to a more central role; grinding more than thrusting; and a move towards more androgynous play. She established the importance of the clitoris for most women forty years ago: and though we may have more of an idea how to find it nowadays, many people still aren't entirely sure what to do with it (or even what it really looks like.)[13]

Many of the fantasies submitted to *Garden of Desires* reflect the desires that Hite identified in her research. Sensual touch is a common desire, foreplay often takes a central role, penetration is far from ubiquitous in female fantasies, and the suggested move towards androgynous play is reflected in the way in which women's fantasies are evolving: now, many of them are the giver as well as the receiver.

While many women did fantasise about oral, anal and vaginal intercourse, penis size was relatively absent in women's fantasies. While the media may perpetuate the myth that a man is his manhood, few women fantasise about a phallus of unusual size – and if they do, they are as likely to imagine it hanging between their own legs as their lover's.

The heteronormative assumption that 'sex' solely entails putting a penis into a vagina is outdated. In fantasy – and indeed, reality – many women are exploring entirely new definitions of sex. The rise in gender fluid fantasies shows that women are increasingly becoming the penetrator rather than the penetrated. As discussion about gender non binary increases, and the concept becomes more accepted, perhaps more women will want to experience a different kind of sex. Others may be entirely happy with their current definitions. Either option is acceptable: it's up to every woman to decide for herself. If the fantasies in *Garden of Desires* show anything, it is that women are diverse and the fruit of their imagination comes in many flavours.

13 blog.museumofsex.com/the-internal-clitoris

Acceptance

Several women surveyed mentioned that Nancy Friday had helped them to accept their sexuality; to learn and grow. They wanted to be part of the next wave of acceptance, sharing their fantasies to help other women feel normal.

Many of the fantasy themes also have acceptance at their core. With submissive fantasy, a woman can accept her sexual side because she has 'no other choice'; in dominant fantasies, a woman may feel accepted because she is being worshipped by an adoring slave. Group fantasies show acceptance of a sexual woman, as do exhibitionist ones.

But even if a woman feels happy to accept and share her fantasies, it doesn't mean she is without guilt. A thirty-year-old librarian said, 'My fantasies elicit pleasure, desire, hope that I will find a lover that is good or experienced in what I desire and need or want – and sometimes shame, particularly if my fantasy involves actual masturbation and I feel I've spent too long in this activity.' There is still stigma attached to female self-pleasure, at least for some. Many women who submitted fantasies asked, 'Am I a weirdo?', or otherwise showed that they felt guilty about their fantasy and hoped to be accepted rather than rejected in sharing it.

Some women said that they keep their fantasies private to avoid rejection from a partner. While certain normalised desires are accepted – and more so in the light of *Fifty Shades* – more taboo fantasies such as bestiality, scat or even BDSM may feel too extreme for a woman to comfortably share. Only in fantasy can she truly accept and explore her desires.

Embracing (A) Sexual Acceptance

O ur fantasies reflect who we are, offering a highly individualised way to enhance our own pleasure. In accepting our own fantasies we accept ourselves; and in accepting other women's fantasies, we support them in their individuality. If, instead, we label women whose fantasies (and realities) are different from our own as 'sluts', or 'whores', we serve to keep women 'in their rightful place' – and in doing so, assert control in a far from feminist way.

Mia More says, 'The Eroticon 2013 conference was so memorable because every woman there wrote about sex and/or sexual fantasy, and yet none of us judged or were judged in turn for it. In fact, the atmosphere was inclusive and nurturing: we were clearly all sexual beings – even those of us who chose not to indulge in sexual practises in our private lives – and the acceptance was infectious.'

This does not mean that sexual freedom requires everyone to shout about their sexuality. Different women have different levels of freedom and some may have good reason to hide their sexuality and keep their desires to themselves. While previous sexual revolutions have focussed on freedom to be sexual, this needs to go hand in hand with the freedom to not be sexual. Around 0.4 per cent of people are asexual, and many more have 'low' libidos (though even that label assumes judgement, given that the nature of sexual surveys means those who are sexually active may be more inclined to participate, making data about frequency of sex unrepresentative).

If we are to have a true sexual revolution, all women's voices need to be recognised: including those who do not have fantasies alongside those who do. Women are not a uniform group. For every woman who feels oppressed by her lack of orgasms, there is another who may feel oppressed by the pressure to present a sexual image that she does not feel comfortable with. For every woman who deems another woman's religion oppressive, there is a woman who sees those oppressions as protections. One woman may feel violated by the existence of pornography, another may get an exhibitionist thrill – or money to pay a mortgage – through starring in an adult film. One woman may have the best sex of her life making her fantasies come true. Another may find the experience deeply traumatic and be unable to enjoy the fantasy again. Only the woman fantasising (or not) has the right to judge whether her desires are healthy or unhealthy. How can you qualify 'normal' without knowing all the situations and experiences that have formed a fantasy – unless you're simply willing to accept the definitions of 'normal' that are spoon-fed by society?

Control comes in many forms and often, opposing views are two sides of the same coin. The woman who wants to keep her private life private should not be considered frigid or repressed; and the woman who wants to talk openly about her desires should not be deemed a 'slut'. Both need to be considered equally for a true sexual revolution to occur: without the option to reject sex without being judged for it, we will never truly accept sex either.

But the first and most important step towards sexual acceptance is accepting ourselves.

Anon, 26, Swedish, white, straight, bilingual. My fantasy has turned into a series of short stories called the Amond Chronicles at etherbooks.com

'I have a fantasy where I am in a city where sex is as natural as having a cup of coffee in the afternoon. Instead of going out for a cigarette every once in a while, the people have sex with each other. It's free, it's happy, it's safe. Entirely lust-driven.'

Part Three

Epilogue: From Fantasy to a New Reality?

Times have changed significantly since Nancy Friday first introduced the idea that women had sexual fantasies, in 1973. Back then, the idea that women not only enjoyed sex but also had their own private erotic imagination was shocking. Before Friday, only a handful of women had written openly sexual material.

Kathleen Winsor slipped sexual intrigue between the pages of *Forever Amber* in 1944, and it was banned in fourteen states for pornography, despite being a relatively tame historical novel about a young woman's social mobility through Charles II's court.

Anne Desclos (better known as Pauline Reage) wrote *The Story of O* in 1954, in response to a lover saying that women couldn't write erotica. Her graphic story of sexual submission and masochism also subsequently faced obscenity charges, but these were thrown out in 1959. However, such was the stigma attached to being a female erotic writer that Desclos didn't admit to writing it until 1994.

Edith Wharton's *Gordon*, containing themes similar to those of *Fifty Shades*, was banned for indecency in 1966.

Jacqueline Susann's *Valley of the Dolls,* also released in 1966, attracted outrage with its tales of sex, drugs and debauchery in the entertainment industry – but was one of the few female-penned sexual books to avoid being banned and has sold over 30 million copies worldwide to date.

However, all these books were fiction. Nancy Friday was the first woman to expose the reality of female sexuality; to show that women had a private sexual imagination; and to popularise the idea that women could like sex too – and not just for procreation.

When her critically acclaimed erotica anthology, *Little Birds*, was published in 1979, Anais Nin said, 'These are my adventures into the world of prostitution. To bring them into the light was at first difficult. The sexual lie is usually enveloped in many layers, for all of us – poets, writers, artists. It is a veiled woman, half dreamed.' By writing *My Secret Garden*, Nancy Friday helped remove that veil – and in doing so, helped many women feel normal for the first time.

Fact vs Fiction

*B*y sharing women's secret sexual thoughts as fact, rather than masking them behind the guise of fiction, Friday helped move the sexual revolution on in a radical way. While fictional sexual accounts could be deemed the work of aberrant women with excessive and wanton appetites, Friday showed that 'normal' women could have graphic sexual imaginations – and in doing so, gave thousands of women the confidence to admit that they had sexual needs of their own.

Since 1973, an entire industry has sprung up around erotic inspiration and stimulation for women, giving a whole new meaning to 'If you build it they will come'. Women now have access to countless erotic books, sex manuals, films, toys, clubs, websites and beyond. E. L. James's sales showed that millions of women enjoy reading sexual material. However, the research for *Garden of Desires* shows that we still have a long way to go before women will truly be sexually free.

Both factual and fictional sex writing have helped drive female liberation. From Alice Walker's *The Color Purple*, which raised awareness of racism, sexism and the effect of gender expectations, to the more recent *Fifty Shades* effect, driving acceptance of BDSM practices, when women talk about sex and write about sex they take ownership of sex. As Nancy Friday said, 'in sharing their sexual stories, women give permission to other women to be open about their own desires.'

These stories also help shed a light on women's sexual reality. Women today are fantasising about power, desire, arousal and acceptance (of diversity). In reality, these are things that many people lack, at least in part, in their real lives. It may seem like we are more sexually liberated than we were forty years ago, but in fact, many women are still only able to be truly honest about what they want in their imagination, outside the constraints of society and the insidious pressure to be 'normal'.

Fantasy vs Reality

Women may now largely feel free to fantasise without guilt but in truth, sexuality – particularly female sexuality – is far from free. Society, government and 'big pharma' have all tried to ensure the garden of desires stays under control by deeming certain desires to be 'normal' or 'abnormal', 'healthy' or 'unhealthy'. Media rarely reflects real sexuality. Instead, it endeavours to define and control it, pushing us to spend to be sexy rather than accept ourselves as we are and acknowledge our true desires. Advertiser-funded sex surveys, inaccurate and misleading sexual definitions, moral panics, medicalisation of sexuality and rhetoric without evidence all stifle the garden of desires, creating a false Eden – a fool's paradise.

While open discussion about sex may have helped free and empower some women to be sexual, it has also been used to manipulate and constrain people within specific boxes, using the tyranny of 'normal' to ensure everyone fits into societally approved roles. Though LGBTQ acceptance has grown over the past four decades, one of the easiest ways for any queer movement to gain acceptance is still through fitting in with heteronormative models: better the 'happily married lesbian' than the 'out proud dyke' – and heaven forbid anyone who is trans but can't 'pass' as their real gender, or who decides to opt out of gender altogether. Though trying to fit in can be a way to avoid, or at least minimise, stigma and violence, in bowing to the pressure to be normal, we collude with the myth that heteronormativity is the ideal rather than accepting that people are different and everyone has a place in society.

It is not always easy to see the pressures we are under – control works most effectively when you don't even realise you're being controlled – but every time we feel bad for looking 'unattractive', feel 'dirty' for having a non-normative desire or even simply fake orgasm, we are buying into the idea that we are wrong if we are not 'normal' – often without questioning who it is that defines normal anyway. As Meg Barker says in *Rewriting the Rules*, 'It is useful for us to identify the rules we are living by, to gently challenge them and open up our options. But the choices about which rules to question and which to reject, are up to you.'

Every choice we make is influenced by the information we are privy to and the experiences we have had. However, these choices can be manipulated and limited through the perpetuation of myths. Moral panics can often be far more dramatically compelling than the truth, but by critically examining evidence rather than blithely believing what we are told, we can start to separate out fact from fiction and take back control of our sexuality for ourselves.

Sexual Politics

*W*hen I started writing this book, I did not intend it to be political. I had wanted to write an homage to Nancy Friday since I did my dissertation on female sexual fantasy in 1994. I thought it would start with a simple history of female sexual fantasy, from Nancy Friday to *Sex and the City* and E. L. James, with a scattering of sexual pioneers mentioned along the way. I thought the bulk of the book would be women's fantasies, with a few words from me in between referencing the research that has been done into the various different fantasy themes. But with every fantasy that came in, I realised that fantasy was far more political than I realised. Women's surveys showed the beliefs they felt stifled by, the realities they felt they had to hide, the encounters which had shaped them sexually and the labels by which they defined themselves.

White middle-class feminists in particular are often guilty of ignoring all but their own voice. While I in no way want to represent 'women', or claim to show anyone's perspective but my own, neither did I want to collude in the erasure of women of colour, transwomen, disabled women, sex workers or any other marginalised group from sexual study. As a result, in addition to considering this when data gathering (see appendix), I also set out to research the histories of all these groups. What I found shocked me. Firstly, the dearth of information showed me just how effectively many women had been rendered invisible. Secondly, I realised how insidious the virgin/whore myth is – and how much it is used to control every woman, particularly those who do not fit into accepted categories of 'woman' (Sojourner Truth's poignant question, 'Ain't I a woman?' is sadly as true today as it has ever been for many women). I also saw how many echoes there are between women's struggles globally, historically and intersectionally. Certain themes kept cropping up again and again. Certain myths kept surfacing which have been used to control women – and female sexuality. As I realised how insidious these myths were, I became angry at the way in which our sexuality has been taken away from us all.

I started taking note of the sexual myths that were particularly insidious and it is these myths that feature below. They all help control our sexuality, whether they have been passed down through the generations or introduced through modern commercial messages. But in rejecting these myths we can take back control over our sexuality for ourselves.

Myth #1: Women Don't Like Sex

The Fantasy: Women are the gatekeepers of sex. Their role is to decline men whose sexual cravings far exceed their own, until such point at which they have secured a romantic commitment. Women have always been more prudish than men – it's only natural.

The Reality: It is commonly accepted that it is the man's role to pursue sex and the woman's role to decline it – until date three at the very least. The idea that a woman might want sex for her own pleasure, rather than using it as bait for a romantic partner is anathema to many (sex between women is, of course, brushed under the carpet in mainstream media as it doesn't fit the convenient heteronormative theory).

However, the idea that men are more sexual than women is a societal belief rather than fact – something that becomes clearer when you study how this perception has changed over time. *Aristotle's Masterpiece* (1684) stated that women 'Have greater pleasure and receive more content than a man . . . whereby she is more recreated and delighted in the Veneral act.' This was based on the belief that both men and women ejaculated in order to procreate – the woman internally, the man externally. (Modern science has found that climax increases a woman's chances of getting pregnant so this is more forward-thinking than it may seem.) And this is far from the only historical text to suggest women are just as sexual as men – if not more so.

Jenny M Bivona says, 'Western culture's treatment of female sexuality, beginning with the story of Adam and Eve, is a history of suppression, incomprehension, suspicion, and denial. This history includes the male fear of women's insatiable sexual appetite, the myth of vagina dentata, the presumed linkage between female witchcraft and wanton union with the Devil, and the Victorian counterassumption that women are asexual beings (Allgeier & Allgeier, 2000; Baumeister & Twenge, 2002).'[14]

Stick a pin in a timeline and women will be presented as either sexual and dangerous or sexless and virtuous. Both of these are equally untrue – and equally damaging.

The Risk: In painting men as sexual and women as sexless, female sexual pleasure is negated and sexual women are placed outside the norm. Slut-shaming is used to justify sexual women's rape, because 'nice girls' wouldn't wear short skirts, flirt or want casual sex. If a woman does, she is considered to be 'up for anything'.

14 Women's Erotic Rape Fantasies, 2008

However, the inverse of this myth is just as harmful: painting women as sexually voracious and men as powerless to their desires has also been used to justify women's rape. Garthine Walker argued that historically, representations of women as libidinous made it hard for women to demonstrate or describe rape. 'There was no popular language of sexual non-consent upon which women could draw.' And these beliefs can still be seen reflected in the way that women of colour, working-class women and trans-women in particular have been hypersexualised, often as a way to justify their sexual exploitation and abuse.

Both positions validate the virgin/whore myth. Both positions help society have an excuse for rape. And in both positions, that excuse is 'women'.

The Solution: We need to put the virgin/whore myth to bed once and for all and admit that female sexuality is just as diverse as men's. In reality, some women are asexual, some are hyper-sexual and some fall in between these two points. The same is true of everyone. Defining someone's sexuality based on their gender (or any other singular trait) rather than assuming everyone is different and taking people on an individual basis places expecta-tions and limitations on our sexuality – and opens the door for judgement, stigma and worse.

Mistress Absolute says, 'I think what makes it so hard to gauge when trying to understand female fantasy is that historically men have been surrounded by permission to have fantasy and in some cases live that fantasy out, whereas women have been given restrictions by society that are aimed at suppressing not only the acting out of any fantasy but aims to nip the very thought of fantasy in the bud. Thankfully this is changing. The internet has helped people share their fantasies. By reading these fantasies from a safe place where anonymity is usually unchallenged, it provides the reader with permission to indulge in their own imagi-nation or find like minds.'

However, with censorship measures becoming ever more strict, there is every risk that sexuality will be suppressed once more. As such, we need to internalise the message that sexuality is individ-ual, not gender based, that women cannot simply be divided into 'virgin' or 'whore', and that there is nothing wrong with being a sexual woman. As 37-year-old Frances says, 'I agree with my husband that I think about sex as much if not more than him sometimes. I also really enjoy watching porn (with or without him) and will also download material for us to watch together. I find it really interesting that there are still questions/opinions that women aren't as sexual as men. It makes me feel that I'm not normal. But then I say, "Stuff it, it makes me feel good so it must be right and I'm not hurting anyone."'

Myth #2: Women Don't Masturbate

The Fantasy: All men masturbate but few women do. Those who do are highly sexual/sluts.

The Reality: Having run sex magazines and websites for women for well over a decade, and seen the letters and erotic stories women have submitted, I find it risible that some people still believe women don't masturbate – particularly when you also consider sales of erotic books and toys to women.

However, male masturbation and female masturbation are still viewed very differently. It is assumed that all men masturbate – to the extent that 'wanker' is barely an offensive term to many people – but a woman talking openly about masturbation is still deemed as sexually wild; as can be seen by the fuss made when any female celebrity mentions using a sex toy.

In reality, while 80 per cent men and 60 per cent of women admit to masturbation, this increases to 95/87 per cent for graduates. As such, education equals masturbation – and women's historic lack of access to education could well explain their different sexual habits (assuming the difference in numbers isn't simply a reflection of women feeling less able to admit to masturbation for fear of being deemed a slut).

The Risk: This myth feeds into the idea that men are more sexual than women. A woman who admits freely to masturbation is thus hypersexualised, with all the inherent risks that that brings. Yet again, lies about female sexuality put women at risk of being judged, slut-shamed or worse. Yet again, the virgin/whore myth raises its ugly head.

The Solution: If you are female and you masturbate, be unashamed about it. That doesn't mean putting your hands down your pants when you're in public (unless that's your thing – and you don't put anyone else in a situation that makes them feel uncomfortable). However, there is no need to feel ashamed about self-pleasure. Masturbation not only helps people relax and get to know their bodies; studies have found that women who masturbate regularly are more likely to get regular smear tests, have more orgasms with a partner and be more sexually confident (though again, correlation does not equal causation). Masturbating in front of a partner can help them learn about the way in which you like to be touched – and often be sexually arousing for your partner too. That's not to say that masturbation is compulsory: if it's not your thing, don't do it – but don't do it because it's your choice, rather than because you believe that women don't masturbate. To be blunt, *that* idea is a load of wank.

Myth #3: Women Have Fewer Sexual Partners Than Men

*T*he Fantasy: Men need to spread their seed and women need to keep one partner close. As a result, men have many more sexual partners than women.

The Reality: Men and women both lie about the number of sexual partners they have had – sometimes even to themselves. In a study into gender differences in number of sexual partners, Brown and Sinclair found that men and women have similar numbers but men tend to over-report and women under-report, generally by judging what counts as sex by different criteria.[15] Men are more likely to include partners with whom they have had

15 Estimating number of lifetime sexual partners: Men and women do it differently, 1999

any sexual contact at all; women are more likely to count only those partners with whom they have had penis-in-vagina sex.

This is hardly surprising. No matter how liberated a society we may pretend to live in, a woman is still considered a 'slut' or a 'whore' if she has 'too many' sexual partners. However, a woman will also be deemed frigid or prudish if she has not had 'enough' experience. And as ever, it is the media that decides exactly where those levels are, fuelling the myth and continuing the stigma.

The Risk: In judging people – of either gender – on the number of sexual partners that they have, it perpetuates the idea that women are virgins or whores (and indeed, that men are studs or losers). Not only does this have all the negatives as detailed above but it also feeds the 'battle of the sexes' by painting a vision of men and women as being far more different than they really are. In turn, this can lead to judgement and resentment – not to mention heterosexual relationship conflict.

The Solution: Forget playing the numbers game. Knowing the number of people that your partner has slept with does not tell you anything about them as a person. What matters is that you know about any sexual risks you are exposing yourself to – and that any partners you have are similarly informed about your sexual health. As was famously said in *The Prisoner*, 'I am not a number. I am a free (wo)man.'

Myth #4: Women Want Romance, Men Want Sex

*T*he Fantasy: All women want candlelit dinners, serenading and flowers. All men hate romance and just want to get laid.

The Reality: Some people want romantic relationships. Some people want sex. Gender is irrelevant. While there are many women who dream of a wedding day with the 'perfect' partner, the same can be said of many men. Similarly, while there are some men whose sexual ideal is having sex with as many people as possible, there are also women who feel the same way: the main difference being that the former are considered to be 'lads' while the latter are labelled as having 'daddy issues' or slut-shamed. However, if a man only wants sex, he can be honest about it. If a woman feels the same way, she is likely to attract stigma if she admits it.

When it comes to sex, it is impossible to remove women – or men – from the society in which they exist so we may never know how much any reported gender differences in libido are a result of gender stereotyping in society rather than biological drives. However, it seems naïve to take the idea that men are more sexual than women at face value. Only when men and women are judged equally for sexual behaviour, in ways that are designed without any gender bias, will we be able to tell how different – or similar – male and female libidos really are.

As to romance, the fantasies submitted to *Garden of Desires* show that, while some women do have romantic daydreams, romance is by no means a ubiquitous part of female sexual fantasies. While it's not quite a case of, 'Forget the knight in shining armour – just bring on the horse,' it's certainly true to say that flogging is mentioned more than flowers, and cocks *much* more frequently than chocolate (though chocolate did crop up once). Conversely, many sex workers say that the most common sexual request they get from men is for the Girlfriend Experience (GFE) – namely, intimate sex with affection and connection – romance by any other name.

Many people want to feel loved. Many people want to feel sexually gratified. As with all aspects of sexuality, how much we want either of those things runs across a spectrum and can't be defined by something as broad-sweeping as gender.

The Risk: Once again, this myth is borne from the virgin/whore myth, and comes with the same array of issues. However, it also places unreasonable expectations on men by feeding the myth that they should spend money on a woman if they want sex. While the honest transaction of simply paying a woman for sex is deemed taboo, the media promotes the idea that real men should buy women expensive presents: one has to wonder how much of Christian Grey's appeal in *Fifty Shades* came from his bulging wallet rather than his bulging package. Again, this helps fuel the 'battle of the sexes' – not least because some women buy into the myth too, which can lead to (rightfully) resentful men.

The Solution: Rather than (literally) buying into the media's idea of what a relationship should be, we each need to decide what a relationship means to us. For me, trust, affection and respect – teamed with a satisfying sex life – are far more important than Valentine's Day celebrations or trinkets. Other people may have a different set of criteria: it is something for every individual to decide for themselves.

We also need to remember that romance is not something that a man does to a woman (with all of the heteronormativity that accompanies that idea). Real romance is showing your partner that you appreciate them, in a way that means something to them. And that has nothing to do with gender but is instead about people's individual wants and needs.

Myth #5: Sex is for Procreation Only

The Fantasy: Sex has one purpose – making babies. If a sexual act cannot make babies, it is not sex.

The Reality: Much as people are more than their body parts, sex is more than just a method of procreation – yet say 'sex' to most people and they'll assume you're referring to penis-in-vagina sex. However, it has not always been defined in such a narrow way. Phillips and Reay say, 'The second half of the eighteenth century saw a privileging of sexual intercourse, a shift towards penetrative sexual culture. Before that, references to kissing, mutual fondling and groping suggest that many unmarried sexual couples may well have limited their sexuality within that frame and that intercourse may not have had the centrality in people's desires that it had in modern sexual cultures.'

And it is not just ancient history that recognised sex as being more than a mere procreative device. After researching and writing her pivotal study into female sexuality, *The Hite Report*, in 1976, Shere Hite called for a redefinition of sex. Women were using the Pill for the first time, meaning that sex and procreation no longer went hand in hand. Hite saw it as a transitional period, in which the rules were still being established, thus giving an opportunity to update traditional definitions of sex. 'Although we tend to think of "sex" as one set pattern, one group of behaviours (in essence reproductive activity) there is no need to limit ourselves in this way.' (p365, *The Hite Report*, 1976)

However, few people paid attention to her. To this day, sex remains broadly defined as 'penis-in-vagina' activity, leaving many women unable to describe the sex they are having in their fantasies as 'sex'.

The Risk: An inaccurate definition of sex controls everyone's sexuality, stifling sexual freedom and accurate discourse. Many survey respondents to *Garden of Desires* felt limited by this. 'I found the phrasing of "sexual" fantasies and fantasies during sex slightly difficult as many of my fantasies (and much of my "sex" life, for lack of a better term) are sadomasochistic and not explicitly sexual. I frequently fantasise about beatings without orgasm or genital contact. Sex in the sense of fucking (fingers, cock, fist) or oral is usually only one component (not infrequently absent) in my fantasies and indeed in my sex life.'

Not only does our current definition limit sex to vanilla heterosexuals, and exclude anyone who prefers non-procreative sex, but it also classifies the 70–75 per cent of women who find it hard to climax through penetrative sex as sexually 'dysfunctional' – whether or not they feel that way. This is demonstrated by a 2008 study that found that, 'females with inhibited sexual desire fantasize less during foreplay, coitus, masturbation and general daydreaming than the controls . . . The females with inhibited sexual desire do not masturbate less often and do not have fewer orgasms through masturbation than the controls. The females with inhibited sexual desire have fewer orgasms through penetrative intercourse alone.'[16]

Despite the fact that these women were able to climax through masturbation, they were deemed to have 'inhibited sexual desire'

16 Sexual Fantasy and Activity Patterns of Females with Inhibited Sexual Desire versus Normal Controls, David E. Nutter MDa & Mary Kearns Condron MSa, pages 276–282

because they didn't climax through penis-in-vagina sex alone. This gives an idea of the way in which labelling can negatively affect sexuality. Women are being labelled as dysfunctional when the real label that should be changed is that of sex itself.

The Solution: We need to throw away outdated preconceptions about sex, start communicating honestly about it and build new definitions that allow space for everyone's sexuality to thrive. Rather than assuming someone to be abnormal for desiring sex without procreation (or non-PIV sex in general) we could instead see sex as a reflection of their personality, no matter what form that takes. Instead of deeming some forms of sex as 'normal' and others as 'abnormal' we could see sex as a communication between all parties concerned that, much like conversation, can go in whatever direction those involved want to take it.

Meg Barker says, 'The psychiatrist Chess Denham says that the way we currently distinguish sexual activities is on the basis of whether they are transgressive or not. Those which transgress current societal norms are the ones we often ridicule, consider to be psychologically unhealthy or even have criminal laws against. What she suggests instead is that we could distinguish activities on the basis of whether they are coercive or not. Does the act involve forcing anyone to do anything against their will or to which they are not able to consent (for example, children, or adults who are drugged). If so then it should be disallowed. If not, then it is really up to the people concerned.'

Myth #6: Women Do Not Pay for Sex

*T*he Fantasy: Men are more sexual than women because they use sex workers. If women liked sex as much as men, they would use sex workers as much as men.

The Reality: While men may form the bulk of sex workers' clients, it is women, not men, who form the bulk of sex toy (and erotic book) purchasers, suggesting that they have just as much need as men to satisfy their sexuality solo – and they're happy to spend money on it too. Indeed, given the amount of money that women spend on massages, it could be argued that they are also happy to pay for sensual pleasure. However, our definition of penis-in-vagina sex as the only true sex allows us to assume that women are not willing to pay for it. If women were offered a 'happy ending' as part of a societally accepted massage, how many would take it? If you've seen the *Sex and The City* episode where Samantha is turned down by the male masseur who sexually services his other well-heeled female clients, you might be inclined to think that it might prove rather popular. Indeed, several women's magazines have featured glowing articles about 'yoni massage' so perhaps it already is.

Maybe the real reason that women aren't buying sex is that they're scared of being judged – or, as yet, no one is selling the kind of sex that they're prepared to pay for. Mia More says: 'If you can now shop for sex toys without stigma, will it eventually be viable for a woman to pay another person for sex, and if so, could patriarchal society be inadvertently overturned in the process? The mind boggles!'

Of course, it could be that the real reason women don't use sex workers is because they can get sex for free much more easily than men (in the main). Rather than being less sexual than men, women simply have more access to sex – and why spend money if you can get it for free?

The Risk: As well as reinforcing the virgin/whore myth, suggesting that men are more sexual than women, and that women need love as a non-optional side order with sex, this myth feeds into the idea that women are the passive receivers of sex rather than the possessors of their own sexual desires. It also reinforces the myth that sex is penis-in-vagina only. In combination, these myths help reinforce heteronormativity – along with all the usual damage that the virgin/whore myth brings, as already discussed at length.

The Solution: Regardless of whether women would use sex workers if they could do so without judgement, we need to remove the taboo surrounding sex work and stop shaming people for the job they choose to do. While capitalism exists, sexual services will be sold along with everything else, and doing so is no more wrong than any other form of labour, as long as it is entered into freely (as with any other job). Research has repeatedly shown that stigmatisation and criminalisation of sex work only increases harm to sex workers. Slut-shaming a sex worker is no more acceptable than slut-shaming any other woman. Indeed, it could be argued that it is only when women stop judging other women as 'whores' – and start listening to each other instead – that we will finally smash the virgin/whore myth – which, as you may have worked out, is pretty pivotal to sexual liberation.

Myth #7: Women Are Less Sexually 'Deviant' Than Men

The Fantasy: Women don't have kinky thoughts and would never cheat on a man. Men have evil, kinky desires and are all cheaters.

The Reality: It's generally assumed that men have kinkier desires than women, and indeed, fetishism is considered to be more common in men than women – though obviously that depends on how fetishism is defined. However, research has found that women have greater 'erotic plasticity' than men, exhibiting more sexual variation over time, and being more able to develop new sexual turn-ons based on social influences, from magazines to friends and lovers.

Further, 'sexual attitude-behaviour consistency' is lower for women than men."[17] This means that women are less likely to behave in the way that they claim or predict they will – particularly if 'social desirability bias' comes into play.

Put simply, if it is socially desirable to be aroused – or turned off – by certain factors, women may (to a degree) shape their

17 Gender differences in erotic plasticity: The female sex drive as socially flexible and responsive. Baumeister, Roy F. *Psychological Bulletin*, Vol 126(3), May 2000, 347–374. *The Garden of Eden or Paradise Lost and Found*, Dodo Press

desires to suit their circumstance.

Further, the fantasies in this book show the diversity that exists within the female imagination, from making love with plants to wild group sex with many men; and porn studies have shown that women respond to a wider array of porn than men. If women really are less kinky than men, how is it that they can apparently become aroused by a greater array of things?

Similarly, while it might be nice for women to believe that they are the more virtuous gender, in reality, women are just as likely to cheat on a lover as men are – if not slightly more so. However, women's magazines are far more likely to run an article about how to spot a cheater than men are – not only giving women a better chance of both catching their lover at it, but also helping them get away with it if they do cheat. If there's an article about cheating in a men's magazine, it's much more likely to be about getting away with cheating – again, reinforcing the gender difference, when in reality, gender has little effect on someone's capacity to cheat.

The Risk: Painting men as 'bad' and 'dirty', and women as 'good' and 'clean' adds more arsenal to the gender war. Encouraging women to perceive men as a flick of a skirt away from cheating only increases the chances of relationship issues: jealousy is far from an attractive trait. Conversely, encouraging men to see women as inherently faithful means that they are more likely to feel like a failure if their partner does cheat – and possibly feel that their manhood has been compromised. And of course, the idea of the 'virtuous' woman feeds into the underlying virgin/whore myth too, but you were probably expecting that by now.

The Solution: We need to accept that people are individuals; that sexual behaviour is about personality rather than gender; and that women can be just as sexually diverse – and open to infidelity – as men.

Myth #8: Sex is a Sin

*T*he Fantasy: Religion and sex positivity cannot go together because sex is an inherently sinful act.

The Reality: Some people use religion to justify shaming those who are sexual – women in particular. However, religion need not be a barrier to sex positivity. Indeed, sex and spirituality have long been linked, whether through rituals, celebrations or the written word (Song of Songs in the Bible is particularly erotic). In 1876, Victoria Clafflin Woodull espoused the idea that the Garden of Eden story was an intricate symbol of the human body, urging, 'Let the sexual act become the holiest act of life, and then the world will start to be regenerated and not before.' More recently, Kelly Brown Douglas says in *Sexuality and the Black Church: A Womanist Perspective*, 'Only when the taboo of sexuality is discarded will Black women and men be free to experience what it means to wholly love and be loved by the lord.' (p143, Orbis Books, 1999). Many spiritual leaders across many different religions now preach sexual tolerance, and are moving away from bigoted views. Being religious does not have to mean being sexually oppressive (though, clearly, our sexuality has been hugely influenced by religious dogma over time).

The Risk: Accepting the myth that sex is sinful can lead to sexual guilt, repression and, at its worst, the murder of those who transgress from accepted norms. Abstinence-based sex education increases unwanted pregnancy and STI rates; people may die as a result of archaic religious laws regarding contraception use; and some people turn to suicide rather than admit their true sexuality or gender to religious family members, or their church. That chilling state of affairs is before you even get into the number of people who are killed as a result of intolerance (bred by some branches of some religions, whether directly or indirectly). In short, intolerance towards sexual diversity can kill, whether perpetuated through religion or other means. Deeming sex to be a sin also paints those who are sexual – particularly women – as sinners. And that brings us back to the virgin/whore myth once again . . .

The Solution: Though some may consider others' religious practices to be an act of oppression, and urge everyone to reject religion and/or shout about sex, there is no shame to be had in wanting to keep sexual expression as a private thing, or a matter between a committed couple. There is no shame in wearing clothes that reflect your view on modesty or that carry special meanings for you. It is only where religious practices cause harm or death – whether through making people have surgical procedures against their will, banning them from using condoms, or insisting that everyone has the same sexuality – that religion clashes with sex positivity. If we could accept that different people have different beliefs, and respect that everyone has a right to choose their own moral code, perhaps we could get rid of the stigma attached to sex, too – and, in so doing, save people's lives. Whether this is possible, given the damage that religious wars have caused historically and the baggage that comes with that history, is something that only religious leaders can decide.

Myth #9: Sexual Content is Corrupting

*T*he Fantasy: Talking about – or worse, seeing – sex leads to the moral collapse of society. Sexual content is responsible for all sex crime.

The Reality: There is an underlying assumption, fed by the tabloid press, that seeing sexual content is dangerous. However, the links between viewing sexual content and increase in sexual harm are tenuous at best, with many studies finding an inverse relationship: namely, that sex crimes go down as porn viewing and access to strip clubs go up. Though correlation does not necessarily equal causation, the fact that this myth is perpetuated despite these findings gives a strong indication of how society is manipulated by those with a 'moral' agenda to push – with potentially dangerous results.

As this book went to press, the British government demonstrated just how deeply this myth has been embedded in society. In July 2013, Prime Minister David Cameron announced that the UK would be introducing opt-out porn filters, saying, 'Many children are viewing online pornography and other damaging material at a very young age and the nature of that pornography is so extreme, it is distorting their view of sex and relationships.' However, there is much evidence to suggest that the 'threat' of porn to 'our children' is actually vastly exaggerated. In an article for *Times Education Supplement*, Alice Hoyle says, 'The EU Kids Online survey of 25,000 young people across Europe found that exposure to pornography – and the level of distress or harm caused by such exposure – was much less than anticipated.'

Many sex educators who work with teens are concerned about the ramifications of this decision. Historically, porn filters have blocked far more material than they are intended to – including sex education sites, LGBT sites, support networks and many other vital resources. Though Cameron did say, 'We need to make sure that the filters do not – even unintentionally – restrict . . . helpful and often educational content,' as yet, no solution has been offered. This raises serious concerns about what will happen should someone search for useful resources – such as bishtraining.com's guide to talking to teens about porn, or Scarleteen.com's guide to negotiating consent – once the filter is in place? What will happen to all the LGBTQ teens – especially those who are unable to talk to their families about their sexuality – if they are blocked from accessing support groups online and consequently realising they are normal? To paraphrase the tabloids: won't somebody think of the children? Further, the negatives do not seem to be outweighed by the positives. As teen sex educator Justin Hancock says, 'There is little reliable evidence to demonstrate that sexually explicit materials can be harmful to young people.'

Though porn is an easy scapegoat for all society's ills, in reality it is a false target. Intolerance, power imbalance and a culture of silence about sex all help perpetuate sex crime, whether indirectly or directly. However, it is much easier to believe that we can stamp crime out by blocking access to sexual content than to realise we have to change many of our underlying societal beliefs.

There is plenty of evidence to show that banning porn does not stop sex crime. In a piece for Policymic.com, Anna Hogeland says, 'In some countries (i.e. India) rapes are even more prevalent than porn-permitting nations. In the US, reported incidents of rape decreased by 85 per cent over 25 years in which [time] porn became more prevalent and accessible. The Atlantic Wire infers, "at best, there's no clear relationship between banning porn and that country's treatment of women and children. At worst, a ban on porn is perhaps harmful."'

Yet, despite all the evidence proving otherwise, it is still commonly accepted that blocking access to sexual content is the pathway to a 'better' society. However, numerous IT specialists have detailed how abusers can easily avoid the ban using the 'dark net'; and pointed out that censoring the internet will not protect children. Talking to the *Sydney Morning Herald* about Iceland's porn ban, Smari McCarthy, of free speech group the International Modern Media Institute, said, 'It is technically impossible to do in a way that has the intended effect. And it has negative effects – everything from slowing down the internet to blocking content that is not meant to be blocked to generally opening up a can of worms regarding human rights issues, access to information and freedom of expression.'

The Solution: Rather than looking at ways to block people from accessing porn, the money that would be used for such technical wizardry could instead be spent on devising ways to distribute free, age-appropriate sex and relationship education to all, thus arming everyone with the tools to defend themselves against sexual predators, and the information to create loving, respectful relationships. In that way, we could genuinely protect our children from the risks of the modern world and give them the tools to recognise, identify and protect themselves from coming to harm.

While child abuse is a hideous crime, and we should do everything in our power to prevent it, blocking porn is not the answer – particularly when every parent already has access to web filtering software, pre-installed on computers for free, should they be worried about their child accessing age-inappropriate content.

Censorship protects no one, prohibition protects no one – and both of these points have been proved time and time again. As Maxine Holz says in *Whatever Happened to the Sexual Revolution*, 'By deflecting fears from the real causes, moral panics exacerbate the anxieties they pretend to address. We need to focus our fear and anger on underlying economic and social problems and not on false targets.'

Myth #10: The Sexual Revolution is Over

*T*he Fantasy: Sex is everywhere. We do not need a sexual revolution because it has already happened.

The Reality: Though some would argue the sexual revolution has already happened, we need much more than the Pill or equal opportunities legislation before things will *really* change. The stigmatisation of sexuality still runs deep in society. There is no one place from which it emanates – an invisible beam of oppression powered by some mighty overlord. Instead, it is insidious, running across media, the government and society. People are criminalised for consensual sex acts, while sexual assault and rape are still alarmingly rife – across all genders – and prosecution rates are low.

Sexual imagery may be more prominent than it has been historically, but the bulk of it does not necessarily reflect reality or liberate anyone. The majority of sexual images reflect 'normal' sex with all the limitations that brings. Studies show that there is little evidence to suggest that seeing sexual imagery is damaging – however, the idea that 'raunch culture' (a term used to describe the increasingly open sexual society) is responsible for all society's ills is widely pushed, particularly by white middle-class feminists. Perhaps as a result, censorship is becoming increasingly prevalent. Within days of the UK porn ban being announced, more censorship campaigns started springing up on Twitter. These calls for censorship have dangerous ramifications. In starting the ball rolling towards censorship, where exactly is it going to stop? We need to stop the hysterical cries of, 'Ban this filth!' and instead focus on equipping everyone with the sexual education they need. Our sexuality is already policed and manipulated on numerous levels – do we really want to hand over yet more control of our intimate lives by allowing ever more heavy-handed censorship measures?

The internet is helping fight the normalisation and control of sexuality – at least for as long as it remains uncensored. While the mainstream depiction of sex is still dominant, reality is slowly beginning to play a larger role in porn. Though there is still a market for mainstream porn, 'real' and 'amateur' are becoming increasingly popular search categories, with sites like MLNP.tv and ifeelmyself.com offering anyone the chance to share their experience of sex. Feona Attwood says, 'The opportunity the Web has provided for people to make and access more diverse representations and views of sex can only be viewed as a positive thing. This doesn't necessarily mean that we are going to like or agree about everything that we find out there, but a grown-up society can find ways of dealing with this. The problematic aspects of any porn – online or offline – remain what they've always been: are the people who work in porn treated fairly? Are they paid properly? Are their working conditions safe? – but these are questions that need to be asked about any form of production and indeed any kind of work.'[18]

It is also important to remember that sexual liberation is not simply about being sexual: it is about having the freedom to be non-sexual too. As I said in the first issue of *Scarlet* magazine, real sexual confidence is as much about saying no as saying yes – if not more so. Fortunately, negotiating consent is both becoming increasingly talked about within sex education circles – as are relationships in general, rather than simply biology. Teen sex educators Scarleteen.com (US) and BishTraining.co.uk (UK) are two of the leading sites helping teens come to terms with their

18 In an interview with Alex Krotoski for http://untanglingtheweb.tumblr. com

sexuality by engaging in honest and open two-way discussion, and taking guidance from their users about what they need to know. Unfortunately, there is little funding for sex education – no matter how economically and socially useful research shows it to be.

In short, we have a long way to go before the sexual revolution is complete, with many battles ahead – but all of us have the power to help evolve attitudes towards sex. As MLNP founder Cindy Gallop told the *Huffington Post*, 'My entire message with MakeLoveNotPorn boils down to one thing: talk about it. Talk about sex. Talk about it generally, openly, publicly, but also personally, intimately.' Only in talking will your voice be heard.

The Risk: Even if you personally feel sexually liberated, assuming the sexual revolution is over ignores vast swathes of society who are still sexually oppressed. People all over the world are feeling pressured to be 'normal', whether or not it suits their (or indeed, society's) needs. People all over the world are being denied agency over their bodies. And people all over the world are being beaten, raped or killed because their sexuality does not fit with the ideals of heteronormative society. These are the casualties of the 'moral majority' – and even when the deaths stop, the sexual revolution will be far from over. Until we have demolished the sex myths that lie at the core of many of our beliefs about sex – and women – the sexual revolution is still in its infancy.

The Solution: While we may have a long way to go before sexuality is accepted in all its glory, more and more individuals and companies are realising that the our attitudes to sex need to change. The sexual revolution is currently progressing not with a mighty bang but with thousands of tiny whispers – and anyone is free to join in.

Every day, activists, fetishists, sex workers and educators are talking to each other through Twitter and other social networks, finding allies with similar aims and joining forces to amplify their message. Sex toy testers such as Blacksilk (http://beingblacksilk. com/) and Nymphomaniac Ness (http://nymphomaniacness.com) are raising awareness of dangerous chemicals used in some sex toys and lubricants – and even banding together to subject sex toys to laboratory testing through dildology.org. Independent inventors such as iGino and Crave are turning to crowdfunding to turn their innovative toy dreams into a reality, as are queer and alternative porn producers.

Trans activists are raising awareness about the reality of gender. Sex workers are challenging outdated stereotypes of 'damaged goods' and 'prostituted women', explaining that the debate is far more complex than it's generally presented and, if you believe a woman has the right to choose what she does with her body, that includes sex work.

More women of colour are becoming sex educators, spurning the stigma traditionally associated with open discussion of sexuality. Disabled people are fighting the stereotype of desexualisation, films like *The Sessions* are helping raise awareness of disabled sexuality – and indeed, many sex workers are particularly vocal about disabled people's sexual rights, as they see how many disabled people have to rely on sex workers for gratification due to society's views of what is and isn't attractive.

There are tiny revolutions going on every day, online, offline and in the privacy of people's bedrooms. If you don't want to be part of the problem, be part of the solution and fight for your sexual freedom – whatever that means to you.

The Danger of Myths

Sexual revolution may seem like a grandiose term. But in reality, it is simply a phrase to describe the changes that need to happen if everyone is to be truly sexually liberated – starting with throwing away the tired old sexual stereotypes and perceptions that control us.

To me, all the above myths are dangerous, stifling women's sexual power and contributing to their control. That control takes many forms, from a woman's own self-perception and self-regulation of her behaviour through to more overt and extreme actions, such as abuse, rape, murder and suicide. Myths breed stigma, and stigma kills – as the number of remembrance days held by marginalised groups, from transexuals to sex workers, shows. Ignorance kills, as the HIV/AIDS public service announcements warned in the 1990s. And moral panics kill – as shown by the UK MMR vaccine scandal, and vigilante attacks on false targets. If we accept these myths, and do nothing in whatever small, individual way we can to combat their effect, we are ultimately complicit in those deaths.

Sadly, these are far from the only damaging myths that exist. It could be that there are other myths that are more important for you personally to counter; each individual must make their own decisions about what they choose to believe. I would ask only this: please consider how the myths we absorb affect those around us – and how much we stymie our own sexuality by passively absorbing the norms fed to us by those in positions of power.

See How the Garden Grows

*B*y writing *My Secret Garden*, Nancy Friday helped women feel normal for having sexual desires. However, over time, 'normal' has become a loaded term, used to shape and manipulate our sexuality. The fantasies submitted to *Garden of Desire* show that there is no such thing as normal. We are all unique and there is nothing to be ashamed of in that.

Today, many women's fantasies challenge accepted notions of gender and sexuality – and even the definition of sex itself. The Pill brought with it the freedom to separate sex from procreation, but we are still largely defining sex under pre-Pill terms. In reality, 'sex' covers a huge and diverse range of activities, and in limiting it to procreative sex alone, we marginalise those who enjoy it in other ways and for other reasons. Everyone is different and there is no reason we should all have sex in the same way – if, indeed, we choose to have sex at all.

However, this diversity does not mean that there are not common sexual struggles shared by many people. For too long, the voices of minorities have been silenced – but now it is easier than ever before for us to find like-minded people, and work together to fight for our rights. As more people share their stories, the more we can recognise shared struggles – and work together to find solutions. The idea of 'normal' is gradually being eroded as more people are open about their sexuality; and every person who adds their voice helps dilute the mainstream representation of sex and replace it with something real.

In resisting the pressure to conform and focusing instead on being ourselves, we put the power of our sexuality back in our own hands, away from the grasp of advertisers and governments. With fantasy, anyone has the freedom to explore wherever their mind wants to go – but with reality, we still have to fight to be free.

Inside the Garden of Desires

How the Research was Compiled

When Nancy Friday wrote *My Secret Garden*, she solicited fantasies by placing classified advertisements in newspapers inviting women to write to her with their fantasies. Critics claimed (rightly) that this made her research unscientific. However, Friday never claimed it was an academic study: more an insight into the fantasy minds of women designed to spread the seed of an idea.

Similarly, *Garden of Desires* is not an academic paper. However, it does draw from a wide variety of data sources to help ensure it presents as balanced and representative a view as possible. A variety of surveys were distributed worldwide via numerous sources including Twitter, Facebook and email, inviting women to answer one of four surveys: a two-point questionnaire for those with limited time; a seven-point questionnaire for those with a coffee break to spare; and two twenty-point questionnaires, one for women in general and another tailored towards erotic writers. Women were instructed to omit answering any questions they felt uncomfortable with answering, both for ethical reasons and to help minimise any fabrication. They were also asked to forward the questionnaire to friends to help reach as broad an audience as possible. Contributors were asked to give a brief biog, describing themselves as they would wish to be labelled and removing identifiable details to protect their anonymity if desired.

The answers from these interviews are interspersed through the book. In addition, a small selection of the full interviews is available later in the Appendix.

In total, 425 surveys were submitted to the book. A handful of men submitted fantasies, which have been set aside for any future work I do on male fantasies (excluding one included in the appendix to show the virgin/whore myth is still alive and well). I used answers from every survey that was submitted in time to meet my deadline, to help show the full range of fantasies submitted rather than introduce any selection bias.

Additional research included:

- Discussions with leading academics in the field
- Interviews with sex bloggers and erotic authors
- Leading books on sexual fantasy and sexuality (*see:* Bibliography)
- Academic research papers (*see:* Footnotes)
- Essays and articles online

While this book only features fantasies from women who have submitted fantasies specifically for it, I also drew inspiration for the themes and topics in this book from the thousands of fantasies that have been submitted to Cliterati and *Scarlet* magazine over the last decade, along with those submitted to previously published sexual-fantasy surveys.

Where available, statistics from academic studies into fantasy are cited to give an indication of the popularity of specific themes. However, research into fantasy is still in its infancy and the diversity already revealed suggests we really have only encountered the tip of the iceberg of female sexuality.

I have not produced any quantitative data from the survey results as my intent was to present rather than analyse the data. However, I have kept all questionnaires so there is potential for future analysis.

Research Issues

*C*apturing an accurate picture of female sexual fantasy is hard. Many people feel that sex is private and sharing intimate details is shameful or inappropriate; and this can be affected by culture, meaning many women remain unrepresented. Any sexual survey can only reveal the sexual desires of those who are willing and able to share, and who have access to the questions being asked, which may or may not be representative of the population as a whole. While it may be possible to give a rough approximation of common themes, there is no way that one survey can reflect the whole of womankind. And that is just one of the problems with sexual research.

People are more likely to admit to desires if they have no fear of judgement, but society tends to judge sex on multiple levels. Religion, gender roles and representations, media and general attitudes to taboos all feed into the fantasies that people report. There is an 'acceptable' level of sexual openness; an 'acceptable' range of fantasy subjects that will be covered in the media; an 'acceptable' way to look; and an 'acceptable' way to be sexual. All these pressures have the potential to feed into our fantasies, whether by creating neuroses or urging us away from our darker, more 'dangerous' desires. These sexual pressures can also affect the fantasies that people share. They breed language that reinforces their message: self-abuse; dirty talking; living in sin. Stigma has been built into many of the words we have surrounding sex; and in using them, we reinforce the stigma.

'Social Desirability Bias' means that people are more likely to share information that they think will be endorsed by the person questioning them. This can lead to over reporting of 'good' behaviour, such as a fantasy which is deemed 'acceptable' by the mainstream; and under reporting of 'bad' behaviour, such as taboo fantasies including incest, bestiality and extreme violence. It is certainly true that there were very few fantasies including these themes submitted to *Garden of Desires*. Whether this is a product of social desirability bias, a flaw in the questioning or a genuine decrease in such fantasies is impossible to tell.

Much sexual research is criticised because it only focuses on people who are white, heterosexual, able bodied, cisgender and middle class, thus capturing one type of experience rather than an accurate diversity. In an attempt to get around this issue, the *Garden of Desires* questionnaire was promoted internationally to groups including sex worker campaign groups, feminist websites, lesbian magazines, trans-women organisations, mother networks, disability groups, women-of-colour organisations, interdisciplinary academic networks and female entrepreneur networks; along with publications and websites including the UK's *Daily Telegraph* and magazines, *Cosmopolitan* online, *Sydney Morning Herald* and US 'alternative' (and female-run) adult site Fleshbot.com, to help attract as representative and intersectional a sample of the female population as possible. A full list of groups targeted, and a more comprehensive outline of the methodology, is included in the Appendix.

I have huge respect, gratitude and appreciation for the women who chose to open up about their fantasies. To share your fantasies is to shine a light on an oft-neglected area: real – and private – sexuality. There is no normal in fantasy – it is our individual place to play and share as we see fit. The beauty is in the diversity: after all, who wants a garden blooming with a single flower?

Selected Interview Responses

Question 1: Describe yourself briefly in the way that you most identify (eg, name, age, sexuality, (dis)ability, cis/trans, ethnicity, marital status, number of children, occupation, academic qualification, hair colour or whatever else is most important to you):

Answer: Even though I do not agree with your identifiers in a way that most identifies myself (Which is that I am Owned), I provide the following. My age is 29, I am bisexual, I have depression. I am Caucasian. I am separated from my husband and living with my Master and his wife. I have one child and he is 27 months old. I work in a call centre. No academic qualifications. I have brown hair. I read extensively and on a daily basis I try and improve myself. Being loved is most important to me.

Question 2: At what age did you first start having sexual fantasies?

Answer: I was ten years old when I had the first sexual fantasy I can remember.

Question 3: Do you remember anything that triggered your sexual fantasies?

Answer: On that specific day, no. But I was sexually submissively inclined for years, if not my whole life. Movies, songs, commercials, stories that featured bondage as a key theme were always something that attracted my attention. It hasn't been until years later that I pieced this together though.

Question 4: What is the earliest sexual fantasy you remember?

Answer: I was on a bus with my class from school going away on an excursion. Myself and two boys from my class who I had crushes on disembarked and they tied me with rope to a sign by the side of the road. They laughed and went back to the bus. I know that doesn't sound particularly sexual, but I remember waking and feeling so energised and like that dream was so special that I wrote in my diary about it. Even at such a young age I recognised that that was something that I enjoyed, even if I couldn't articulate why.

Question 5: Have your fantasies changed over time?

Answer: Oh most definitely. When I first started looking into BDSM I filled out a checklist about likes, dislikes, things I haven't tried and want to, things I never want to try. That list was so limited, I really only liked bondage. These days I rather like objectification, orgasm control, bondage, chastity, service, puppy play, etc.

Question 6: What was your most recent fantasy?

Answer: I welcome my Master home kneeling in the doorway, arms bound behind my back with an armbinder. I have my hood on my head, which only has a mouth hole. My breasts are bound and sensitive, my nipples are pierced with the thick rings my Master likes so much. My labia are also pierced with those thick rings and padlocked closed – a reminder of my Owner's control over my sexuality and my orgasms. I follow him to his chair and he pulls his pants down and has me kneel and throat his cock in silence. It's very messy because he likes that. While he enjoys my mouth-hole he tells me how pleasing it is to have me chaste for his pleasure, so that I become more focussed in my service to him. By this stage I have not had an orgasm in quite a while and it doesn't look like I'm going to have one any time soon. I like knowing that soon afterward he is going to fuck any one of my holes and cum in it, that I will be able to feel all of the pleasure and have to control myself that I do not disobey his wishes and cum without permission. That, to me, is lovely service. Giving all that you can towards someone's pleasure without the expectation of receiving what you desire in return.

Question 7: What is your favourite fantasy?

Answer: Being reduced to little more than three holes. Usually this is by wearing a full latex suit, including my hood so that I am dehumanised. Usually my arms are bound behind me and at times I am hobbled. I have a ring gag in my mouth to keep it open and accessible. My genital area is able to be opened by a zipper in the latex suit. It is merely my fantasy that my Owner uses me in any hole, anytime his whim takes him.

Question 8: What feelings do your fantasies elicit whether positive, negative or both?

Answer: It depends on my emotional scope for the day. As stated previously, I have depression and I am struggling with how my father may have had a large impact upon my inherent submission. I detest that he may have shaped me that way through the abuse I received in my early years. Mostly I am happy to be a slave to my Master, but there are times where I loathe my weakness and my need to be controlled.

Question 9: Do you use fantasies when you masturbate?

Answer: Yes, though mostly it's about serving my Master. I am not allowed to orgasm without his permission though, so I rarely masturbate unless edging for him so that I am wet and ready. He likes this.

Question 10: What purpose do sexual fantasies serve in your life?

Answer: They are something that I desire to see become reality at some stage. It's not vital though. My sex life keeps me quite fulfilled.

Question 11: Do your sexual fantasies influence your sexual reality?

Answer: I think it's the opposite. I think my sexual reality influences my sexual fantasies.

Question 12: Does your real life (whether sexual or otherwise) influence your fantasies?

Answer: Yes, because I live in a 24/7 TPE relationship with my Master. I am intrinsically submissive and it has a very heavy emphasis on the way my personality is shaped, how I communicate with people and how I serve my Master. It seems the more dominant my Master is, the more I crave to be dehumanised, objectified and humiliated.

Question 13: Do you use fantasies during sex with partner(s)?

Answer: My Master often talks to me about how he looks forward to my labia being pierced for him. He also talked last night about looking forward to whipping, bruising and marking me in a few weeks when we have the house to ourselves. It's not so much fantasies, I guess, because they are going to happen. If this question is about my escaping inside of a fantasy when my Owner is fucking me, then no. He is so great in bed (and outside of) that I have no need to.

Question 14: If you do use fantasies when you have sex with partner(s), what are your reasons for doing this?

Answer: See above.

Question 15: If you do use fantasies when you have sex with partner(s) how often and do you share the fact that you are doing so with your partner(s)?

Answer: See above. If I have any fantasies, usually I tell my Owner about them. I do not need the cover of the darkness of the bedroom to tell him – I am quite open with him about my needs and wants and desires. We are currently writing a story between the two of us, exploring as we go the concept of new things that we want to try or that are erotic.

Question 16: If you do use fantasies when you have sex with partner(s), have you told them that you are doing so? If not, why not?

Answer: See above.

Question 17: If you do share fantasies with partner(s), what is their response and has it affected your attitude to your fantasies?

Answer: My Master is so welcoming and amazing, that he makes me comfortable in my own skin. I don't feel afraid to tell him things, even the things that are touted to be taboo or extreme. When I'm play-acting as a puppy he makes me feel so loved and cherished that I don't feel stupid or embarrassed. He is very good about making sure that I am able to express myself and my sexual desires.

Question 18: Have you made any of your fantasies come true and if so, how did you feel about it?

Answer: Living with my Master and having him fuck, love, guide and control me is my fantasy. I am very lucky and outside of my depression and battling the issues that stem from my past, I am so very happy and proud and grateful to be so.

Question 19: Have you made any of your partner's fantasies come true and if so, how did you feel about it?

Answer: One night my Master wanted me to piss my bed. I did so and with great difficulty slept in it. I had anticipated him coming into my bedroom at night and praising me and telling me what a good girl I was. Instead he came in about 5a.m, by which time I'd pissed the bed twice (so very hard) and fucked me and then told me he couldn't sleep in bed with me because it was too uncomfortable to do so in wet sheets and that he needed a shower and would go and sleep with his wife in his bed. That was a horrible experience and I still feel soiled thinking about that experience. I feel dirty at times. Other than that I know that he has fantasies about cutting, which he has done on me on numerous occasions and I feel proud. I feel proud that I am able to serve him even if I don't necessarily enjoy the acts themselves.

I'm 31, have a doctorate, think bisexual is the best word available to describe my sexuality but also think it's a dumb word. I'd prefer to just be 'sexual', or maybe 'omnisexual' because it sounds playful and open-minded. I'm single, though I've mostly been in relationships over the past 13 years – usually lasting between two and four years each. Always guys, though I have slept with a woman once too. I'm white and I think it's a strange survey that lets you pick your own categories! Very qual. [qualitative – referring to a type of research]

Question 2: At what age did you first start having sexual fantasies?

Answer: 17

Question 3: Do you remember anything that triggered your sexual fantasies?

Answer: No.

Question 4: What is the earliest sexual fantasy you remember?

Answer: It was very inarticulate – this was when I was seventeen. It basically involved a room so steamy you could hardly see – and a naked male body. I'd had elaborate romantic fantasies since I was much younger – about 11, but 17 was the first time they took a sexual turn.

Question 5: Have your fantasies changed over time?

Answer: Hugely.

Question 6: What was your most recent fantasy?

Answer: Fucking a man I know but have not slept with yet – I was taking a dominant role.

Question 7: What is your favourite fantasy

Answer: Probably a fantasy that I am a man, and am either masturbating, or fucking a woman. Sometimes a man.

Question 8: What feelings do your fantasies elicit whether positive, negative or both?

Answer: Almost always positive. I use fantasies to excite me when I masturbate, or when someone's going down on me – if the fantasy doesn't excite me I cast it aside and look for another. Occasionally they turn a little violent and I feel bad when that happens.

Question 9: Do you use fantasies when you masturbate?

Answer: Always.

Question 10: What purpose do sexual fantasies serve in your life?

Answer: To make masturbation and oral sex more pleasurable. I don't usually fantasise when I'm having actual sex. I prefer to concentrate on fantastic reality when that's happening.

Question 11: Do your sexual fantasies influence your sexual reality?

Answer: A little bit, but not as much as I'd like.

Question 12: Does your real life (whether sexual or otherwise) influence your fantasies?

Answer: Definitely. Almost all of the men I fantasise about are real people. (I'm more likely to make the women up.) I often re-live actual sex I've had, or imagine sex with real people I'd like to fuck.

Question 13: Do you use fantasies during sex with partner(s)?

Answer: When I'm receiving oral sex. Not otherwise.

Question 14: If you do use fantasies when you have sex with partner(s), what are your reasons for doing this?

Answer: I find oral sex quite boring unless I'm fantasising. It would take me a long time to come if I didn't bring my imagination in on the game.

Question 15: If you do use fantasies when you have sex with partner(s) how often and do you share the fact that you are doing so with your partner(s)?

Answer: I've only had one partner who asked me about my fantasies and I actually found it a little draining. It's nice to have sovereignty over your fantasies, and not have to open your head for your lover to peer inside. On the other hand it's also nice to feel able to share fantasies, if and when you want to.

Question 16: If you do use fantasies when you have sex with partner(s), have you told them that you are doing so. If not, why not?

Answer: These questions aren't phrased very well. I don't share because I'm afraid my fantasies will scare my lovers. Telling a guy that I'm imagining I'm a guy, having sex with him – isn't going to go down well with many Kiwi men.

Question 17: If you do share fantasies with partner(s), what is their response and has it affected your attitude to your fantasies?

Answer: With the one guy who I did this with – he was excited by them, but I felt I always had to provide him with a certain sort of fantasy (i.e. my fantasies about women) and I found I resented that a bit. It felt like he was taking my fantasies away from me – appropriating them, and demanding more at a rate I wasn't able to supply.

Question 18: Have you made any of your fantasies come true and if so, how did you feel about it?

Answer: Yes, a few. I slept with a woman once and a few of my boyfriends have allowed me to digitally penetrate them. Always awesome. In my lucid dreams I live them all out.

Question 19: Have you made any of your partner's fantasies come true and if so, how did you feel about it?

Answer: Dressing up is fun. I don't mind being tied up as long as I'm treated with respect – and if I'm being teased then I love it. I won't do threesomes. I think sex is a two-way street, and two-way only, or else there will be ugly crashes and no one will know which direction they are supposed to go in.

Question 20: Is there anything else you would like to add?

Answer: Good on you for doing this project! It's something we, especially women, but both women and men, are poor at talking about, and it's an immensely important subject that affects all our lives. This seems like a strangely organised survey, though – if you have the money you should consult someone who knows about surveys for advice. I'm saying this not to be annoying but because I think this is a very important subject and the research should be gathered carefully. Thank you!

No. Females like you have daddy issues and should stop with this whorish character of yours.

Question 2: Describe your most common fantasy.

Answer: Please stop making promiscuous, you're going to be in your thirties without children.

Question 3: Where do you think your fantasy comes from?

Answer: Nobody loves a woman with a vagina that's been plummet by a hammer five thousand times.

Question 4: Do you fantasise during masturbation?

Answer: Please lady you're probably in your fifties you're about to die.

Question 5: Do you fantasise during sex?

Answer: You're too old for this lady.

Question 6: How close are your fantasies to reality?

Answer: Yep.

Question 7: Do you have anything else to add?

Answer: Yep, yep if you want to contact me, email me or call me out.

26-year-old, cisgendered, brunette graduate student

Question 2: Describe your most common fantasy.

Answer: They usually involve some sort of equal power dynamic; one person in charge, the other person at their mercy and begging for more. I don't explicitly visualise myself in either role, but I imagine the experience from both points of view.

Question 3: Where do you think your fantasy comes from?

Answer: I'm a Type-A perfectionist and I think that makes me more interested in this power dynamic scenario, either imagining being fully in control and all-powerful, or completely letting go and letting someone please me.

Question 4: Do you fantasise during masturbation?

Answer: 99 per cent of the time. I can't get off if I don't.

Question 5: Do you fantasise during sex?

Answer: I'd say about fifty per cent of the time. It depends on the situation and how turned on I feel initially. Sometimes I need some mental stimulation to get my body going.

Question 6: How close are your fantasies to reality?

Answer: My fantasies include some extreme scenarios, including borderline rape, that would absolutely NOT be sexy in real life. But I don't mind a little bit of power-play when I'm having sex.

Question 7: Do you have anything else to add?

Answer: I've only ever had sex with men, but my fantasies involve both men and women freely. In fantasy land, anything goes.

Librarian, 30

Question 2: At what age did you first start having sexual fantasies?

Answer: Pre-teen/teen years.

Question 3: Do you remember anything that triggered your sexual fantasies?

Answer: Books that had more explicit content than I'd known about, boys and girls kissing and groping.

Question 5: Have your fantasies changed over time?

Answer: Yes. Pornography and erotic novels as well as my sexual experiences have changed a lot of the fantasy settings and have broadened what I find attractive, but I do have some of the same fantasies regarding my current lover doing things I've enjoyed.

Question 6: What was your most recent fantasy?

Answer: I don't know that it counts as a fantasy given that it was me remembering a pornographic lesbian video.

Question 7: What is your favourite fantasy?

Answer: Anything where I'm receiving oral sex, being told I'm naughty.

Question 8: What feelings do your fantasies elicit whether positive, negative or both?

Answer: Pleasure, desire, hope that I will find a lover that is good or experienced in what I desire and need/want, sometimes shame, particularly if my fantasy involves actual masturbation and I feel I've spent too long in this activity.

Question 9: Do you use fantasies when you masturbate?

Answer: Yes.

Question 10: What purpose do sexual fantasies serve in your life?

Answer: For arousal and masturbation. Sometimes as a way to bond with my partner.

Question 11: Do your sexual fantasies influence your sexual reality?

Answer: Not really.

Question 12: Does your real life (whether sexual or otherwise) influence your fantasies?

Answer: Yes.

Question 13: Do you use fantasies during sex with partner(s)?

Answer: Sometimes sharing fantasies with a partner we act them out.

Question 14: If you do use fantasies when you have sex with partner(s), what are your reasons for doing this?

Answer: In order to bond with and pleasure my partner or for him to pleasure me.

Question 15: If you do use fantasies when you have sex with partner(s) how often and do you share the fact that you are doing so with your partner(s)?

Answer: I don't know how often, but, yes, I will share the fantasy . . . to me fantasies are often things that aren't done in our everyday sex life, so he would know it's something I fantasise about. Or do you mean am I fantasising while I'm having sex with a partner, if that's the case, then, not often if I do it's usually to get myself to climax more quickly and I don't share that I'm fantasising.

Question 16: If you do use fantasies when you have sex with partner(s), have you told them that you are doing so. If not, why not?

Answer: No. It would serve no purpose. It's just so I can climax more quickly. Usually it's just me thinking I'm naughty or about to be caught or that he's about to ejaculate.

Question 17: If you do share fantasies with partner(s), what is their response and has it affected your attitude to your fantasies?

Answer: My partners have always been curious and receptive.

Question 18: Have you made any of your fantasies come true and if so, how did you feel about it?

Answer: Yes. Nervous initially that it wouldn't go well, but pleased my partner was willing to try.

Question 19: Have you made any of your partner's fantasies come true and if so, how did you feel about it?

Answer: Yes. Initially nervous that I really wouldn't enjoy myself, but willing to try in order to please him.

Female heteroflexible, married, one child, 49. I am a submissive and play BDSM games in secret with a number of doms. I'm educated to MA level, and own a small business.

Question 2: At what age did you first start having sexual fantasies?

Answer: The first one I remember is aged 3 or 4.

Question 3: Do you remember anything that triggered your sexual fantasies?

Answer: Stories, often fairy stories, where anybody got chained up or similar.

Question 4: What is the earliest sexual fantasy you remember?

Answer: You can read about it here: http://stillostandhumiliated. tumblr.com/post/44633606369/my-first-sexual-fantasy.

Question 5: Have your fantasies changed over time?

Answer: When younger I probably augmented my core diet of BDSM fantasies with vanilla fantasies about film stars etc, but I doubt that I would have 'got off' on these. Over time have incorporated more activities into my basic repertoire, but there is a core of sure-fire fantasies I still retain from adolescence. I have some quite subtle ones now, some very complicated ones involving large groups of people, weird steam punk machines etc. For example: http://stillostandhumiliated.tumblr.com/post/42193375193/ victorian-whores-humiliated-on-bikes.

White, uni-educated female, 26, lefty, renting, single but not celibate, mainly straight, had a Christian upbringing

Question 2: Describe your most common fantasy.

Answer: Dirty talk from my partner, or if more extreme, rough sex.

Question 3: Where do you think your fantasy comes from?

Answer: I think sex is dirty! I also like to have verbal communication during sex.

Question 4: Do you fantasise during masturbation?

Answer: Yes.

Question 5: Do you fantasise during sex?

Answer: No – I'd like to though.

Question 6: How close are your fantasies to reality?

Answer: I've had rough sex before and my most satisfying partner talked dirty to me. However I also fantasise about women and that's not what my real sex life looks like!

Question 7: Do you have anything else to add?

Answer: Look forward to reading the results!

Patricia, 27, straight, cerebral paralysism, single, marketing tecnic, Masters, white, red-haired

Question 2: Describe your most common fantasy.

Answer: Being handcuffed and or blindfolded and being told what to do/ control and dominate one's moves and pleasure.

Question 3: Where do you think your fantasy comes from?

Answer: Imagination, movies/books, friends' experiences.

Question 4: Do you fantasise during masturbation?

Answer: Yes.

Question 5: Do you fantasise during sex?

Answer: No.

Question 6: How close are your fantasies to reality?

Answer: Close, because I try to make them come true.

Glossary

It's hard to discuss sex in any detail without using some language that may be unfamiliar to many people. Some words and phrases used to describe sex acts and sexualities may seem crude or academic. However, in learning their meanings, it makes it easier to understand shades of nuance and the true diversity that surrounds us.

This is by no means a comprehensive glossary. I have only included words and phrases used by women in their responses to this survey and any terms I have used that may need clarification.

I have also included my definition of 'woman', 'partner' and 'normal', as used in this book, for reasons of clarity.

24/7: Someone who assumes a particular sexual role all the time, most commonly used to refer to people who are submissive or dominant 24 hours of the day.

Agency: Power and control over one's own – or another's – life.

Androgynous: Someone who dresses and/or feels as if they are neither male nor female, or who celebrates both their masculine and feminine traits.

Asexual: Someone who does not feel sexual desire. They may or may not feel romantic desire. As with all aspects of sexuality, asexuality falls along a spectrum.

Aromantic: Someone who does not feel romantic desire. Again, this falls along a spectrum.

BDSM: Bondage, domination, sadism and masochism.

Boi: A term generally used to describe young, butch lesbians. It is also used to describe a female-bodied person who does not identify as being female and may also be used to define a young transman who is in the earlier stages of transitioning.

Bottom: Someone assuming a sexually submissive role during sex play (and sometimes outside sex play – see '24/7')

Bukkake: Numerous people ejaculating over someone at the same time – generally numerous men ejaculating over a woman. Porn producer Kazuhiko Matsumoto is credited with creating the bukkake genre in 1998 as he was unable to show penetration due to censorship laws but there was a loophole allowing ejaculation. It means 'to heavy splash'. Though some claim it was created as a punishment for infidelity, this is widely disputed and believed to be urban myth created to add a sense of history to the act.

Cis: Identifying with the gender that you are assigned at birth. If you feel like a woman and were viewed as a girl (due to your body) you are a cis woman.

DFAB: Designated female at birth.

Dom/Domme: Someone assuming a dominant or 'top' role during sex play. 'Dom' refers to a man, 'Domme' to a woman. Some people capitalise 'Dom'/'Domme' as a mark of respect/submission. (These words may be used interchangeably with 'Master'/'Mistress' or 'Top' – all of which may also be capitalised by some as a mark of respect.)

DP: Double penetration, generally referring to simultaneous penetration of the anus and vagina. This was a particularly popular feature in porn films of the 1990s, and often features in gang bangs, which have also featured more frequently in porn over the last decade.

DS: Domination and submission.

Edging: Originally referring to knifeplay, edging is now commonly used to refer to sex play that is 'on the edge' or 'extreme' – as considered by the person using the term. It may include acts such as fisting (vaginal and anal), asphyxiation, play piercings, needle-play or branding, or none of these and numerous, entirely different acts: everyone defines 'the edge' in their own way.

Electro: Using electricity in sex play. This is done using specially designed equipments such as TENS machines or violet wands, and should never be undertaken using mains electricity.

Ethical Slut: A term created by Dossie Easton in her book of the same name, referring to someone who has a non-monogamous lifestyle but conducts themselves in an ethical and honest way (not cheating, for example).

Femme: A feminine lesbian. Sometimes also used when people deliberately dress in a very feminine style in order to demonstrate that gender is a performance rather than 'natural'.

Fisting: Inserting the fist into the vagina or rectum. This should be done slowly and carefully to minimise risk of bruising and/or tearing. Despite the name, the hand is not formed into a fist but instead the fingers are bunched together to ease entry. Lubricant is essential.

Frottage: Sexual stimulation by rubbing the genitals against another person, also known as 'dry humping'.

Gender Non-Binary: The idea that gender does not easily split into male and female, and gender is actually a spectrum in a similar way that Kinsey's sexuality scale shows sexuality is a spectrum, and/or something that we perform in different ways in different situations.

Girlfriend Gaze: A more recent term than male gaze, this refers to the judgemental gaze of other women which may be used to manipulate women's self-perception in much the same way as the male gaze.

Genderqueer: Most commonly used to describe someone who feels that they fit outside the gender binary (see gender non-binary), sitting between or outside 'boy'/'man'/'male' and 'girl'/'woman'/'female'.

Intersectionality: Recognising that different people have different experiences, opportunities and (dis)advantages that need to be taken into consideration when developing an argument or policy. For example we might speak of 'intersections' between race, age, sexuality, gender, disability, class etc.

Heteronormative: The assumption that heterosexuality is the normal and natural state of things: that people are either men or women and are attracted to either men or women. Heteronormativity is reinforced through the media and society in numerous ways, from unequal marriage rights (particularly for transgender people) to depictions of romance in the media.

Heteromantic: Being romantically attracted to the 'opposite gender'.

Homoromantic: Being romantically attracted to the 'same gender'.

Informed Consent: Being willing and able to offer consent freely without being rendered vulnerable by outside influences (eg. drugs, alcohol, peer pressure or a lack of information about what an act entails).

Lipstick Lesbian: A feminine lesbian and/or a woman who engages in flirtatious behaviour with other women in order to attract male attention.

Male Gaze: A term first introduced in film theory, this refers to the assumption that a viewer will be male and, as such, the tailoring of images to suit his desire. This is often cited in reference to media depictions of women.

NC: Non-consent. 'CNC' refers to consensual non-consent, in which people role-play non-consensual activity but give their consent in real life.

Normal: Conforming to societal norms. Described in the Urban Dictionary (urbandictionary.com) as 'A word made up by this corrupt society so they could single out and attack those who are different.'

Omnisexual: Attraction towards all sexualities and genders, often used interchangeably with 'polysexual' and 'pansexual'.

Orgasm Gap: Research shows that men in heterosexual relation-ships have three orgasms to every one their partner has. This is known as the 'orgasm gap'. Lesbian relationships do not show the same disparity.

Partner: A person with whom you engage in romantic or sexual activity, whether once or on a longer-term basis. However, having sex with someone does not mean they must be defined as a partner.

Pegging: Anally penetrating a partner using a strap-on vibrator or dildo.

Polyamorous: A form of openly non-monogamous relationship that can involve loving and/or sexual relationships with multiple partners. Polyamorous units tend to be governed by their own rules and boundaries depending on the people involved and rela-tionships desired.

Polysexual: See 'omnisexual'.

Pro-Domme: A professional Dominatrix who charges clients to dominate them.

RACK: Risk-Aware Consensual Kink – ensuring anyone taking part in an activity (generally BDSM-related) is aware of any risks involved and willing and able to choose to take those risks. This has replaced 'SSC' (Safe, Sane and Consensual) as a guideline for some, as the word 'safe' was deemed limiting.

Queer: Although it is often used to mean gay, this is becoming an umbrella term to cover anyone who does not identify within a heteronormative framework.

Sex-positive: The belief that sexual expression is healthy and should not be stigmatised or repressed as long as it is consensual and all parties concerned have the education/information required to ensure they are making an informed choice.

Sex Worker: Someone who sells sex. This can take many forms. Many sex workers object to the term 'prostitute' as it does not acknowledge that selling sex is work, much as any job. 'Prostituted' is a similarly controversial term as it removes the agency of the sex worker and victimises her against her will.

Scat: Sex play involving fecal matter.

Seeker: A person that seeks.

Spitroast: Group sex involving two people simultaneously penetrating the mouth and vagina or anus of a third party.

SSC: Safe, Sane and Consensual – a common guideline followed by people involved in BDSM activity.

Sub: Someone assuming a submissive role, generally during sex play.

Top: Someone assuming a dominant role, generally during sex play.

Trans: Not identifying with the gender that you are assigned at birth. If you were viewed as a boy at birth and are a woman you are a transwoman. If you were viewed as a girl at birth and are a man you are a transman (although the 'trans' part is only relevant if you are specifically talking about something to do with being trans, otherwise you are simply a woman or a man unless you choose to label yourself otherwise). If you were viewed as either a boy or girl at birth but have a non-binary gender you might also see yourself as trans (see Gender Non-Binary).

Tribbing: Also known as tribadism or scissoring, this is a sex act involving two people with vaginas grinding against each other with their legs scissored together.

Vac Rack: An inflatable latex envelope sometimes used in BDSM play. A person gets inside the envelope which then has all the air sucked out of it, making the latex cling tightly to the person's skin. Some vac racks include a tube for the person inside to breathe through. Other models allow the person inside to breathe through a gas mask incorporated into the vac rack. Some enjoy asphyxiation play, whipping or spanking through the bed as part of the experience. A vac rack should only be used with at least one other person in the room to assist in getting out of the vac rack as the person inside cannot break the vacuum.

Vanilla: Someone who prefers their sex without any 'different flavours' – often used to describe people with a heteronormative 'normal' sex life. It is sometimes used in a disparaging way. However, this is no better than slut-shaming and should be avoided.

Woman: Anyone who identifies as female or leans towards female on the gender non-binary spectrum and uses the term. Ciswomen and transwomen are both included in the term 'woman'.

Womanism: A term created by Alice Walker to describe a 'black feminist or feminist of colour'. This was created in response to feminism's racism and lack of intersectionality. Beauboeuf-Lafontant (2005) describes 'womanism' as a 'theoretical perspective focused on the experiences and knowledge bases of Black women [which] recognizes and interrogates the social realities of slavery, segregation, sexism, and economic exploitation this group has experienced during its history in the United States.'

W/S: Watersports, also known as 'golden showers' – urinating on a partner or being urinated on by a partner. It may also refer to simply watching a partner urinate or being observed urinating.

Yaoi: A form of Japanese erotica targeted at women and gay men, and featuring homoerotic and homoromantic love stories. Also known as 'Boys' Love' (BL). Eighty per cent of Thai women are thought to read Yaoi, and it is generally most popular with teenage girls and women.

Bibliography

History of Sex

The Perfumed Garden of the Shaykh Nefzani, translated by Sir Richard Burton (Grafton, 1963)

The Kama Sutra, Translated by Sir Richard Burton (Penguin Popular Classics, 1994 – first published 1883)

The History of Sexuality: An Introduction (Volume One) Michel Foucault (Vintage, 1990)

Sex Before Sexuality: A Premodern History, Kim M Phillips and Barry Reay (Polity, 2011)

The Garden of Eden; or The Paradise Lost and Found, Victoria Claflin Woodhull (Dodo Press, 1876)

Sex and Gender Research

Arousal: The Secret Logic of Sexual Fantasies, Dr Michael Bader

For Yourself: The Fulfilment of Female Sexuality, Lonnie Barbach Ph.D (Signet, 1976)

The Intimate Adventures of a London Call Girl, Belle de Jour (Weidenfeld & Nicolson, 2005)

Rewriting the Rules: An Interactive Guide to Sex, Love and Relationships, Meg Barker (Routledge, 2012)

What Do Women Want? Adventures in the Science of Female Desire, Daniel Bergner (HarperCollins, 2013)

Sex, Work and Sex Work: Eroticizing Organisation, Joanna Brewis and Stephen Linstead (Routelege, 2000)

Why is Sex Fun? The Evolution of Human Sexuality, Jared Diamond (Phoenix, 1997)

My Secret Garden, Nancy Friday (Virago, 1973)

Men in Love, Nancy Friday (Hutchinson, 1980)

Women on Top, Nancy Friday, (Arrow, 1991)

Beyond My Control, Nancy Friday (Sourcebooks inc, 2009)

Healing Sex: A Mind-Body Approach to Healing Sexual Trauma, Staci Haines (Cleis, 2007)

Honey Money: The Power of Erotic Capital, Catherine Hakim (Allen Lane, 2011)

The Hite Report, Shere Hite (Macmillan, 1976)

Sexual Honesty, Shere Hite (Arrow, 1982)

The New Hite Report, Shere Hite (Hamlyn, 2000)

Who's Been Sleeping in Your Head: The Secret World of Sexual Fantasies, Brett Kahr Ph.D (Basic Books, 2007)

Girl with a One Track Mind, Abbey Lee (Ebury Press, 2006)

The Sex Myth: Why Everything We're Told is Wrong, Brooke Magnanti (Phoenix, 2013)

Private Thoughts: Exploring the Power of Women's Sexual Fantasies, Wendy Maltz and Suzie Boss (New World Library, 2008 – new edition))

Why Women Have Sex, Cindy Meston and David Buss (Vintage, 2009)

Naked Ambition: Women Who are Changing Pornography, Carly Milne (Carroll and Graf, 2005)

The Butcher, the Baker, the Candlestick Maker, Suzanne Portnoy (Black Lace, 2013)

Whipping Girl: A Transexual Woman on Sexism and the Scapegoating of Femininity, Julia Serran (Seal, 2007)

Your Brain on Sex: How Smarter Sex Can Change Your Life, Stanley Siegel, LCSW (Sourcebooks Casablanca, 2011)

Where Their Feet Dance: Englishwomen's Sexual Fantasies, Rachel Silver (Century, 1994)

Sexual Fantasies for Women and By Women, edited by Lisa Sussman (Thorsons, 2001)

Womanism and Feminism

Sexuality and the Black Church: A Womanist Perspective, Kelly Brown Douglas (Orbis, 1999)

Black Feminist Thought, Patricia Hill Collins (Routelege, 2009)
Communion: The Female Search for Love, bell hooks (William Morrow, 2002)
All About Love: New Visions, bell hooks (William Morrow and Company, 2003)
Female Chauvinist Pigs: Women and the Rise of Raunch Culture, Ariel Levy (Pocket Books, 2006 – new edition)
Who Stole Feminism? How Women have Betrayed Women, Christina Hoff Sommers (Touchstone, 1994)
Antiporn: The Resurgance of Anti-porn Feminism, Julia Long (Zed Books, 2012)
When Chickenheads Come Home to Roost: A Hip Hop Feminist Breaks it Down, Joan Morgan (Touchstone, 1999)
Meat Market: Female Flesh Under Capitalism, Laurie Penny (Zero Books, 2010)
After Pornified: How Women are Transforming Pornography and Why it Really Matters, Ann G Sabo, Ph.D (Zero Books, 2011)
The Female Woman, Arianna Stassinpoulos (David Poynter, 1973)

Fiction

Story of the Eye, Georges Bataille (Penguin Modern Classics, 2001 – originally published 1928)
Sex and the City, Candace Bushnell (Abacus, 2008)
The Bitch, Jackie Collins (Simon and Schuster, 2013)
Lace, Shirley Conran (Penguin, 1983)
Riders, Jilly Cooper (Corgi 2007 – new edition)
Fifty Shades of Grey, E.L. James (Arrow, 2012)
Scruples, Judith Krantz (Crown Edition, 1978)
Little Birds, Anais Nin (Star, 1980)
The Wicked World of Women, Erin Pizzey (1996)
The Story of O, Pauline Régae (Olympia Press, 1970)
Valley of the Dolls, Jacqueline Susann, (Virago, 2003, copyright 1966)
Gordon, Edith Templeton (Penguin, 1966)
The Color Purple, Alice Walker (The Women's Press, 1983)
Forever Amber, Kathleen Winsor (Penguin, 2002 – new edition)

Useful Websites

Sex and Gender Education

Scarleteen.com
Bishtraining.co.uk
Dildographer.org
Mygenderation.com
brook.org.uk
itspronouncedmetrosexual.com
aasect.org

Erotica and Sex Blogging

Cliterati.co.uk
Blacklace.co.uk
Literotica.com
Musingsofemilyrose.blogspot.co.uk
Maggiemcneill.wordpress.com
Annaspansdiary.com
Beingblacksilk.com
Candidaroyalle.com
Cliterati.co.uk
Counterpunch.org
Daisydanger.com
Desirealliance.com
Drunkenslutmum.co.uk
Erikalust.com
Feminisnt.com
Janesguide.com
Lovehatesexcake.com
MLNP.com
Msnaughty.com
Nymphomaniacness.com
Poisonthorns.blogspot.com
Rebelsnotes.com
sexonomics-uk.blogspot.co.uk
Titsandsass.com
Tinynibbles.com
Xcitebooks.com
Writesexright.com

Acknowledgements

In addition to the books and websites listed in the bibliography, many people and organisations helped this book come to fruition including academics, sex workers, erotic writers, therapists, sex bloggers and friends. Whether through their Twitter timeline, email and phone conversations or wine-fuelled conversations – sometimes all three – everyone mentioned below has fed into this book, and all are well worth following online. This book was woven together from many people's brilliant thoughts and works rather than being simply the product of my own imagination, though any conclusions drawn are, of course, my responsibility. I am hugely grateful to have had access to such kind people with brilliant minds.

Particular thanks go to Mia More, for taking time to read the book and add her thoughts when the deadline was looming, and helping in every way she possibly could. Tom Rea was similarly wonderful, spending hours debating, reading what I'd written, helping me hone my arguments and supporting me in more ways than I could list. This book would not have been the same without either of them. Thanks to Chelsey Fox and Kate Moore for helping this project come to fruition, and Diana Colbert for helping spread the word about it. Abi Jenkins, Rose Crompton and Alyson Fixter deserve particular thanks for hand-holding my way through the entire process and being prepared to engage in discussions about gender, sexuality and fantasy versus reality at all hours of the morning particularly when, in some cases, it was the last thing that they wanted to be doing. Writing is a lonely task and having loved ones who are prepared to support the process – even when that entails having a philosophical discussion at four a.m. – is a privilege. I feel lucky to have you in my life. Robin Sweet, Susan Quilliam, Raphael Fox and Hannah Platt were also integral to the researching and writing process, debating key issues with me to help me unpack what I learned. Meg Barker, Gemma Ahearne, Brooke Magnanti, Ronete Cohen, Robert Page, Richard Robinson, Flic Everett, Karen Krizanovich, Caroline Walters, Zoltan Dienes and Emma Mornington all provided invaluable support, and numerous Twitter followers helped lead me through the research into female sexuality and navigate its complexities. And of course, the biggest thanks of all go to the women who kindly contributed their fantasies to the book, and Nancy Friday, for writing *My Secret Garden* and inspiring me in the first place. Without her seed, there would be no *Garden of Desires*.

So many people gave their support to this project that it's impossible to thank everyone due to the limitations of my memory. If you contributed in any way and I haven't mentioned you, please see that as a result of a brain frazzled from immersing itself in fantasy research for months on end rather than any lack of gratitude, consider yourself included in these acknowledgements and I'll buy you a drink the next time I see you.

Twitter

@bmagnanti
@drpetra
@remittancegirl
@megbarkerpsych
@dildographer
@princessjack
@Mabsolute
@bishtraining
@gradientlair
@irregularvoice
@curvecoouture

@blacksilk
@cheekyminx
@Mia_More_UK
@Nichihodgson
@scarleteen
@Obscenitylawyer
@BBWMelody
@NymphomaniacNes
@makelovenotporn
@Dustylimits
@Pastachips
@Notahappyhooker
@redlightvoices

Websites

Mygenderation.com
Facebook.com/robinsweetsexpert
Rosemcrompton.com
Mia-More.co.uk
Gradientlair.com
Susanquilliam.com
Loversguide.com
Brightonscience.com
Malcolmvandenburg.co.uk